A NEW AMERICAN CREED

A NEW AMERICAN CREED

THE ECLIPSE OF CITIZENSHIP
AND RISE OF POPULISM

David H. Kamens

STANFORD UNIVERSITY PRESS
Stanford, California

Stanford University Press
Stanford, California

Printed in the United States of America on acid-free,
archival-quality paper

Library of Congress Cataloging-in-Publication Data

Names: Kamens, David H., author.
Title: A new American creed : the eclipse of citizenship and rise of
populism / David H. Kamens.
Description: Stanford, California : Stanford University Press, 2019. |
Includes bibliographical references and index.
Identifiers: LCCN 2019005083 (print) | LCCN 2019006599 (ebook) |
ISBN 9781503609549 (e-book) | ISBN 9781503604964
(cloth; alk. paper) | ISBN 9781503609532 (pbk.; alk. paper)
Subjects: LCSH: Political culture—United States. | Citizenship—
United States. | Individualism—United States. | Populism—United States. |
Social change—Political aspects—United States. | United States—
Politics and government.
Classification: LCC JK1726 (ebook) | LCC JK1726 .K358 2019 (print) |
DDC 320.56/620973—dc23
LC record available at https://lccn.loc.gov/2019005083

Cover design: David Drummond

Typeset by Newgen in Sabon 10/15

Contents

Preface

This book is the result of many years of conversation with Ron Jepperson on American political development. We both lived through the 1960s as students and saw the start of an episode of democratization, as a wide variety of disenfranchised groups successfully challenged classic legal and social restrictions against them. These successes, however, were quickly followed by countermovements aimed at de-democratization. One sign of the latter was the wave of voter demobilization that occurred after the 1960s (Burnham, 1984). This was an anomaly, and a puzzle for political scientists, because it occurred simultaneously with rising popular education levels, which typically increase electoral participation. Declining participation seemed to be a sign that many people were ignoring conventional politics. Meanwhile, bitter conflict was surfacing in the political system. White Southerners were turning Republican in response to President Johnson's and the Democratic Party's stance on civil rights. Racial resentment among white working-class voters in the north was also surfacing. Their migration to the Republican Party was beginning and later became a stampede. And the Democratic coalition was crumbling. Clearly from the viewpoint of the 1950s, something had changed for the worst as society appeared to go from consensus to paralyzing conflicts around fundamental issues.

How to theorize this dramatic change became our challenge. We knew of significant research on many pieces of this puzzle, but neither sociology nor political science had convincing answers at the macro level of how such changes could come about so dramatically and quickly. Many of the contemporary arguments did not seem up to the scale of the problem. Not only were individuals changing, but organizations, communities, and the political system itself were undergoing reorganization. S. M. Lipset's (1996) argument comes closest to a satisfactory explanation. Lipset recognized that the changes were systemic and proposed an argument suited to the scale of the problem. It invoked the dramatic challenges that the

Great Depression, World War II, and the Cold War posed for American exceptionalism. Lipset argued that in response to these developments, governing elites and their constituents suspended many of the tenets of classic American political culture. However, once American hegemony had revived a sense of "normality" in society, public support for these changes weakened. Classic American exceptionalism reemerged as a political response. I have built on this insight and have sought to show how the changes provoked by these developments in state and society led to the current political crisis.

This insight also led to the realization that these earlier crises had produced national responses that were deviations from the normal path of development that the American political system would have followed—and major segments of society believed *should* have followed—at the time. One of Ron Jepperson's particular contributions was the recognition that the 1930s were a "collectivist moment" in American history. Global crises and developments drove many of the changes in American politics. An ongoing crisis arose when, to cope with these shocks, elites introduced adaptations that challenged key narratives of American exceptionalism. Such deviations produced a dialectic in which the changes introduced, such as big government, became sources of conflict when normality reemerged. Important political factions then denounced these changes as "un-American" or "socialist" and demanded a return to small government and deregulated capitalism. Business groups, for example, considered the experiments of the 1930s a complete mistake. Similarly, ideological conservatives saw the developments in the 1960s as preludes to anarchy and disaster for society. Many joined the chorus crying for "law and order." American society became divided between the pro-1960s factions and the anti-1960s ones.

American hegemony in the 1960s and early 1970s opened the door for these reactions to develop and flourish. Classic American responses to these changes began emerging in this period: anti-elitism, anti-intellectualism, and populism. People were angry at political elites and their allies. The South was in revolt against government intrusion. Many resented "big government" and the gains of minorities. These post-1960s developments were not new, but they were more extreme versions of classic American responses. How these responses developed and intensified is one of the central subjects of the book.

We also realized that given the scope of change in society, any explanation had to be one suited to the scale of the problem. Change had occurred at multiple levels: individual habits and attitudes changed; communities had undergone reconstruction; and society itself had changed. Big government, big science, and a big military were part of the new normality. Realization about the scale of the problem was slow in coming, in part because the literature was itself fragmented.

Yet, as we began to grapple with the scale of change, we also recognized that there had been a major shift in authority in society. Many institutions and norms suffered diminished authority or lost it. Citizenship was one but there were many others, including families, communities, ethnic/racial groups, and the nation-state itself. The *responsibilities* conventionally associated with the key role of citizen morphed into *options* for the liberated person (Janowitz, 1983). Military service, voting, and religious observance, for example, declined once they ceased to be the obligations of respectable citizens. Other facets of the traditional citizen role—like local community participation and volunteer work—also became obsolescent or, at least, optional. How this happened is an important subject of the book.

As a result of these changes, American political culture evolved in an important way. The "individual" became framed as the key agent of society. Charisma shifted from institutions to "persons" in dramatic fashion. This new cultural framing of authority in society threatened to vitiate that of *all* elites in society. It also dramatically enhanced the power of public opinion in society. The authority of science, medicine, law, the media, the state, and education were all weakened by this change. Virulent anti-intellectualism gained legitimacy under this redefinition of authority in society, freeing populism from constraints, and providing justification for a growing public disdain of elites. These changes created new problems for democracy. How to curb the anarchy that enhanced individualism licenses is one. Another is the question of whether enhanced individualism can be the basis for a communal ethic and social solidarity? (Bell, 1973). I address both issues.

Given this framing, the narrative focuses on long-term sociocultural processes rather than on short-term political ones. It also takes a macro societal view. Once we had developed these ideas, Prof. Jepperson developed an outline of the argument in the summer of 2013. This was a significant point in the development of the book.

Numerous people have helped realize this project. Prof. Ron Jepperson has been a long- term collaborator and friend. Many of the central ideas of the book were developed in discussions with him. He, unfortunately, was unable to participate in writing the book. Nevertheless, his fingerprints are all over the work. Doubtless, it would be better had he been able to continue participating.

We also received strong encouragement and help from many others. John W. Meyer has been an important mentor to us both. Over the years he read drafts and commented in ways that helped keep our enthusiasm intact and pushed us to keep thinking theoretically about these problems. He pushed us to think about macro social processes comparatively that work out over long time periods. He also cautioned us to act like anthropologists. His advice was to view Americans as natives acting out social rituals linked to major societal myths (narratives) rather than as enacting their own personal action repertoires. This led us to think about how transformations of society affect the citizen role. The eclipse of traditional citizenship became one of the themes of the book.

In addition, through his seminar at Stanford we developed strong bonds with many of his graduate students who were generous with their time in reading and critiquing drafts. Early versions of the first draft circulated among this group, and their insights and critiques were helpful. Members of the seminar included Frank Dobbin, Michelle Lamont, John Boli, Phyllis Riddle, and Francisco Ramirez.

John Boli was an early member of this group, and he has been especially generous in reading and critiquing the current manuscript. His efforts helped me reorganize the original architecture of the book and to extend the analysis of neoliberalism. He commented extensively on all the chapters, identifying weaknesses wherever he found them. Whatever faults remain are despite his wise counsel.

Francisco Ramirez was influential in both his work and conversations with us over the years. In some of his own work he focused on an important feature of American exceptionalism, namely how embedded the American state is in civil society from a comparative perspective. His display of the utility of this idea gave us a valuable tool in our analysis of the evolution of the U.S. polity. His comparative work also helped us put the United States in international perspective.

Ann Swidler was one of the early supporters of the project, and her enthusiasm was a source of strength. She continued to encourage us long after the initial phase and at points when anyone else would have imagined that the project was dead. Early on she helped organize a faculty seminar at Stanford where I presented an early version of the project.

Two other friends and colleagues were influential. Charles Cappell, a longtime colleague and friend, taught me most of what I know about modern methodology and worked with me on empirical projects highlighting the growing polarization in American politics. His influence has been substantial and his friendship sustaining.

Jeff Mirel is an American historian and colleague whose work and conversation have tutored me on many subjects, particularly those concerned with American educational history. His monograph is featured prominently in the book as a major study of one strand of American history, that is, rising social libertarianism and tolerance for pluralism. His friendship has been invaluable in surviving academia.

I owe two other colleagues an enormous debt for encouraging Stanford University Press to back the project with a book contract. One is David Frank of the University of California at Irvine and the other is an anonymous reviewer. Both wrote extremely useful and detailed comments of an earlier version of the manuscript. I owe them immense gratitude for their interest and the care they took to constructively critique the manuscript.

David Baker is another longtime colleague and friend who was helpful. He deserves thanks for encouraging the project and for the many conversations we have had about education and national development that helped shape this project. His own work has been influential in tutoring me on international development, particularly in Europe. I also want to thank him for introducing me to Stanford University Press and its editor, Kate Wahl. My own editor at the press, Marcela Maxfield, has been extremely helpful in suggesting changes that have made the text more intelligible and accessible. I have been lucky to have such an astute editor.

My wife, Beth, was a staunch supporter and participant in the project. She helped edit the manuscript. More important was her acceptance of my multiyear commitment to the project. Her patience and positive outlook have been remarkable. In addition, her experience as historian, as editor and publisher of *In These Times* in Chicago, and as senior staffer at the Institute for Policy Studies and Every Voice in Washington, D.C., gave her insights into American politics that she generously shared with me. She was also instrumental in introducing me to people and viewpoints I would not otherwise have experienced. James Weinstein, historian and founder/publisher of *In These Times,* and the late Marcus Raskin, a Kennedy administration veteran, critic, and founder of the Institute for Policy Studies, were two of the many whose comradeship supported and informed me. I am grateful to Beth for surrounding me with intellectually informed practitioners of politics whom I otherwise would not have known. Beth and my stepdaughters, Anna and Claire, have also provided a family life of adventure and pleasure that has been sustaining and kept my curiosity alive.

A NEW AMERICAN CREED

CHAPTER I

Introduction

I AM CONCERNED in this book with the future of democracy in the United States. This requires coming to grips with two issues: the decline of the traditional citizenship role and a corresponding rise in populism. Both processes have undermined consensus in the political system about how to confront present and future challenges. This stalemate has also stymied efforts to extend democracy and fostered both a backlash and a leadership vacuum. Nativism is now rampant and overt. Mass movements have neutered political elites and undermined their authority. I am convinced that accounting for these developments requires a more realistic analytic narrative of the evolution of the American polity and political culture in the post–World War II period than exists in the literature.

This project involves limning a "big picture" of American change, synthesized from a generation of historical and sociopolitical scholarship. Most accounts feature shorter-term explanations. For instance, the distinguished political sociologist Michael Mann (2013) has recently argued that post-1970s American politics primarily reflects a series of successful short-term right-wing political surges. He does not address longer-term causation. I make the case for the influence of long-term cultural and institutional change.

Institutional adaptations to the Great Depression of the 1930s, World War II, and the Cold War produced a new political system. Citizens adapted accordingly and began to reference new political problems, such as "out-of-touch elites." Meanwhile, patriotism declined, and citizens revised their political action repertoires to adapt to the new politics—for example, by engaging more in social movement orientations and less in electoral participation. In short, the "civic culture" of the 1940s and 1950s went into eclipse (see Almond and Verba, 1963). Academic discourse began to cite new notions such as the "end of ideology," "mass society," and "downsizing democracy" (Bell, 1960; Goldfarb, 1991; Hamilton and Wright, 1986; Crenson and Ginsberg, 2004). A good deal of effort went into analyzing why political participation was declining after the 1960s (Teixera, 1987; 1990; Burnham, 1975; 1984). The major paradox for political scientists was: why would voting decline when popular education levels were rising (Brody, 1978)? In the past, they had risen in tandem.

The big-picture approach has several virtues. Those of us seeking to analyze change in the American polity have struggled to establish an appropriate baseline for comparison over time. The tendency to normalize and idealize the historically peculiar post–World War II period has hindered us. Many features of this period—World War II solidarity and the postwar U.S. international dominance that followed, Cold War tensions, and the subsequent postwar prosperity—combined to produce an imagery of American consensus. Memories of the conflict-ridden 1930s disappeared—a significant act of forgetting in much of the subsequent literature and theory. Characterizations of the United States as a uniquely "civic culture" supported by a consensual society, experiencing an "end of ideology," became prominent in both intellectual discourse and popular culture (Almond and Verba, 1963; Bell, 1960). Scholars have noted that such reifications have often accompanied hegemonic position—as with the hyperconfidence and idealized tradition of imperial and post-imperial Britain (Bell, 1973; Krucken and Drori, 2009: 296–320; Mann, 2012; 2013).

This largely fictional baseline has endured. It impairs discussion of sociopolitical change. How problematic this imagery is becomes apparent in the *imagined* contrast between the current period of bewildering discord and decline and a more authentic and virtuous past. These idealizations are present in civics texts and have become part of folk, ideological, and even academic descriptions of American society and polity. They remain with us to this day (Jepperson and Meyer, 2011).[1]

We need to develop explanations that are appropriate to the scale of the problem. A proper analysis of change in American institutions must take account of the fact that shifts have occurred at multiple levels. Individual behavior and outlooks have changed. Boycotts, social actions, and social movements have become common. These action repertoires displace electoral activity (Kamens, 2009; Tilly, 1979). Citizens' trust of each other has also plummeted (Paxton, 1999; Pharr and Putnam, 2000; Kamens, 2012; T. Smith, "Trends," 2012). Many imagine that members of the opposing political party are untrustworthy and less rational than themselves. They also see them as enemies of the country instead of compatriots with different opinions (Pew Center Report, 2014).

There has also been dramatic change in collective action (Skocpol and Fiorina, 1999). Local generalist community organizations are decaying while special-interest groups are becoming dominant (Walker, 1991). National political organizations with paid staffs are displacing local political organizations. And the organization of the state has undergone dramatic change.

National government has grown and become a major center of resources and authority. Government regulation of many areas of life has grown enormously since the 1950s (Pierson, 2007; Pierson and Skocpol, 2007). Many more people have become "clients" of the federal government, including much of the population (via programs such as Medicare and Social Security); corporations (as in the military-industrial complex); and state governments (e.g., public school and higher-education budgets, interstate highways, and Medicaid).

But at the same time, there is growing popular disdain for political elites. They are under increasingly fierce populist attacks (Judis, 2016). Conservatives are waging a successful battle against government and collectivist solutions to social problems (Judt, 2012). Higher education is under attack and has undergone a prolonged period of defunding. The public, particularly conservatives, contests the legitimacy of science. Government officials and politicians also increasingly disdain and attack it (Gauchat, 2012). For example, at this writing, the current president, unlike his predecessors, has yet to appoint a national science advisor. Meanwhile, political discourse teems with conspiracy theories, hateful references. and nasty language, to an extent not seen since before the Civil War (Shea and Sproveri, 2012). Political partisanship burgeons in Congress and in the country (Andris et al. 2015; Pew Research Center, 2014). Gridlock has become routine. The nation appears to be in a legitimacy crisis.

Such large patterns of change demand explanations that are appropriate in scale. Demographic and organizational-level theories seem inadequate explanations for this kind of seismic change (Stinchcombe, 1968). While demographic accounts of declines in patriotism across generations are useful, changes at the individual level are not adequate to explain the large-scale changes in state and society (e.g., Putnam, 2000; Janowitz, 1983). The same is true for theories that focus on changes in organizational fields and the death of local community organizations (Skocpol and Fiorina, 1999). Such theories are too narrow in scope to account for the big and multifaceted changes in political institutions that are occurring at different analytic levels across American society. In short, only analysis at very macro levels seems capable of accounting for such a bewildering array of changes.

THEORETICAL STANCE

The stance I take is a common one in institutional analysis (Brubaker, 1992; Meyer et al., 1997; Baker, 2014). I assume that society and state are not just organizational structures. They also incorporate narratives and myths that legitimate or define members of society, provide descriptions of how society works, and create the boundaries between the state and other social institutions. Such stories constitute cognitive maps that describe the foundational elements of a society. These cultural premises become institutionalized in society and state as a civil religion (e.g., Bellah, 1975; Cole, 2012a). These conceptions persist because they are part of the design of state and society. They also determine the purview of the state and the role of civil society.

Secularization has affected both the state and civil society. This process involves the relocation of authority and charisma (Shils, 1958). Rising secularization of society in the eighteenth and nineteenth centuries initiated a historical transition in authority that continues. The emergence of nation-states from empires entailed a radical shift in authority. Units like families and guilds lost charisma and authority as their power shifted upward to nation-states and their elites. Authority also shifted downward in society to individuals. Through citizenship, individuals gained rights at the expense of families and other units (Daalder, 1987; Bendix, 1964; Marshall, 1963). Individuals and families also became subordinate to the nation-state in this process.

As secularization has advanced, even nation-states are losing authority (see Ramirez, 2006). This is happening at two levels. As globalization advances as a cultural and social project, larger global society supplants the authority of nation-states (Meyer et al., 1997). World models of society, including the ideology of human rights and its reification in transnational human rights treaties, create new models of social organization, transcending the nation-state. Increasingly, people have rights, independent of their citizenship status, creating, as Cole (2012a) argues, a new civil religion. It endows all individuals with rights that nation-states agree to honor and to implement.

This process also enlarges citizen rights (see Boli-Bennett, 1979). For example, a common assumption is that all children should have the right to education. Nation-states are under mounting pressure from both their own populations and external agencies to provide more education to their populations or lose aid and international standing. Children and their parents are now responsible to participate in formal education. In many nations, failing to do so has become a crime.

At the same time secularization also imbues individuals with more authority. As Durkheim's ([1912] 1961) "cult of the individual" develops, individuals accrue more authority and rights at the expense of the nation-state and other social units such as families. Women's and children's rights, for example, supplant monolithic patriarchal family authority. Both the expansion of education and the ideology of human rights have driven this process (Krucken and Drori, 2009: 280–296; Cole, 2012a; Ramirez, 2006; Habermas, 1991; Frank and Meyer, 2002). As national and, increasingly, global citizens, individuals become responsible for enacting both *rationality* and societal *morality*. A society's primary duty becomes the imperative to socialize individuals to ensure that they are aware of and attached to their collective responsibilities as citizens of the nation and the world.

A series of macrosocial changes associated with globalization have thus altered American conceptions of citizenship. I *do not* take the position that these changes undermine political participation or interest. But I do propose that patterns of participation have changed, along with increases in conflict and polarization. As individualism has been culturally enhanced, individuals have gained more authority vis-à-vis society (Janowitz, 1983). "Dutiful citizenship" has declined. Activism, including resistance to social authority, has increased. The huge surge in rights cases that overwhelmed U.S. courts in the 1960s and 1970s was one harbinger of this change (Pierson, 2007). More rights have been legally established, exemplified by the nongendered right to marry.

Other changes have surfaced. Contemporary politics now takes the form of social movements and more populist expressions of discontent (Kamens, 2009; Judis, 2016; Gitlin, 2012). Civic duties have become civic *options*. This set of changes has enlarged the power of public opinion while the influence of experts and leaders of all kinds has diminished. Unvetted public opinion now thrives and enjoys legitimacy. The public downgrades knowledge in this contest, and real expertise loses out in public forums.

Changing models of citizenship have generated other institutional consequences that are also the subject of the book. Importantly, growing hostility to government, per se, has facilitated resistance to the creation of a modern social welfare state. Much of society no longer finds the ideology at the heart of the modern welfare state plausible (Judt, 2012). In general, fear of the state and of collective solutions to societal problems has escalated.

Meanwhile, as citizen authority has grown, so have assaults on elites. The historic anti-intellectualism long associated with the American creed has not only thrived but grown (Hofstadter, 1962, 1965). Attacks on rationality and science have had a serious growth spurt, particularly among Republicans and conservative elites. Science itself has become suspect (Gauchat, 2012). The result is a growing disdain for knowledge and experts in the political system coupled with the rising power of public opinion, rendering both traditional media and new social media outlets newly important drivers of U.S. politics.

These changes have helped delegitimize national political elites and undermine public support for political institutions. Thus, during the fiscal crisis of 2008 and the ensuing Great Recession, government—rather than business and the patently culpable banks—received the lion's share of blame and the public's anger (Martinelli, 2008; Kamens, 2012; Brooks and Manza, 2013). Part of the burden of the book is to clarify this institutional logic convincingly.

The eclipse of citizenship in the late twentieth century via the larger forces of individualism and globalization represents a pivotal moment in the development of American political culture. Evidence of the change is visible in the decline of classic civic consciousness that included such elements as elevated levels of local volunteering, voting, local political participation and organizational memberships, and a sense of solidarity that "we're all in the same boat" (Janowitz, 1983; Putnam, 2000; Crouch, 2004; Mann, 2013). While others have noted this change, no one has yet sufficiently analyzed it (Crouch, 2004; Janowitz, 1983). I try to provide a more satisfactory explanation of these changes in the book.

DISTINCTIVE CULTURAL NARRATIVES AMID INCREASING GLOBALIZATION

An additional purpose of the book is to dispel the idea that Americans' political dispositions are becoming like Europeans' because of the spread of globalization and individualism. Institutional differences appear perfectly capable of coexisting with the widespread global borrowing and diffusion that is occurring under intensified globalization. To take one example, American politics are different from those of Europe because Americans have not had institutions that promoted collectivist notions of the polity, exemplified by Christian democracy, socialism, or traditional British Tory ideology (McKenzie and Silver, 1968). Only in the context of the Great Depression did collectivist ideologies gain strength, but they lost traction after World War II with the return of prosperity.

Nationalism in the United States is "tamed" but nevertheless is alive and well (Meyer et al., 1997). Global narratives accompany the diffusion of key institutions across societies, but much of the rhetoric underlying them concerns the wider purposes that modern societies should pursue: health for all via modern medicine and science, education for all via public schools and universities, and so on.

Global narratives are less likely to describe the form of these institutions, how they will operate, and which practices will be effective in different country settings. While there *are* emerging notions of global "best practices," such procedural recipes leave a good deal of room for local and national content to fill in the empty spaces. This vacuum opens opportunities for local and national cultures to intercede with their specific narratives of how to organize roles and lines of action. Thus, the French are likely to construct more centralized school systems while Americans favor more decentralization (see Baker and LeTendre, 2005).

American society illustrates this point because it has not taken the path predicted by modernization theories or mass society arguments (Inglehart, 1990; Wilensky, 2002; Kensworthy, 2014). As some in the 1970s predicted or feared, the United States has not become a European-style welfare state despite the staggering level of state expenditures (Steinmo, 2010; Lowi, 1978b). Instead, the U.S. welfare state lags internationally. Collectivist political ideologies do not gain traction in the political system, as responses to the fiscal crisis of 2008 suggest.

Wealthy democracies have many similarities, and this may increase as globalization intensifies. All have large-scale economic and political bureaucracies, expanded educational systems, and a large, well-funded, scientific-technical sector (Collins, 1999). But their political cultures are different and remain so, despite the spread of modernization. Almond and Verba (1963) made this point emphatically and it is still true (Jepperson, 2002).

One result is that American political culture impedes movement in a European direction. For example, there seems little chance of a full-fledged American social welfare state emerging in the near future. Fragmented centralization is still the rule and will probably impede such development (Scott and Meyer, 1983; Katznelson, 2013). Enhanced individualism also fosters fear of an expanded state and a regulated economy. Future development will therefore likely entail increasing civil libertarianism. Legal and civil rights will expand. But the extension of social welfare rights will continue to be contested terrain because it involves government regulation of the economy and higher taxes. This development may lead to an unstable form of democratization if the middle class diminishes amid extreme and deepening inequality. And it could undermine democracy itself if it entails a continuing increase in populist politics. Under these conditions U.S. democracy may not survive persistent legitimacy crises.

NATIONALISM IN A GLOBAL CONTEXT

My account of U.S. political development emphasizes the enduring effects of American nationalism and institutional design (see also Pierson, 2004). But it takes seriously the impact of extranational events and forces in accounting for features of the system that have more recently emerged. These changes are increasingly under attack as illegitimate deviations from American *exceptionalism*. They include a stronger national state, the rise of a national political class with pretensions of expertise to govern, and the rise of U.S.-based "world-class" universities whose members seek to use scientific knowledge to guide public policy. The political right characterizes these developments as socialist and "un-American" while the left regards them as undemocratic and anti-egalitarian.

Even as globalization intensifies, much space remains for national narratives to operate and stimulate national variation. National narratives are unlikely to die, though they may be "tamed" in periods of rapid global integration when global economic and political institutions appear to be "working" (Meyer et al., 1997; Wuthnow, 1980). However, in periods of disintegration or conflict, the myths of specific nation-states can resurface forcefully, along with their ugly consequences. Brexit is one reaction, but hopefully not the future of Europe. Regardless, nativism is a powerful narrative for large minorities across Europe and America.

The larger point is that the rise of right-wing attacks on government and the rise of populism are not short-run political processes but outcomes of a persisting institutional system. I focus the narrative of the book on two historic elements that have driven the American polity. First, such political reactions arise from features of the classic American tradition that constitute the basic institutional elements of the political system.

Second, globalization generates important effects by producing challenges that political elites must respond to. My analytical framework is therefore one that emphasizes the evolution of the larger world system. Tracking how American elites have perceived and adapted to it is part of the narrative frame I use in surveying the zigs and zags that the American polity has taken since the 1930s.

A major point is that globalization has produced developments that were atypical of the classic narratives surrounding the American polity. Of note is the highly unusual collectivist moment in U.S. history, produced by the tight temporal sequencing of three major events: the Great Depression, World War II, and the Cold War. Big government and other developments arose from responses to these challenges. Many still do not sufficiently appreciate this break within the American political tradition and the broader atypicality of the postwar period despite the stress placed on it by such prominent scholars as Seymour M. Lipset (1996) and Ira Katznelson (2013).

These developments produced conflicts that continue. After the shadow of the Cold War receded, U.S. political culture *reverted* to its historic conflictual, populist, individualist, and anti-statist characteristics.[2] A renewed focus on American exceptionalism produced conflicting interpretations of the institutional legacies of the Great Depression, the New Deal, and the Cold War. The political question that arose was this: were these developments deviations from the American tradition or proper extensions of it? Different sectors of American society came to different conclusions on this question.

Globalization affected this development by increasing the economic, social, and political uncertainties the United States faced after a period of world hegemony. The new interdependencies and uncertainties—and perceived loss of control—have stimulated different would-be "revitalization movements" that present *competing* visions of an authentic American way forward. An overarching Cold War nationalism, parochialism, and economic dynamism—and quasi-imperial hubris—previously *dampened* this ideological competition. With the decline of these threats and the solidarity they produced, conflicting visions of an appropriate way forward have multiplied in number and intensity.

In addition, wartime and postwar rhetorics of freedom, democracy, and human rights unleashed powerful cultural logics that have propelled individualism and populism forward, with tremendous momentum.

One significant development that has heightened conflict over the direction of society is that of enhanced individualism in the United States. This has long been a constituent element of the American creed and part of American exceptionalism. But under the challenge of globalization it has intensified to the point that it eclipses citizenship as the key social construct of American society.

INTENSIFIED INDIVIDUALISM AND THE ECLIPSE OF TRADITIONAL CITIZENSHIP

Lipset (1996) identified the resurgence of individualism as a key cultural development in the United States once the shadow of the Cold War passed. The Great Depression, World War II, and the Cold War had produced a regulated form of capitalism that suppressed it. For a brief period, collective, though nonsocialist, solutions to the problems presented by these events emerged. Government efforts during the New Deal exemplify such attempts to cushion the impact of capitalism's collapse (Katznelson, 2013). This scenario subdued classic features of the American creed. Individualism and populism went into remission.

As the United States emerged from World War II victorious and the world's hegemonic power, a tamer "civic culture" developed (Almond and Verba, 1963). The postwar nuclear standoff between the United States and the USSR had sown fear and terror (Gaddis, 2005). But there was also high confidence in America's political institutions and citizenry. Manifest destiny, imperial hubris, and xenophobia prevailed and reigned during this period of the Cold War.

By the 1960s, urgent fear of nuclear war morphed into a relatively stable Cold War international order among the great powers. Conflict continued but elites deemed it manageable. The Cuban missile crisis reinforced this attitude. Soviet and American leaders had narrowly averted nuclear war.

Under these conditions classic individualism reemerged. With the spread of education and a high-technology economy, fueled by the national security state, the properly socialized individual became the key player in the American social narrative—a shift that ramified throughout the polity (Meyer, 1986; Meyer and Jepperson, 2000). As a result, the 'individual' was endowed with charisma and authority that was historically associated with religion, the family, the nation-state and other institutions.

This change undermined classic civic orientations of Americans. The generations from 1896 to 1940 were the most traditionally patriotic and collectivist, though not socialist (Janowitz, 1983; Putnam, 2000). Voting, volunteering, country loyalty, and a sense of common destiny prevailed among these generations (see also Mann, 2013). This ethos declined in succeeding generations. Robert Putnam blames the decline of community and the subsequent loss of collective social capital for this change. Morris Janowitz focuses on the decline of the "citizen-soldier" ideal, the decline of conscription and decreasing alternative opportunities in school or society for civic participation, producing a notion of citizenship that emphasizes rights at the expense of responsibilities.

I am more sympathetic to the latter argument, but I locate the cause of these changes in a much wider, global context. What has changed is the enhanced significance that political elites, and now the public, attach to education and properly socialized citizens for achieving national economic and political goals. This is happening elsewhere as well and is now part of global culture. This institutional change is one of the reasons that the citizen-soldier ideal has declined. Shils (1971) pointed out that there is now no salvation without education, especially higher education. It was always a key component of the American creed, but it now plays a highly enhanced role.

In the dominant narrative of society, education is now the paramount institution charged with producing rational and morally responsible citizens. As a result, it is especially significant as the dominant socializing agency in society. The job of other institutions such as the family is preparing children for success in school. In this view, highly educated people will be the military and economic warriors of society. They will be the sources of future societal success. Elites and the public believe that they will need people with such skills in all sectors, from the military to the economy. The modern world economy is similar in requiring people with advanced literacy and numeracy skills.

The United States has historically placed a high value on literacy and numeracy (Tyack, 1975). In a country where evangelical Protestantism was prominent and later became part of Republican Party ideology, leaders took common schooling for granted as the major way to train future citizens (Thomas, 1989). Elites regarded reading and arithmetic as essential skills (Cohen, 1982). Morality depended on citizens' ability to read the Bible and other moral literature. And secular progress required them to know how to count properly to benchmark the achievement of social goals. In this worldview, being a citizen meant being capable of rational and responsible action in pursuit of shared societal goals. These included the subjugation of nature and the marginalization of those opposed to Protestant ideas of progress, such as Native Americans, Catholics, and others deemed un-American.

Changes in the post–World War II era expanded the role of education in constructing society. Education spread widely and rapidly at all levels. More important, it has become a critical component of civil religion, not just in the United States but globally (Baker, 2014; Meyer et al., 1992). In national and global ideology there is no (secular) salvation without higher education. Political elites in the U.S. took this injunction seriously, and higher education surged in the 1950s and 1960s, beyond levels seen after the 1944 passage of the GI Bill (Schofer and Meyer, 2005).

At the heart of this modern version of education is the *individual* as the primary social actor. The nation, and state, lose potency in this contest. The socialized individual becomes the principal driver of economies and the significant actor in democratizing political systems. The perception of the individual has always been part of the American political tradition, but in the context of global competition it has become all-encompassing.

One direct result has been the escalated value placed on the performance of schoolchildren. It is common to imagine that their success in school will shape the future of the country. Human capital theory and modern discourse both encourage this conception of society.

Schooling, then, becomes the primary social *duty* of children and young adults, as well as a key responsibility of parents. Truancy in the early years has thereby acquired quasi-criminal status in law and social practice. The failure to participate becomes a significant social problem precisely because, according to both elites and parents, societal success depends on schooling (see Baker, 2014: 219–246). It is the modern initiation ritual: an introduction to rational myths (narratives) of society and the corresponding social responsibilities of citizens.

Other aspects of modern education, meanwhile, emphasize *individual* achievement. Such achievements gain weight and significance when viewed as indicators of the future success of both the student *and* society. Test scores and grades become critically important not just for individuals but as indicators of the talent of entire generational cohorts. Higher average scores signal that a society has a bigger stockpile of highly rational individuals, socialized to pursue collective goals. Hence society gains more human capital (Becker, 1994; Schultz, 1961). For example, despite the evidence, political elites worldwide believe that international test scores predict the future economic prowess of their nation. The same is true for schools at the state level. Grades signify not just a student's progress but also the success of individual teachers, classes, and the school itself. Low grades and test scores indicate *failing* schools and *failing* societies (see Baker, 2014).

Studies of textbooks show that in the United States and elsewhere, teaching has become more focused on individual student growth and achievement (Bromley et al., 2011). Teachers and parents now expect students to participate more in class and to be critical of texts they read. Curricula place less emphasis on memorizing, dates, and the feats of historical figures and more on social explanations of the country's history. History, civics, and geography, for example, have now become combined into social studies in the United States and elsewhere, and social science models of explanation have become common (Wong, 1991). Schools place much less stress than in earlier eras on nationalism and patriotism. Both are alive and well, but they exist within a context of more rationalized explanations of society and nature as high schools and universities increasingly elevate hard science as well as social science (see Frank and Gabler, 2006).

In this new frame, nations are part of a global economic and political order. A nation's success depends on its ability to compete in this world order on its terms. This understanding increases the value of acquiring world languages; achieving competency in science and technology skills; and gaining enough familiarity with other national cultures to facilitate commercial, political, and other interactions. Under the canopy of such a rationalized curriculum, patriotic absolutes such as "my country right or wrong" subside, without disappearing.[3]

In addition, high school students start to become specialists in specific areas of the curriculum and extracurriculum as schools aspire to produce differentiated *individuals* with distinct profiles and constellations of talents. Students and their families see schooling as a chance to build résumés that make them attractive to colleges and employers, striving to match their talents and interests with activities and classes where they can excel. This behavior parallels adult behavior in the community at large, where generalist voluntary associations have lost out to more specialized ones (Skocpol and Fiorina, 1999).

These trends undermine the ability of schools to inculcate a generalized civic consciousness among all students (Janowitz, 1983). But this *taming* of nationalism does not destroy it. Individuals may still be patriotic but more restrained in their enthusiasm for the nation and more committed to key institutions of law and justice. Meanwhile, those with less education remain most committed to traditional forms of nationalism that are exclusionary in terms of ethnicity, race, religion, and other characteristics (see Bonikowski and DiMaggio, 2016; Inglehart, 1990).

Given the prominence of education in constructing the modern individual, societies now tend to severely punish people who do not achieve elevated levels of education. The public has long valued education for its role in increasing people's skill sets and as a fair way of selecting the most productive people. Yet the practical implication of that value became much more pronounced in the 1970s when the pay differentials for college-educated versus non-college-educated workers widened substantially (Geiger, 2009). Since then these differentials have only increased. Copious research has documented the strong link in the United States between educational attainment and economic success, occupational attainment, and political success (Collins, 1979; Nie et al., 1996).[4]

The new predominance of the individual as society's primary agent reduces the salience of other institutions traditionally engaged in citizenship education, such as the military. Education enjoys both critical attention and a huge infusion of resources at the local level. Education is usually the leading item in city and town budgets. Local governments spend 45 percent of their revenues on education budgets, while the individual states assume 47 percent of the cost. The federal government pays the rest—a mere 8 percent (U.S. Census, 2016, Tables 5, 8). Education is also expensive. In 2016, the average cost per pupil for elementary and secondary education (K–12) was $11,762 per year. High-tax states spend even more, with New York weighing in with the highest costs at $22,366 per pupil.

Moreover, with the rise of the high-tech national security state, education has also become associated with national defense. Indeed, Congress enacted the most significant legislation vis-à-vis higher education in 1958 and called it the National *Defense* Education Act. In this context, formal military service represents just one option alongside other opportunities—like the Peace Corps—for civic participation. This is true even in the post-9/11 era, when warfare has become a staple of U.S. foreign policy. Even before the elimination of the draft in 1972, educational status was a common source of deferments. In the Korean War and the early years of the Vietnam War (1964–1971), local draft boards considered enrollment in post-high-school education as reason enough to exempt people from the draft.

The rise of the individual has clearly undermined traditional expressions of patriotism. Other bases of solidarity have evanesced. Secularization has supported individuals' personal pursuit of secular as well as other-worldly salvation (Baker, 2014; Putnam and Campbell, 2010) Religion has adapted by becoming organized around individuals' pursuit of authenticity (Boli and Elliot, 2008). It is by no means dead, but it has changed in adapting to modern society.

The new primacy of the individual has also shaped the contemporary evolution of democracy in American society. Individualism as ideology is a force for extending legal and political equality. Women's rights, LGBTQ rights, and civil rights for other historically marginalized groups have expanded significantly since the 1950s. This part of classic liberalism coexists well with the elevation of the individual as a principal social actor.

Conversely, the advance of individualism has proven to be a power-ful force *against* democratization in social welfare rights. A strong suspi-cion of state power in the private affairs of individuals and communities remains firmly embedded in the modern American creed. When the in-dividual becomes the key source of charisma and legitimacy in society, fear of the state as an enemy of personal freedom *intensifies*. American political parties, especially the Republican Party, have sanctioned and institutionalized this notion, making it a key element of neoliberalism. This cultural development undermines support for the extension of social welfare rights that rely on active state regulation of the economy and the redistribution of its benefits.

With these diametrically opposing effects on democratization, indi-vidualism has played an important part in polarizing political culture. Support for broader individual freedoms antagonizes moral conservatives and the religious wing of each party but wins the support of liberals and much of the business community. The new individualism's suspicion of the state also reinforces neoliberalism when it comes to the issue of gov-ernment regulation of the economy. This angers those concerned with the growing inequality in society but satisfies business elites, evangelicals, and traditional conservatives (e.g., Lowi, 1996).

The net result is a society where majorities highly value personal free-doms and civil rights but are willing to tolerate the exceedingly high levels of inequality and poverty that result from the unregulated market power of corporations (Reich, 2007).

Individualism has also had far-reaching consequences for political institutions. It *accelerates* a long American tradition of delegitimizing the power of *all* elites. That tradition is now operating in the extreme, diminishing the role of expertise and knowledge in political affairs. It frees public opinion of the obligation to rely on verifiable information in debates and it licenses fraud, lies, and deception across media plat-forms. In this way it helps undermine traditional civic consciousness and democracy (Janowitz, 1983; Putnam, 2000; Zukin et al., 2006; Hacker and Pierson, 2005, 2010).

A political consequence of enhanced individualism is to provide niches for populist politicians of all stripes. Politics has now become organized around social movements that can successfully control major political parties as captives of populist politicians. It also supports very radical forms of populism in which all elites in society are suspect, including those in education and science, as well as politicians and bankers.

This trend magnifies the classic forms of anti-intellectualism and populism built into the American political tradition. The new American creed turns them into viral plagues that leaders cannot counter by rational debate and inquiry. This form of populism has grown and undermined the role of parties and their ability to produce reforms that the populace craves. This change also aggravates cynicism and enhances the conviction that political institutions are inherently ineffective and illegitimate (Cappella and Jamieson, 1997). In short, it has helped produce the legitimacy crisis that American society now faces.

The individual chapters in the book flesh out these arguments and examine the supporting evidence.

METHODOLOGICAL STANCES

In this book I try to maintain an anthropological distance from the American polity, given the all-too-frequent tendency in U.S. social science to normalize it. Such a stance and the distance it creates from the subject focuses attention on the evolving mythologies and grand dramas that constitute the United States' distinctive political world. It encourages one to see people—both the mass public and elites—as natives, enacting the culture's grand dramas in their postures, rhetoric, and practices. Citizenship and individualism are, after all, highly scripted roles. These are part of the political system, co-evolving with other elements of the political system. It turns out to be much more realistic to interpret individual political behaviors and attitudes as ritualized enactments of mythologies and dramas, as opposed to autonomous reactions to, or autonomous reflections upon, the political system. Americans' political participation has changed markedly because the political system has changed so much, including the role and status of the individual within it. And Americans' political attitudes have changed markedly, because individuals are reporting on a different political system and are enacting changed roles within it.

Such an approach emphasizes that people's embeddedness in the institutionalized narratives of their political culture has strong effects on their behavior and patterns of thought.[5] One example of this argument comes from opinion poll surveys of Americans and Europeans. The Pew Research Center studied adults in nine European countries and the United States on reactions to immigrants (Pew Research Center, July 16, 2016). Americans responded more favorably to immigrants than Europeans did in answers to the following question: "Do you think that having an increasing number of people of many different races and nationalities in our country makes it a better place to live, a worse place to live or doesn't make much difference?"

Given the dismal state of race relations currently, and the political attacks on immigrants by politicians, this seems a strange, unbelievable finding. However, it makes sense if one presumes that participants are articulating one of the main narrative myths of American society instead of giving well-thought-out private opinions.

People learn these narratives in the family and at school. The data show that those with more education had the most favorable view of immigrants. Political institutions are also sources of such narratives. In this study, those with more leftist political views were also more favorable toward immigrants in the United States and elsewhere. Both education and political party ideology are heavily influenced by global culture, particularly ideas about human rights. Thus, in all countries those with more education and with leftist views have more favorable attitudes toward immigrants. But U.S. adults in this survey in all cases have *more* favorable views of immigrants.

"Mouthing" the culture, of course, does not predict behavior or even people's private attitudes in given situations. Implicit racial bias, for example, is widespread in the United States. So is intolerance for religious groups such as Mormons, Muslims, and non-Christian religions (Putnam and Campbell, 2010). Anti-immigrant sentiment is also growing and has now become a mainstream political phenomenon. Despite this, given the generality and facelessness of immigrants presented to them by the surveys, Americans can more easily imagine that immigrants are a lot like themselves, unless otherwise directed, than Europeans can. American civil religion has created a culture that is more amorphous and less bounded by cultural specificities like nationality, ethnicity, and place of birth (see Chapter 2).

The next chapter describes the American polity in comparative perspective. It highlights the differences that make U.S. political culture exceptional and provides empirical evidence that this is still the case. A focus on the content of American nationalism is important for understanding how the United States has adapted to the challenges of globalization and the limitations it imposes on this process. It is also necessary background for understanding why the United States is unlikely to become a modern social welfare state.

CHAPTER 2

The United States in Comparative Perspective

GLOBALIZATION AND MODERNIZATION have not erased the salient differences between Americans and wealthy, European democracies. Though structurally similar (Collins, 1999), their political cultures differ. That was the point of Almond and Verba's (1963) classic, *The Civic Culture*. As many have noted, institutions bear the imprint of the era of their founding (Stinchcombe, 1965; Pierson, 2004). American political culture and institutions are no exception. Initial conceptions of the state, the nation, and citizenship endure. This chapter outlines the dominant narratives of American society that make up the cultural blueprint of how the United States "works." It also offers comparative evidence that highlights the enduring differences between the United States and Western European democracies.

An important part of this effort requires understanding the cultural assumptions underpinning the American idea of nationhood, the state, and citizenship. Nations in this view are "imagined communities," not mere territorial and functional arrangements of governance (Anderson, 1983; Brubaker, 1992). They depend on a common set of understandings about who are legitimate members of the community, what holds them together as a community, the proper role of citizens, and the role of the state in developing social solidarity and prosperity. For example, Germans believe that society created the state and that both are held together by bonds of common descent and ethnicity. Under this understanding, only

Germans can be proper citizens. Turks who have lived in Germany for thirty years do not fit this description of a proper citizen and are not easily assimilated. On the other hand, Germans in Siberia and Eastern Europe do fit this view of German citizen and were until recently offered citizenship if they moved to Germany. This occurs even though they have never lived in Germany and do not know the German language.

The French, by contrast, imagine that society is a creature of the state. Society is therefore a territorial community open to all legal inhabitants (Brubaker, 1992). People who are legal residents of France, whatever their ethnicity, are regarded as proper citizens. The state and common conceptions of acting "French" are the glue that holds society together. Public displays of religiosity, for example, violate these rules. The formal idea of *laïcité* dictates that symbols of diversity that undermine national solidarity are not permissible in public. Wearing burka-type bathing suits on the beach is therefore controversial. Bikinis, and even partial nudity, are not.

THE AMERICAN NATION-STATE

The United States was a new nation and a frontier society that had to create a distinct set of cultural understandings concerning citizenship, the nation, and the role of the state (Lipset, 1963). Since it had rejected European models of state and society (Hartz, 1955; 1964), diplomats and leaders had to invent new myths of nationhood and narratives of agency in society. These became blueprints for the design of the state and its relationship to society. This process also generated "recipes" for how society would be constructed to achieve these goals, including the proper role in society for citizens.

The new society had to confront two important and related issues. First, it had to construct new citizens capable of functioning in this new society (see Boli, 1989). This meant creating new narratives of the role of "citizen." And secondly, it had to design a society and state that would create space for such citizens to flourish. This meant imagining a new kind of nation and a state that would be compatible with such a citizenry.

THE NATION AND MYTHS OF AGENCY

In his classic book Anderson (1983) observed that nationhood requires the invention of an "imagined community" among key groups in society.

This involves valorizing the national experience of key groups, such as Creoles in Mexico and Latin America, as well as the *creation* of a shared sense of the past and the future that is uplifting. It also involves *suppression* of memory of past hatreds among groups in society. In the case of the European Union there was and continues to be the task of submerging past enmities among nation-states into a common, sanitized history.

Nations and nationalism, like all religions, require creation myths and a history of how such charismatic authority was born and endured. They need a pantheon of founders, a catalog of the battles they fought, and the names of the villains they faced. Hence, the importance of the literature created by writers and historians as well as the depictions of the national community by artists, novelists, and musicians. Maps, the national currency, the creation of national institutions (e.g., national museums, symphonies, zoos, universities) all symbolize this emergent entity and delimit its boundaries and geography.

American nationhood is no exception. While immigration to the United States has been part of the positive story of the nation, the resulting ethnic and racial diversity has not. The American myth of nationhood suppresses this unpleasant fact. The main narrative in the United States has been that it is a melting pot, not a mosaic of nationalities and cultures. Assimilation to a common American culture and identity has been the dominant narrative. The metaphor of the melting pot suggests that Americanization boils out diversity and produces homogeneous citizens with a common culture. In practice, however, ethnic diversity was important and recognized as such. For example, many major immigrant communities in American cities kept their language and culture intact. But U.S. institutional structure and its political culture were not grounded in this set of facts.

Only recently has ethnic diversity become culturally valorized along with gender and other identities. One upshot of that development, identity politics, is a recent phenomenon. Instead, historically U.S. national identity has been built on *suppressing* ethnic and racial differences in pursuit of a common, sanitized American identity. There was, and still is, debate over this characterization of the nation, but historically the melting pot narrative won out (see Mirel, 2010). As the election of 2016 indicates, conflicting narratives about the nation are still in play. At present, the war over hyphenated identities is, by and large, over, but the battles continue.

The United States suppressed religious and ethnic diversity as the narrative of nationhood for a variety of reasons. Religious diversity was a practical fact on the ground. The religious diversity among the original thirteen colonies dictated that there could be no national religion. The political compromise that emerged in the Constitution was the doctrine of separation of church and state. While this preserved the argument that the United States is a Christian civilization, freedom of religion as a constitutional right meant that there was to be no preeminent, official religion that represented the nation-state as a community.

Tolerance for religious diversity allowed the society to maintain the narrative that Christianity was a foundation of American civilization and that personal religiosity was a civic duty. Freedom of religion also created both individual choice and a competitive market for different faiths. One result was increased religiosity since no religion had a monopoly as the national religion (Baker, 2014; Stark, 2005). Given the historical demography of the United States, these were acceptable premises since they did not require the acceptance of a specific religious theology or practice.

This contradiction endures. Religion is valued and was long thought of as a civic duty. On the other hand, no given religion can act as a national source of solidarity. On the first point Howe (1965), a constitutional scholar, observes that the early prevailing theory of disestablishment *disabled* the state from forcing any one religion, but it also *enjoined* religion as a *popular duty*. This conception of the role of religion held steady through the 1950s (Putnam and Campbell, 2010). Howe again notes the early evidence for this case. The framers of the Massachusetts Declaration of Rights made this clear in the following sentence: "It is the right as well as the duty of all men in society, publicly, and at stated seasons, to worship the Supreme Being, the great creator and preserver of the universe" (quoted in Howe, 1965: 25). Additional facts support this point. In New England ministers were paid out of the public purse since good order and stable civil government was deemed to depend on piety, religion, and morality. Similarly, in many early cases judges made decisions on the theory that Christianity was part of the common law inherited from England.

And judges also took the view that the "morality of the country is deeply engrafted upon Christianity" and therefore it is safe to assume that "we are a Christian people" (see Howe, 1965: 28–29).

In American ideology, individual voluntarism happens because the differences that might be caused by ethnic and religious variation are undercut by an ideology declaring that Americans are united by a common American creed that is independent of these variations. This creed enshrines individualism and voluntarism as national values, reinforced by commitment to a common set of understandings called the "American way of life" (Fischer, 2010). This narrative has generated an enormous amount of collective activity in the United States and institutional-legal support for voluntarism. Contributions to charities and religion, for example, are tax deductible. And secondly, voluntary associations have long been a major way that communities get important tasks done. They are easy to form and there are many more of them in the United States than in many other industrial countries (Schofer and Fourcade-Gourinchas, 2001). In France, they are objects of suspicion both by the state and by ordinary citizens as centers of corruption and particularistic (often unsavory) interests. Therefore, there are many barriers to forming voluntary groups and they are comparatively rarer. The state rather than such voluntary citizen groups is the main agent of society.

The ideology of Americanism, however, does not produce either a notion of social rights or of society as a collectivity with superordinate interests. Margaret Thatcher's comment on England also fits the United States. As prime minister, she asserted: "There is no such thing as society. There are only individuals and families." The only caveat is that in the United States even families are imagined as contractual entities. Only individuals have such primordial status (Varenne, 1977; see chap. 6).

Despite the prominence of religion and religiosity in American society, these features did not lead to collective representations that "we are all in the same boat" or that many social problems are so big that they require collective solutions. In part, this is because religious market competition that Stark (2005) chronicles undermined this prospect. Religions gain by "polishing their brand" and noting the differences, not by pushing for common solidarity. Similarly, voluntarism and individualism are not ideologies that produce such an understanding either. They simply commit individuals to short-term cooperation for the achievement of limited collective purposes. This kind of belief system instead is the basis for a social movement society.

CITIZENSHIP

The U.S. model of citizenship is distinctive. It is not based on descent or ethnicity, nor is it based on a state-based territorial arrangement and civic culture. Instead, it is rooted in adherence to a loose nondenominational civic religion (Bellah, 1975). Historically America had few requirements for entry and for becoming a citizen. Place of birth, ancestry, and culture were not among them. Disease and criminality were the main disqualifiers. This changed in 1922 when Congress introduced quotas that favored Western Europeans. Even now with anti-immigrant fever spreading and tougher eligibility rules to become prospective citizens, the actual tests for citizenship in the United States are much easier than in Europe. The tests are designed to favor inclusion. Following five years of legal residence in the United States, prospective citizens must pass a civics exam and a written and spoken English test. On the civics test, test takers must answer six out of ten questions on U.S. government correctly to pass. Recently, 92 percent of those who took the civics test passed it in 2014 (Christian Science Monitor, 2011). On the English test, one must (1) write down one to three sentences in English that are given in an oral interview; (2) read aloud one to three sentences provided by the interviewer; and (3) talk with the interviewer in English about the information on your application. There are exemptions for disability and for people over age fifty. By all accounts, the required English test is extremely easy compared to required language tests in European countries and Canada.

By contrast, the tests for citizenship that are required in Germany, Denmark, Canada, and much of Europe are designed to be exclusionary. Recently, for example, Denmark has designed new written tests for prospective citizens. They are so difficult that most Danes could not pass them. Over two thirds of the immigrants who took the test failed it in the most recent testing.[1] When questioned about the test, the Danish integration minister said that being Danish is "very special" and that "citizenship is something you have to earn."

Germany exhibits a similar pattern of exclusion. Until recently (1999) German ancestry was a requirement of citizenship. Now prospective citizens must pass difficult tests requiring high levels of competence in both the German language and German culture (Kamens, 2012: 179). Since local governments administer the tests for citizenship, this often means that questions are asked regarding a person's cultural practices, such as treatment of women. Some answers may disqualify a person for citizenship because the practices admitted to are "un-German."

Formal cultural literacy is less important in the United States as qualifying one for citizenship. What is important is that prospective citizens accept the American creed. This is the civil religion the United States invented to represent its distinctive form of solidarity. It embodies accepted notions of what it means to be an American.

THE AMERICAN CREED

Robert Bellah (Bellah and Tipton, 2006) and many others have noted that the United States evolved a civil religion that promoted a diffuse solidarity. For example, according to a recent Pew Research poll, Americans are much more comfortable with the idea that diversity "in our country makes it a better place to live" than are Europeans (Drake and Poushter, 2016). But consistent with other American traditions, Americanism is a highly individualistic and populist religion, based on Protestant folk epistemology that fused into a diffuse civil religion.

An important part of the American creed is disavowal of ideas of a natural leadership elite. American civil religion does not include visions of a sacralized leader or guardian caste viewed as having special knowledge and capacities (Eisenstadt, 1987). The Calvinist idea of predestination and an "elect" of the saved quickly crumbled in Massachusetts and led to the slow decline of Puritanism (Bailyn, 1967). Other ideologies that featured elitism also died lingering deaths. Any lingering Federalist notion of an elite educated ruling class (a natural aristocracy) was demolished by the Jacksonian Revolution of the 1830s (Schudson, 1998a; Meacham, 2008).

Built into this ideology was the "cult of the common man" (Tocqueville, 1945; Kluckhohn, 1958). This view lent populism important legitimacy as a theory of the role of the public in the polity. And it provided support for both an extension of the franchise to those without property and later to many other groups. This theory of society has also led to popular attacks on other aspects of the polity viewed as undemocratic, such as the selection of political leaders by political parties and the electoral college.

High valorization of the "common man" also meant that popular opinion was given important weight. Anti-intellectualism, as an aspect of anti-elitism, therefore became a key part of the American creed as well (Hofstadter, 1962, 1965). Attacks on science and scientific theories have been regular features of American political life, exemplified by the current antivaccination movement.

Anti-intellectualism follows from the anti-elitist narrative of society. Ideas that are not conventional stir suspicion because there is no legitimate space in society for people who are different or think differently than others (Meyer and Roth, 1970). Babbittry thus holds sway. Unpopular ideas arouse antagonism and accusations of "thinking you're better than other people." This is particularly true in the political system, where economic interests often coincide with egalitarian culture. Accounts of global warming, the dangers of tobacco, and intimations of pacifism have all been met with hostility, derision, and calculated disbelief. Anti-intellectualism has also provoked attacks on scientists and science as well as efforts to defund scientific research on some issues, such as gun violence and climate change. Political attacks on teachers and intellectuals for political beliefs have also been common (e.g., Lazarsfeld and Thielens, 1958).

Another feature of the creed is the idea that progress comes from collective social action. In this view citizens, not the state, are responsible for building a Christian civilization on Earth. Such emphasis put a premium on civic morality and the religious nature of the polity. While no one religion could have priority, religiosity of some kind was a moral duty (Thomas, 1989). The United States has defined itself as one nation "under God." Furthermore, as Max Weber ([1922] 1963) stated, nineteenth-century Americans regarded sectarian membership as evidence of good character.

Religion was important because creating the millennial society required moral citizens who would create moral institutions to bring this transformation about. Given its anti-elitist stance, American society required appropriately indoctrinated citizens to carry out the task of building a Christian civilization on Earth. Evangelical religion was a major carrier of this ideology in the nineteenth century, and its influence crossed all Protestant denominational boundaries (Thomas, 1989: 68ff). Society was to be a continuing revitalization movement aimed at eradicating social evils and converting sinners. And for this purpose, revivalism brought with it a variety of social innovations aimed at creating the millennial society.

Foremost among these innovations was the common school. Education was to induct students into Americanism and give them the tools to enact citizen roles. Besides moral education and religious training, there was a strong emphasis on literacy and counting. Schools devoted much effort to teaching arithmetic and literacy since both were deemed important skills in a society run by ordinary citizens (P. Cohen, 1982). One way to measure progress in this view was to count. Numerical counts of everything from the number of drunks and prostitutes to the number of safe births became important evidence of progress or the lack of it in towns, cities, and counties in nineteenth-century America (P. Cohen, 1982). Reading was also important because it opened access to the Bible and other moral literature. Like numeracy, it was also useful in commerce.

Many other institutions were born under the influence of revival religion, all of them efforts to reform and revitalize American society. This included the establishment of Sunday schools and public schooling for all children, temperance movements, societies for the abolition of slavery, juvenile courts, antiprostitution societies, and shelters for abused women (T. Smith, *Revivalism*, 1957).[2]

Civil religion also helped define the mission of the nation as millennial. It was to be a "redeemer nation" that would show the world how to cultivate the "garden" and lead the world out of the "wilderness" (Tuveson, 1968; Howe, 1965). Theological opinion differed as to whether this would happen in this world or the next (Thomas, 1989). Nevertheless, this ideology put a strong premium on revitalizing American society as a model for the world. And it produced a wave of reform movements bent on establishing God's kingdom on Earth (T. Smith, *Revivalism*, 1957). The temperance movement, abolition, prison reform, and a variety of other reform movements flourished as efforts to revitalize American society.

The creed also built in millennial aspirations vis-à-vis the larger world. Reconstructing other societies such as the Philippines and Cuba by force (Mann, 2012) became an appropriate goal and policy under this construction. In this view, America had a moral duty to spread its institutions and faith across the world. American missionaries, for example, were active and prominent throughout the third world, trying not only to convert souls but also to reconstruct the societies they lived in. These missions were privately supported by individual denominations but were generally lauded as moral enterprises. These millennial instincts are still with us in the ideology and policies that have led to "incoherent empire" (Mann, 2005). Proponents of interventions in Vietnam, Iraq, and Afghanistan have often cited nation building and the responsibility to spread democracy among their justifications.

While the United States was founded as a religious enterprise, it was also a business venture. Frontier capitalism became part of the creed. Virginia, for example, started as a business organization and developed into a society (Diamond, 1958). The whole point of British colonization was to establish economic and political dominance in the new world. This was to be accomplished by chartered groups of entrepreneurs, supported where possible by the British army and navy. Capitalist culture is, therefore, part of the American creed.

A key feature of the American creed is laissez-faire capitalism that valorizes individual effort and property rights. The creed put great emphasis on individual rationality and the conquest of nature. Both are prized as goals and also as moral duties. This view of society led to support for voluntarism in the economy and elsewhere. It also instilled in the public a belief in the inviolability of contracts and property rights. Underlying these doctrines was a materialist view of societal success and individual worth. These ideas developed in the nineteenth century under the canopy of evangelical Protestantism (see Thomas, 1989). The result was a polity built around individualism and property rights. Religiosity and materialism were conjoined in the creed.

The fusion of religion and secular ideology gave capitalism American style enormous sanction.[3] Religious revivalism provided an important source of legitimacy by defining the nation as a community of individualistic strivers, whose efforts and moral discipline would make the nation a "garden in the wilderness" (Thomas, 1989; Howe, 1965). Religion thereby transformed capitalism from a purely economic doctrine into a potent moral one in which individual economic effort and free markets commanded religious sanction.[4]

CONSEQUENCES OF AMERICAN CIVIL RELIGION

One important consequence of having the sense of Americanism grounded in a diffuse ideology rather than an ethnic community or a territorial state is that the boundaries of who is a legitimate American can become blurred, particularly in times of conflict. During World Wars I and II, for example, those of German descent were suspected of disloyalty and often harassed. In World War II the federal government interned (read imprisoned) much of the Japanese population on the West Coast. Currently, there is a campaign to stigmatize immigrants as dangers to society, particularly if they are Hispanic or Muslim.

American nationalism has two contrasting sides: (1) an openness to immigrants and a willingness to accept and integrate them into society, and (2) a deep fear of "others" because they might be a source of "un-American" narratives and values (Judt and Snyder, 2012: 325). Historically the political system has oscillated between these perspectives. When faced with geopolitical threats, or perceptions of them, politicians have often used fear of immigrants as "un-American" to stir popular anger. During these periods, the fear of being an outsider also drives natives to strive for public conformity to avoid the taint of association with such un-American sentiments.

The recent Trump campaign is just one example of how nativism is used by movements and enacted by ordinary citizens.[5] Any communal identity can become suspect if it is based on unpopular ideas. Majorities of the U.S. population, for example, still view Mormons and Mormonism with suspicion. Islam and atheism face the same stigma of being alien and "un-American" (Putnam and Campbell, 2010). Large sectors of the public have also defined socialism as an alien ideology. Such views have led to the persecution of people espousing these views both by their neighbors and sometimes by the state itself, acting in response to populist pressure.

The narratives of agency contained in the creed have also had consequences for the political system considered broadly. We discuss the most important ones next.

A. The Paucity of Ideological Alternatives[6]

Under these doctrines of nationhood and statehood, the historic suspicion of government has reigned without competitors. This gave way to eighteenth- and nineteenth-century philosophies of "boycotting government" (R. Williams, 1997), "nullification" (Mann, 2012), and the nineteenth-century ideal of limited government. The result was an early amalgam of laissez-faire, Social Darwinism, and religion, contested partly by a secondary more "liberal" social gospel (e.g., R. Williams, 1997). The United States became a classic liberal polity (Hartz, 1955).

The "American creed" (Myrdal, 1944; Lipset, 1963, 1996) became dominant largely because of the *absence* of more collectivist representations—for example, various ideas of corporatism and socialisms. American leaders viewed old-world models as threats to freedom and popular democracy (e.g., Lipset, 1963; Mann, 2012). Both Catholicism and Judaism, for example, were suspect because elites and the public viewed them as harboring more collectivist views of society. Unions, political radicalism, and a rebellious working class were some of the outcomes associated with what elites regarded as "un-American" belief systems. The presidential campaign slogan "Rum, Romanism and Rebellion" in the 1884 presidential campaign epitomizes this fear of the negative impacts of both religious and ethnic collectivism.

The public also rejected some attempted elitisms like the Whig notion of a natural aristocracy. In addition, the absence of a labor party or a strong labor-farmer alliance meant that such alternative conceptions had little sustained social basis of support.

There are secondary traditions that partly contest or modify the dominant liberal tradition, but arguably they do not displace it (Timothy Smith, 1957). The labor movement, the populist movements in the Midwest, and the New Deal articulated more distinctively collectivist views of the role of the state in society and the rights of groups such as labor as opposed to individuals. But business and other elites have hotly contested these ideas. As a result they never became commonly taken-for-granted assumptions about how society should, or does, work. Egalitarian movements have also been prominent (Wilentz, 2016), but these did not contest the basic organization of society. They were generally reformist in their stance to societal organization.

The widespread acceptance of this credo as the "American way of life" severely limits the space for alternative ideologies.[7] While this civil religion has provided a basis for social solidarity, it has not supported strategies for collective action. One result is that the United States is devoid of conflicts common in Europe between secular versus clerical factions; socialists versus Tories; Christian Social Democrats versus left-wing labor parties; and so on.

On the other hand, this narrative provides little support for the idea of a competent state as an independent agent to act on behalf of the nation. It frames collective action as the result of individuals uniting voluntarily with others to produce common strategies and solutions to problems. This is the logic of a social movement society.

B. The Lack of Secular versus Religious Conflict

The lack of an official state supported religion also produced a culture in which there is little division between secular and religious groups in the polity. While conflict between religions has been common, anticlericalism has not. With no established church linked to the state, there is no central target for anti-religious or anti-statist sentiment. Furthermore, given the hegemony of religion in the culture, there has been little room for political parties or social movements that attack organized religion in the name of secularism. Until recently, the bulk of the population claimed a religious affiliation, and the proportion of atheists in the population remains historically low, currently around 5 percent (Putnam and Campbell, 2010; Pew Research Center, 2014).

C. Anti-Elitism, Populism, and Conformity

Egalitarianism acclaims the virtues of the "common man" as opposed to elites. It empowers the "people." The result historically has been a groundswell of grassroots organizational activity and movements. The lack of strong national elites has leveled the playing field for organized economic and social activity. The narrative of voluntarism legitimates it. Voluntary associations thus proliferate. All studies since Tocqueville have pointed to the ubiquity of voluntary associations in the United States (Schofer and Fourcade-Gourinchas, 2001; Curtis, Grebb, and Baer, 1992; Curtis, Baer, and Grebb, 2001). The society has also generated numerous social movements (Meyer and Tarrow, 1998). They are a major source of change in the absence of strong governmental institutions. Many of these movements are anti-elitist in ideology and purpose.

Populism supports associational activity because it endows individuals as agents of society. But the same ethos and institutional structure that promotes social movements also sanctions pervasive attitudinal conformity. Under egalitarianism no group has the standing to be different (see Meyer and Roth, 1970; Hofstadter, 1962). Meritocracy is lauded primarily for the practical benefits it produces in agriculture and manufacturing. And science is appreciated and supported because of its association with technology. But public rejection occurs when it leads to questioning either religious or social conventions. Darwinism, for instance, was historically problematic on religious grounds. It still is among large sectors of conservatives and evangelicals (Froese and Bader, 2010). Similarly, science is often rejected when it suggests that collective action is needed to deal with the external effects of corporate activities, such as pollution and climate change (Gauchat, 2012). Hofstadter (1965) noted this characteristic of American society and called it "backwoods paranoia."

Tocqueville (1945) made similar observations. He observed that while everyone in America was opinionated, the range of opinions was narrow indeed. He believed the source of this pattern was the community peer pressure that equality produced. There were no institutions like Catholicism, socialist political parties, or an aristocracy to support dissonant social and political beliefs. Political equality generated a public opinion that was homogeneous and intolerant of deviant ideas in many realms (Meyer and Roth, 1970). One was left to the conventional judgments of local peer groups. Like Japan, the nail in the American public that stood too tall was hammered down by local public opinion. It was safer to adopt the strategy of conformity, masked by trivial differences.

D. Status Politics and Revitalization Movements

Social movements often become the vehicles of agency and social change in modern societies. But one of the unusual features of American society comparatively is that many of these movements in the United States take the form of revitalization movements aimed at purifying society at large rather than as policy-targeted movements (Beer, 1971; Shefter, 1977). American movements often have ideologies that are diffuse. And many define opponents as members of larger elites who are "corrupting" society. President Andrew Jackson, for example, saw banks and bankers as such threats and denounced them in his farewell address (Commager, 1960: 98). In the ideologies of these movements opponents are often demonized as traitors or representatives of greed and/or other forms of immorality.

One consequence is that such movements turn normal politics into a zero-sum game. Hence, Seymour Lipset (1963), Richard Hofstadter (1962), and others coined the term *status politics* to describe these movements. And they have been a constant feature of American political life (Meyer and Roth, 1970; Hofstadter, 1965). Given the zero-sum nature of the demands often made by such movements, they tend to generate polarized politics. The result is that a good deal of nonrational discourse and scapegoating flourishes around them. Conspiracy theories are common since these movements are intent on locating sources of evil they believe must be eradicated. To outsiders they have a paranoid character (Hofstadter, 1965). Placing the blame for imagined societal evil also becomes an important part of the mission. Scapegoating is common, and the targets picked are frequently too weak to effectively fight back against such organized politics, for example, the "witches" in Salem; welfare recipients in the 1980s, and university professors in the 1950s (Lazarsfeld and Thielens, 1958).

Wuthnow (1980) has argued that these movements are often responses to globalization. The increasing penetration of economic markets and political institutions in societies creates "winners" and "losers" within societies. Two kinds of movements emerge in these circumstances. The "winners" in this contest often develop reform movements that attempt to accommodate global challenges. They want to incorporate society into the larger world that has engineered these changes in local institutions. Such movements are reformist, aimed at incorporating society into the wider world society by reconstructing it from within. The antislavery movement in the nineteenth century is one such example. Slavery had become a global issue in the West. Religious movements in the United States were intent on cleansing American society of this scourge as the British had done earlier. The purpose was to align U.S. institutions with those of other civilized countries.

The "losers" are likely to reject these models of society altogether in favor of radical alternatives. These movements are reactive, opting out of the world order altogether rather than trying to incorporate themselves within the existing society and world order. Historically utopian religious movements and minority religions in the United States tried this option by withdrawing from the wider society to create a purer alternative within it, for example, the Shakers, Oneida Colony, and Brook Farm. The Nation of Islam under Elijah Muhammad also tried this strategy in the 1950s and 1960s as a response to American racism. It envisioned a black nation featuring his version of Islam as its religion, carved out of the old Southern states.

U.S. populist traditions are strong breeding grounds for such movements. American anti-elitism and the weakness of the center creates an ecology favorable to such movements in moments of crisis. The religious and millennial character of American society also adds plausibility to the purposes and intent of such groups. These factors have aided the emergence and legitimacy of such groups.

SUBNATIONAL CULTURES: COMPETITORS TO NATIONALISM

One of the cultural problems that the United States faced historically was the difficulty of developing a common "imagined community" in the presence of many regional and ethnic cultures. There have been fierce debates throughout U.S. history over whether this is a multicultural nation or a melting pot (Mirel, 2010). But nationalist imagery of the nation has always been complicated by the fact that there have always been many subnational social identities and imageries that were often as powerful as national ones.

This fact has led to recurring contests and crises in American political development over conceptions of nationhood. Regionalism, sectionalism, and states' rights (essentially regional party systems and political cultures) have all been viewed as foundational to the American polity. A recurring question has been: in what sense is the United States a nation (Huntington, 1968; Dahl, 1971)?

The Civil War resolved only part of this issue. It ruled out the idea that the nation was a contract among otherwise sovereign states who could voluntarily nullify the contract at will. But it did not resolve the other issues of regionalism, sectionalism, or states as contestants for primacy in the popular imagery of the nation. These alternative loyalties diminished the sense of nationhood. Regions, states, and localities have historically proudly hailed their distinctive histories, cultures, and ways of life.

However, the importance of these regional differences has lessened. After World War II regional differences, while still important, diminished (J. Freeman, 2012: 24). The war had subordinated local loyalties and differences to larger national ones. In addition, World War II brought a sense of common purpose and a renewed feeling of confidence after a long depression. It ushered in a period of optimism, confidence, and trust—what has come to be known as the "civic culture" (Almond and Verba, 1963). While this culture was short-lived, the changes that produced it have undermined regional cultures and produced a national cult commonly known as the "American way of life."

Race, ethnicity, and religion have also subsided as sources of imagery of nationhood, especially among younger age cohorts. The idea that the United States is a white, Protestant nation is losing ground. Both demography and the culture of the nation are changing, as secular trends increase and religion itself becomes highly rationalized around individual and societal goals. As a result, individual diversity and ethnic pluralism have become prominent descriptions of society, though these ideas are still contested. The imagery of a melting pot has given way to the idea of the nation as a mosaic of cultures that are merged into a national one—"patriotic pluralism" is Mirel's (2010) description of the evolving outcome.

The downside of this development is that it has undermined national unity by championing the idea that the United States is composed of many distinctive communities with their own cultures. The public image that all Americans share a common culture with core values has declined, giving way to views of a society racked with conflict (see Chapter 10).

RECENT COMPARATIVE EVIDENCE

This section asks whether this exceptionalism is currently evident in the attitudes of American citizens compared to those from other democracies in Western Europe; the new nations of Eastern Europe; and for comparison purposes, the Islamic nation-states. If the major narratives about the American nation that we have described are still dominant, we should find that Americans' attitudes about the polity differ substantially from those of Western Europeans and others.

To do this we mined recent public opinion data from the 2005–2007 World Values Surveys of forty-five countries. Relevant data are available on twenty-five countries. We look at three issues: (1) the significance of religion as part of political culture, (2) citizen perceptions of the responsibilities of the state vis-à-vis society, and (3) views of economic opportunity and success. The question is, is the United States exceptional on these dimensions?

The first issue is the significance of religion as part of political culture. The United States began as a religious (and business) enterprise. God and godliness were and are important parts of the national narrative. Much of the public expects political leaders to be religious and to sanction religiosity. The first issue concerns whether belief in God is a prerequisite for political leadership. The World Values surveys asked respondents to disagree or agree (on a five-point Likert scale) with the following statement: "Politicians who do not believe in God are unfit for public office." The results show that citizens in the United States agree with this statement more than other rich Western nations. For example, 38.5 percent of Americans agree or agree strongly with this statement compared to 11 percent of other Western democracies, including Catholic countries. Eastern Europeans, however, have a similar outlook to Americans: 42 percent support this requirement. Islamic societies are

TABLE 2.1 Data on American vs. Other Political Cultures: Means on 8 Items

Variables	USA	Rich Western Democracies	Eastern Europe	Islamic Nations
1. RELIGION:				
a. Deism	2.58	2.06	3.18	3.88
b. Clerical Influence	3.18	3.75	2.72	2.19
c. Pluralism I	2.57	1.96	2.11	2.25
d. Pluralism II	2.84	2.08	2.20	2.47
2. GOVERNMENT RESPONSIBILITY				
a. Help People vs. Self-Help	6.01	5.34	4.35	4.09
b. Income equality vs. Inequality	6.18	5.26	5.87	6.47
c. Private Sector vs. Public Sector	3.60	4.87	5.51	6.19
3. INDIVIDUALISM				
a. Hard Work vs. Luck/ Connections	3.87	4.64	4.66	3.55
N (nations)	1	10	8	6
N (people)	1,193	11,546	8,821	6,623

Source: World Values Survey, Wave 1 through Wave 5. www.worldvaluessurvey.org.

1. The multivariate tests for the equality of means, assuming equal variances, are significant in all cases at $p > .0000$. The means are therefore significantly different from one another.
2. The individual Ns vary slightly with each item.
3. The countries in the samples are:
* Rich Western Democracies: Italy, Spain, Canada, Australia, Norway, Sweden, Finland, Switzerland, Andorra, Germany
* Eastern Europe: Poland, Slovenia, Bulgaria, Romania, Ukraine, Serbia, Moldova, Georgia
* Islamic Nations: Turkey, Indonesia, Egypt, Morocco, Jordan, Malaysia

the outliers: 69 percent of their populations assent to this statement. The Scandinavian countries, on the other hand, are the outliers in the West. Only 6 percent of their populations agree with this statement. And even in Catholic Italy and Spain, only 12 percent and 11 percent agree with this proposition, respectively. In the West, the United States is the outlier.

The next metric deals with popular beliefs about the separation of church and state—a key American belief. It asks respondents' agreement with the following statement, using a five-point Likert scale: "It would better for (my country) if more people with strong religious beliefs held public office." The data show that Americans are a little more skeptical of this proposition than other rich Western democracies. For example,

57 percent of Americans agree with this statement compared to 63 percent of Western Europeans. The difference is small but significant.

Two points are important. First, majorities in the United States favor religion as a support of democracy. But Americans are a little more skeptical of the idea of endorsing a specific religion. It is arguable that in the context of religious pluralism, large sectors of the public feel that injecting religion overtly into politics is dangerous, since it raises the question of whose religious beliefs will dominate. For example, Frank Bruni, a *New York Times* columnist, argues that distancing religion from politics is "not an affront to the faithful. It's actually more respectful of religion than not, because letting the government and its servants go too far in celebrating one religion over others creates the possibility of looking up someday to find that the religion being promoted isn't your own" (Bruni, 2012).

In mono-religious cultures in Western Europe the main divide is between the secular population and those who hold to the dominant religion. Many of these states have official religions. The idea of political elites being overt about their religious beliefs seems less troubling to public opinion there[8] than in the United States.

American pluralism also reduces public support for religious elites participating directly in politics or in government decision making. The surveys asked respondents to respond to the following statement (Item 3 in Table 2.1): "Religious leaders should *not* influence how people vote in elections." Item 4 asks respondents to respond to the following statement: "Religious leaders should *not* influence government decisions." Contemporary Americans are more skeptical on both of these issues than their European peers (as the higher means of Americans indicates). For example, 38.7 percent of U.S. respondents agree with the first statement compared to 11.4 percent of Western Europeans. And 49.2 percent in the United States agree with the second statement compared to 13.8 percent of their European peers.[9]

On the issue of the role of the state, the American public has quite different perceptions of the state's responsibilities than all other groups. Item 5 asks about the role of the state. Low scores indicate respondents who agreed with the following statement: "The government should take more responsibility to ensure that everyone is provided for." Higher scores indicate support for the following belief: "People should take more responsibility for themselves." The American *mean* on this item is significantly higher than that of all other groups. And Americans also tend to be more extreme on this than all others. Over 13 percent of Americans score 10 on this item versus an average of 5 percent for Western Europeans, Eastern Europeans, and members of Islamic societies.[10] Americans endorse self-help rather than government action on issues such as poverty.

Americans are also more individualistic and less enthusiastic about state policy when it comes to income inequality. The ten-point scale for Item 6 states: "Incomes should be made more equal" (1) versus "We need larger income differences as incentives for individual effort" (10). The American mean of 6.18 is significantly higher than that of Western Europeans and Eastern Europeans. Only Islamic societies believe that more inequality would be better for society (a mean of 6.47).[11]

Americans are also more addicted to *private sector* rather than public sector growth. Item 7 asked respondents to respond to the following statements: "Private ownership of business and industry should be increased" vs."Government ownership of business and industry should be increased." Again a ten-point scale was employed, with 10 being extreme support for government sector growth. The American mean on this item is significantly lower than that of all other groups.[12] Americans *distrust* government action in the economy more than all three other groups of nationals.

Not surprisingly, ex-socialist countries and the developing countries of the Islamic world are highly favorable to public sector growth. So is Western Europe. Socialist narratives there have had an impact on public opinion despite the spread of neoliberalism. Americans, to the contrary, are very suspicious of public sector growth and a large state.

The last issue concerns the narrative of individualism as a source of success. Item 8 consists of the following two statements: "In the long run, hard work usually brings a better life" versus "Hard work doesn't generally bring success—it's more a matter of luck and connections." A ten-point scale was employed, with 10 being extreme support for the role of luck and connections. The American mean is significantly lower than that of Western European—and Eastern European—publics. And there is more convergence in the United States around this mean.[13]

This evidence indicates that there are significant continuities in political culture that distinguish the United States from Western European, Eastern European, and Islamic societies. The low variance around the means in the American case also suggests that the U.S. public is now "tainted with ideology," contrary to Philip Converse's classic suggestion. These narratives of how society works—and should work—are in fact ideologies. They describe both how people think American society works and ideals of how it should work. Clearly these attitudes describe an ideology of American exceptionalism that is distinct from those of Western Europeans and those in Eastern Europe. Large parts of the American creed are still intact.

The prevalence of these narratives assigns a limited role to the state as a source of collective goals and action. The next chapter argues that the design of the American state embeds the state in society—a design that curtails and inhibits state action and makes for furtive policy making with little transparency.

CHAPTER 3

The Embedded State

THE AMERICAN CREED PERSISTS because elites have embedded these narratives of society and citizenship in law and in the state itself. While the structure of state and society have changed over time, these narratives have remained remarkably stable. The design of the state is therefore an aspect of American exceptionalism. As noted earlier, this design is based on distrust of government and anti-elitism.

DISTRUST OF GOVERNMENT AND EMBEDDEDNESS: UNITED STATES VERSUS FRANCE

Nineteenth-century conceptions of the American nation left little room for an activist state with authority over society. The main concern was to prevent *unwanted* government intervention in the public's private affairs. There was nothing wrong with government activism per se, but Americans objected to unsolicited government intervention in private affairs. They associated such action with tyranny (Dobbin, 1994: 35). They also regarded uncircumscribed private authority, exemplified by religious "tyranny," with suspicion.

The state at all levels in this view was to be the handmaiden of the nation. In the language of social science, the founders, reinforced by later developments, embedded the state in society, rendering its boundaries porous and its authority widely dispersed across national government, between states and the national government, and between states and local communities. The purpose was to severely limit government's independent authority and inhibit its activity. In S. E. Finer's (1970) telling expression, the American state is "self-stultifying." Americans know this and value limited government.

Like other natives, U.S. citizens learn the key narratives of society and facts about state accessibility by participating in it. American schoolchildren learn early on how embedded the state is in society. By observation of their parents' behavior, for example, they find out that participation in local civic organizations involved with schooling is an important way to improve schools and help with their funding. They learn this lesson at home and from the school itself via its plethora of student organizations and their own participation.

By contrast, French schoolchildren learn a different lesson. By participating with their teachers and parents in yearly national strikes against the National Ministry of Education and its local representatives, they learn that organizing nationally against the national ministry of education is the only effective way of changing local schools.

The point here is that different narratives of action embed different forms of participation in the structure of political institutions. The French are different because they learn different civic lessons in their daily lives (see E. Weber, 1979; Lamont, 1997; Prasad, 2005). They learn that the national state is the source of almost all local authority. Americans, on the other hand, learn that "all politics is local," with national authority embedded in a web of decentralized relationships involving the states, local communities, and citizen groups like school boards and citizen groups within communities.

They also learn that government officials and politicians have little insulation from the citizenry and must respond to citizen requests and complaints. And they know from observation that organized citizen action can easily penetrate all these units. No strong elite civil service stands between them and various agencies of state. The civic lesson they imbibe is that citizens who organize can compel government agencies to bargain with them; witness the student-led marches in early 2018 against gun violence and for gun control laws and the early effects of that organized effort in Florida.

French students learn that they must organize on a national level to have any effect. And furthermore, they know that the state must recognize their organizations as legitimate for them to have any standing to bargain. France is relatively hostile territory to citizen voluntary associations. The state is suspicious of them and citizens have learned to associate them with corruption and antisocial purposes, such as enabling religious elites to assert illicit public authority (Schofer and Fourcade-Gourinchas, 2001).

These differences between French and U.S. students are outcomes of variations in the design of their respective nation-states. One significant difference is the degree to which each polity embeds the state in society. Many have commented on the porous character of the American state and its many points of entry (e.g., Wilson, 1981). In rejecting European models of state and society, the founders built this characteristic into the design of the American state (Hartz, 1955; Lipset, 1963, 1996). France did not, and it remains a society where the state is an important, and relatively autonomous, actor.

AMERICAN STATE DESIGN

The purpose of this section is to show how exceptional the American state is because of its deep embeddedness in society. As the political scientist S. E. Finer (1970) observed, the founders designed the American state to be "self-inhibiting" in its ability to act, and "opaque" in terms of its processes. The upshot is that gridlock and lack of transparency are endemic (see Fiorina, 1996; Norris, 2017; Mettler, 2011). Legitimacy crises are also chronic features of American politics. Populist accusations that the state is either unresponsive to citizens or too overbearing in its behavior also create periodic crises and lead to support for insurgent third parties (Huntington, 1981; Rosenstone et al., 1996). Thus, the current wave of populism is not a new phenomenon, though its intensity and radical critique of all elites is new.

The Constitution sets out the design of the state in procedural terms, delineating the powers of various branches of government. It does not specify what government should or must do. Nor does it specify what rights citizens should expect of government, other than negative ones, for example, that the state should not abridge their freedoms of speech and religion. It also prescribes procedures for protecting these rights via legal redress or the threat of violence, for example, the second amendment and the right of states to develop a "well-regulated militia" to be used if the federal government oversteps its authority or if enslaved people or Native Americans threaten local white settlers.

It is a document compatible with a social movement society. The presumption is that if a large segment of society is in favor of some action, such as prohibition or abortion, the Constitution provides a blueprint of how to translate such sentiment into legislation. And it sets up the Supreme Court as the ultimate authority of what activities are or are not in accord with the Constitution. But it does not specify anything that government must do or specific substantive rights that citizens have, such as rights to health care or education. This is an important form of exceptionalism. The constitutions of Western Europe and even new nations in the third world typically specify such rights (Boli-Bennett, 1979). The newer the nation-state, the more formal rights (and duties) of citizens these documents confer, although these rights may not be implemented or protected in practice, such as access to medical care.

Another key point that many analysts have made about the American state is that its design is one that insures that *politics* outweighs governance and administration. This occurs because government infuses society. Banfield and Wilson (1963: 1) make this point emphatically: U.S. government "is permeated with politics. As they put it, "our constitutional structure and our traditions afford individuals manifold opportunities not only to bring their special interests to the attention of public officials but also—and this is the important thing—to *compel* officials to bargain and to make compromises. . . . There is virtually no sphere of 'administration' apart from politics." The traditional American polity was the quintessential representative of "politics" rather than "administration." This has changed but only by degree (see Chapter 6).

The following complaint about American government by Columbia University economist Jeffrey Sachs illustrates the preceding characterization of the American state:

Effective governments in well-run countries (such as Sweden, Norway and Singapore) prepare white papers, make plans, set targets, prepare medium-term budgets and create innovative new agencies to address novel problems like low carbon energy, efficient health care and lifelong education, and they do it with a strong sense of the power and positive contribution of private business which creates jobs, fosters innovation and pays taxes.[1]

The (U.S.) government is mostly led by appointees or elected officials with little technical knowledge, less management experience, and an expected job duration of a few years at most, often culminating in a lobbying position on K St. after leaving government. . . . The year 1981 was a milestone on the retreat from government. . . . We need to reinvigorate government for the 21st century (Jeffrey Sachs, *The Economist*, February 2–8, 2013: 64–66).

The point of American state design was to hobble and inhibit its action. S. E. Finer (1970), for example, calls the American state "self-stultifying." Others like Nettl (1968) view it as an exemplar of a weak state. Unlike European states, thanks to another aspect of this design, American state actors have little buffering from the demands of civil society. The boundaries of the state are porous at every level and there are many points of entry (J. Wilson, "The Rise," 1981). Furthermore, the state lacks an official cadre of managers who are autonomous from politics and have a distinctive esprit de corps and culture (Heclo, 1977; Aberbach et al., 1981).

Checks and balances that disperse veto power widely, across both government agencies and other actors, including the public, limit all authority. The result is that there are many points at which influential veto groups can exercise influence to change, challenge, or demand legislative initiatives or bureaucratic policy making. Influential business folk or other constituents routinely vet proposed legislation. And lobbyists for these groups often help write it.

The U.S. state is also exceptional compared to its European counterparts in its frequent inability to act or to effectively monitor and administer programs and policies that it does establish. Frequent gridlock at both the state and national level inhibits the ability of states to initiate policy or programs at all (Fiorina, 1996).

Interested constituencies can actively resist effective monitoring of established programs in terms of usual accounting standards: needs, costs, and the distribution of benefits. This has been true of both the military-industrial sector and of corporate subsidies in general. The openness of government has allowed important constituencies to capture regulatory agencies set up to monitor them and to develop strong congressional support through a variety of strategies to undermine effective policing of their behavior (Friedberg, 2000). This has been common throughout American history (Weinstein, 1968).

THE HIDDEN STATE: INVISIBLE
PROCESSES AND OUTCOMES

While the design effectively restrains state action, unless requested, it has had another consequence as well. The widespread distrust of the state institutionalized in society has led state actors to shroud their actions from public visibility.

Many observers describe U.S. policy making as "furtive" and opaque (Finer, 1970; Mettler, 2011). Its processes are frequently invisible to the public and to many in government itself. And the outcomes are often baffling. Individual members of Congress, for example, often do not know the detailed content of the legislation that they voted on, such as the recent tax law lowering income taxes on corporations and the rich. These tendencies are chronic and nonaccidental, though the current polarization of politics has arguably accentuated these tendencies.

Social scientists have argued that this pattern of decoupling processes and outcomes often is an organizational strategy for dealing with uncertainty or legitimacy crises. It obscures the links between rules, the authority system, and results (Meyer and Rowan, 1977). Decision makers then judge managers and entire agencies based on conformity to bureaucratic regulations, rather than their effectiveness at accomplishing goals. In fact, the goals themselves may be so diffuse as to defy clear operational directives for their accomplishment. In some cases, this happens because the means to accomplish goals are uncertain, such as increasing student test scores. In other cases, it is a way to sidestep controversy among conflicting factions. In defying transparency, all parties can claim success because subordinates adhered to standards of performance, such as bureaucratic rules of procedure, without having to consider whether their activities produced concrete achievements.

Action by the expanded American state frequently depends on decoupling process from outcomes. For example, legislators who believe that the public will not accept tax cuts for the wealthy or health care legislation that requires all to be insured have strong incentives to decrease transparency and obscure the real contents of legislation. Witness the late 2017 tax bill. Once the bill passed, the system requires no review of the link between the policy and its actual results. Popular ideology, rather than evidence, drives the public narrative about its effectiveness.

The problem is that alternative processes of governing require a good deal of confidence and trust among those involved. They require public trust and confidence in the expertise of politicians and civil servants to effectively conduct the public's business. And they also require clear lines of authority between agencies and trust among them. These conditions do not exist in the United States and have currently gotten worse. For example, much of the public believes that running government well takes little more than average common sense, and little training or experience. This was historically part of the logic of the spoils system of government (Shefter, 1977). It continues as attitude research shows and the current wave of radical populism demonstrates. This is the American creed in action. Furthermore, low levels of rationalization of authority between agencies undermines trust among agencies and the public. "Iron triangles" and bureaucratic infighting are so common that constituents require high-priced guides like policy operatives (often former members of Congress) and lawyers to get them through these labyrinths.

Indeed, the design of the state *compels* government at all levels to negotiate and bargain with citizens and other constituencies over legislative outcomes, a process that suggests faith in the democratic process but ultimately renders rational outcomes and transparent procedures even more unlikely (Banfield and Wilson, 1963: 1, chap. 2). Much lawmaking therefore involves citizen groups and lobbyists negotiating the outlines of bills with legislators and cooperating in writing the bill itself. This process generates enormous possibilities for conflict and zero-sum games among participants. It incentivizes legislators to paper over these disagreeable realities to make the bill acceptable to the public.

One way to accomplish this is to decouple the purposes of legislation from the means to achieve them. Those claiming to fix the health care system, for example, may accept in the ultimate legislative package a set of funding mechanisms that are inadequate for, or even irrelevant to, these purposes. Success therefore requires a good deal of effort to obscure these conflicts through outright secrecy and lack of transparency. Legislators themselves are often unaware of the contents of legislation and simply follow the lead of their staffs and party leaders in voting.

The point is that the *hidden welfare state* is an endogamous feature of the U.S. polity. It is a form of decoupling that has emerged to resolve the persistent legitimacy crisis that big government faces (Meyer and Rowan, 1977). The solution to government's lack of legitimation has been to make its decision making and consequent legislative outcomes less visible to the public. This is one major source of the disconnect that many have noted and that populists have seized on as their issue (Crenson and Ginsberg, 2004).

Congressional lawmaking is a case in point. Congress often passes legislation that is vague in principles and instructions. Lawmakers fill the bills with hundreds of pages of detailed specifications to address the complaints of many actors. This forces administrative agencies to iron out the details of federal regulations in bargaining sessions with those subject to the regulations. Agencies, and their inevitable constituencies, must then clarify and codify the specific intent of the legislation.

The resulting legal complexity often papers over inherent conflicts. This generates lengthy legislation, another major difficulty. Given the length of bills and the speed with which legislative teams must rush them through the U.S. Government Printing Office so Congress can read and vote on them, sloppy language and errors proliferate. For instance, the recent Dodd-Frank bill regulating the finance and banking industries is two thousand pages long. Errors of language give opponents grounds to contest the legislation or major parts of it in court. For example, both Obamacare and the Clean Power Act now face court tests because of such issues.

Given the length of these documents, individual members of Congress also typically do not know all the provisions of legislation or even the most salient ones. Nor are they privy to the detailed negotiations between agencies and the industries subject to their authority. Members of Congress can thus claim to have done something about a problem, while leaving much of the actual lawmaking to negotiations between federal agencies, industry lobbyists, and other constituencies. The same members of Congress can later decry parts, or all, of the ensuing administrative interpretations of the bill if they disagree with them. This is a common spectacle in American politics—Congress passes legislation and then members later denounce its specific provisions, by claiming that this was not their intent.

As a result, Byzantine policy processes and nontransparency reign. The government acts like a Rube Goldberg machine to all but insiders, and policy mystification prevails. When polarization between political parties intensifies, so does lack of transparency. The debate on the new Republican tax overhaul is an extreme example of this point. Republicans negotiated the bill in secret, holding no public meetings with expert testimony. The bill is quite long, running five hundred pages, and filled with last-minute loopholes designed to entice the votes of reluctant senators. Most legislators saw the written version only a few days before the scheduled vote. Given the combination of rush and secrecy, moreover, no agency had time to score the bill. Such rushed production too often leads to errors, prompting subsequent litigation. There were also no credible figures on who benefits and whose taxes will increase, and on how much it will cost in terms of an increased deficit. Much of this procedure was purposive so the bill would pass with an all-Republican majority in both houses.

Other examples of the Byzantine character of government are numerous and include the nontransparent and policy-overloaded tax system (Bartlett, 2011; 2012), evasive fiscal policy generally, mystification of core policies (e.g., Social Security), underacknowledged corporate welfare and "socialism for the rich," and citizen unawareness of government benefits that they are eligible for or are receiving (Mettler, 2011). Most people also have little idea of their own or others' federal tax rate.[2]

Citizen mystification of government action is a major product of this design. For example, when Cornell University political scientist Suzanne

Mettler (2011) asked a sample of 1,400 people whether they had ever used a government program 57 percent said they had not.[3] When she read off a list of twenty-one programs and asked the question again, 96 percent reported that yes, they had used a government program. These included the student loan program, home mortgage interest deduction, Medicare, Social Security, public housing, and food stamps.

While people value these programs, many do not even associate them with government. This finding partially reflects the fact that once established, citizens do not think of these benefits as government programs. They become cherished rights that governments are not supposed to alter. One of the favorite Tea Party movement chants, for example, was "Do Not Touch My Medicare" (Skocpol and Williamson, 2012).

One consequence of the mystification of government is that recent generations have learned not to associate benefits and collective goods with government. This is a new development. The generations who experienced the Great Depression and World War II had positive views of government action to solve collective problems like poverty (Putnam, 2000; Janowitz, 1983).

LACK OF COST CONTROL AND ACCOUNTABILITY

Because politics invades all aspects of government, American government programs are frequently more expensive than those of European states and are often less effective in terms of outcomes. Constraints on U.S. government hinder efforts to control costs and ensure that legislation achieves intended outcomes. Cost control, evaluation, and monitoring are often weak, for example, in military spending, Medicare, and federal taxation. The Internal Revenue Service, for example, has the fewest tax collectors per capita of any major country.[4]

The fact that attention to *politics* outweighs governance in the United States is a direct result of the embeddedness of the state in society and the ability of organized groups to penetrate government and demand voice. Effective administration and cost control are therefore secondary issues. Polarization arguably accentuates this problem in a system that tends to gridlock. Getting the votes to pass legislation is often so difficult that it entails adding many amendments to a bill that industry and other constituency lobbyists want. These add unknown costs and may divert benefits from those that lawmakers pledged to help.

President George W. Bush's effort to include prescription drug coverage for seniors in part D of Medicare in 2003 provides a strong object lesson. The proposal represented the largest expansion of Medicare in history, and many fiscally conservative Republicans hesitated to sign on. But when bill sponsors amended the bill, allowing hospitals to appeal the rate (determined by the labor costs in a hospital's geographic area) at which Medicare reimburses them, they secured the votes of enough holdouts. The new provision gave the executive branch considerable discretion in granting and determining the size of the increase. Researchers have found that hospitals in districts represented by a Republican member of Congress who voted for the bill were seven times more likely to have a waiver request granted than those in districts of members who voted against it. They further found that hospitals used the extra cash, at least partially, to give big pay increases to hospital CEOs. In cost terms, these accommodations necessitated spending an extra $1.25 billion, 25 percent more than originally allocated for these hospitals. In addition, there was no evidence of improved quality of care or medical outcomes. But legislators in later years who were in districts with such hospitals did see a 65 percent increase in campaign donations from the health care sector.[5]

Passage of a bill, however, is not the end of the process. Bargaining over its implementation ensues between government agencies conducting oversight and the industries or interests involved. In the process of bargaining over their enforcement, interest groups tend to capture their respective monitoring agencies. Business interests often successfully dominate inspection/evaluation processes. This can alter the intent of legislation or lead to avoidance of effective program evaluation altogether, such as Pentagon spending. This has been a persistent feature of American government at all levels historically (Weinstein, 1968). For example, defense industries often operate on cost-plus contracts with few controls and no external evaluation of results (Friedberg, 2000: 9–34, 81ff). One result is unnecessary or defective weapons systems like the F-35 fighter jet or the M-16 rifle used in Vietnam that tended to jam in battle situations. Another result is lack of budgetary restraint due to the lack of external controls.

The invisibility of government simultaneously produces unacknowl-edged or *hidden* successes. These are programs that work but remain sub-merged from public view. Examples include Head Start, Save the Children, Medicare; the GI Bill and the GED exam, student loan programs and Pell grants, and the Federal Deposit Insurance Corporation.

The opaqueness of government makes it difficult to pinpoint responsi-bility for both good and bad legislation and decision making. The result is that it is hard for politicians and the public to separate the successes from the failures on grounds other than political ideology.

One consequence is widespread cynicism about government. Good de-cisions and programs as well as bad ones seem to be a matter of chance, not concrete choices made by specified elected officials or agencies. When things go badly, the public's response tends toward throwing all incum-bents out and turning government over to neophytes with no or little experience. Another remedy often proposed is term limits on legislators and/or staffing cuts to make government cheaper. These options have the same effects, that is, lowering the aggregate experience levels of legisla-tors and their abilities to legislate effectively.

Given tendentious politics and a skeptical public, it is easy for oppo-nents to argue that most programs are examples of government waste, ineffectiveness, and/or corruption. Witness the recent efforts to obscure and deny the success of the Affordable Care Act in providing health ac-cess to many Americans who had not had it before. The nontransparency of government adds weight to these charges.

OUTCOMES: HIGH COSTS AND PARTICULARISTIC BENEFITS

Many economists recommend that social policy makers rely on broad-based taxes and universalistic social expenditures as predicates, because they have good incentive effects and promote a sense of even handedness (Lindert, 2012: 3). This is critically important and is a sensibility that the American public lacks. Bartlett (2012) argues convincingly that Americans increasingly feel that they are paying for benefits that other people get.[6] Note that Medicare, Social Security, and the Defense Department are the major components of the federal budget. The old, the military, and major corporations in the military-industrial complex are thus the major beneficiaries. The public senses unfairness in who benefits, and this feeling furthers massive distrust of government and undermines collective solidarity.

The cost of U.S. government programs is also comparatively high (Steinmo, 2010). The benefits tend to be particularistic. This picture of high costs and restricted benefits is generally true of American government programs. They also disproportionally benefit wealthy Americans.

Scholars who include all these benefits in measures of social spending (as a percentage of gross domestic product, GDP) have shown that the United States has a welfare state similar in size to most wealthy European countries (Steinmo, 2010).[7] As a share of GDP, U.S. net public social welfare outlays consumed 27.2 percent of GDP in 2005. This percentage is well above those for countries usually thought of as big social welfare states. Denmark comes in at 25.7 percent, Finland at 24.4 percent, and the Netherlands at 25.8 percent. In fact, the U.S. ranks sixth among Organisation for Economic Co-operation and Development (OECD) countries (Bartlett, 2012: 93, table 10.2).[8]

In addition, policies are not rooted in broad-based taxes and universalistic benefits. The consequence is that an invisible welfare state has developed, one whose benefits are narrow and specific. Lobbyists often manage to hide these in the tax code in ways that disproportionately benefit the wealthy, the elderly, and/or corporations. As a result, the population at large gets burdens while the old and the rich get benefits (Bartlett, 2012).

Health care is a case in point. The lack of broad-based government-funded services means both that health care is more expensive in the United States and that fewer people have access to it, even with Obamacare. Currently around 32 percent of the population gets medical services through some form of government program (Attewell, 2012: 13). The United States spends about 17.6 percent of GDP on health care, including both public and private spending. And our health outcomes are no better than, say, Britain or Norway, each of which spends about 8.5 percent on health care (Reid, 2009).

Furthermore, 50 percent of health care expenditures come out of the federal budget, dwarfing the costs of all other entitlement programs. Access for minorities and the poor is severely rationed. The National

Research Council and the Institute for Medicine, for example, report that the United States ranks last among seventeen wealthy countries in life expectancy (Meyerson, 2013). The death rate for Americans under age fifty is unmatched by any other wealthy nation and is growing. American health outcomes are comparable to those of third world countries (Reid, 2009: 240ff).

This is a result of many factors, but inadequate preventive health care and lack of access to primary care are clearly major ones. Staring at age seventy, American mortality rates shift dramatically downward. This is the point at which those who have survived this far now experience the benefits of a national health care program—Medicare. And at age eighty, U.S. citizens have some of the longest life expectancies in the world (Meyerson, 2013).

THE U.S. STATE IN COMPARATIVE PERSPECTIVE

This design and conception of the state is different from those prevalent in Western Europe.[9] There are different ideologies of statehood between these countries, but all picture the state as a legitimate representative of collective interests in society and grant it more agency as an actor.

Both Scandinavia and Western Europe had powerful institutions that supported the view that society is a "collective entity" (see Brubaker, 1992; E. Weber, 1979; Boli, 1989). Lutheranism, as well as Catholicism, institutionalized this view of society. They imagined society as an organic community, embedded in nature itself. Later, socialism transformed this belief into a secular doctrine.

These ideologies see individuals as embedded in an organic community. In this perspective, citizen rights flow from membership in the community. When they emerged from empires, European nation-states inherited this image of society. In this view, the state represents the collectivity and has the duty of articulating citizens' rights/obligations and implementing them in concrete programs.

In the American narrative, individual rights do not flow from membership in an organic society. They are *natural* rights to individual liberty and freedom from oppression. There are few collective rights, save those to "life, liberty, and the pursuit of happiness."

Individuals must earn other rights in the competitive struggle to sub-due nature. In this analysis, poverty is a natural product of competition rather than a product of societal organization. This conception is part of the American creed that arose out of evangelical Protestantism (Thomas, 1989).

STRENGTHS AND WEAKNESSES
OF THE AMERICAN STATE

All democratic nation-state elites confront two issues they must resolve if they are to remain in office. The first concerns their ability to act in ways citizens consider useful and effective. The second involves successfully re-solving challenges to their authority and avoiding legitimacy crises. On both counts the U.S. state has been exceptional.

First, given the embeddedness of the American state in society and the constraints this produces, it is extraordinary how *activist* the Ameri-can state has been. Contemporary commentators forget the essential plebiscitary nature of the U.S. polity because the current presence of the state in American life has become so large. But its growth obscures two patterns that Huntington (1981) reminded us are writ large in American history. First, Americans have been good at *state building* and mobilizing to achieve important societal goals. A state dependent on populist sup-port can mobilize quickly if such support exists or if leaders can gener-ate that support, as was the case during the Great Depression and with the Iraq war. The post office; the land grant college system; the Federal Reserve banking system; the New Deal; and mobilization for the Civil War, World War I, and World War II are all monuments to this zeal and creativity. So are the various "wars": on crime, drugs, poverty, and so on, since the 1950s.

The federal government, while weak, was also active in promoting capitalism through policies that had a broad consensus (Mann, 2013). It supported westward expansion, for example, the Louisiana Purchase. And under early presidents the government was heavily involved in inter-nal improvements and road and canal building. Later it helped establish intercontinental railways by generous land grants and military expedi-tions against Native Americans. It also supported practical science and technology via the land grant college system. Institutions like the U.S. Postal Service supported capitalist enterprise by expanding communication and keeping it cheap via subsidies, such as cheap rates for advertisements and newspapers.

Second, Americans have been equally good at *deconstructing* state ventures and "old" institutions when popular enthusiasm wanes. Populism as the basis for state action produces a lot of erratic and unpredictable behavior by public bodies. It is not the basis for building a competent, governing state. Planning and evaluating the usefulness of institutions for given purposes is not a strong point of such societies. There are many instances in U.S. history of populist sentiment turning on institutions that once enjoyed wide approval. For example, the federal government abolished pension systems established for veterans of the Civil War (Skocpol, 1992). Congress and states have also slashed funding for the land grant college system drastically over half a century (see Chapter 7). Efforts to repeal much of the New Deal have been underway since the 1950s and 1960s. Both Democratic and Republican administrations have overseen significant defunding and downsizing of many established federal programs including the post office, the National Science Foundation, and the Export-Import Bank (see Chapter 5). Agency managers can no longer assume that the budget process will generate adequate funds for even the most basic maintenance and infrastructure of key government services— including the national highway system, railroads, and the Internal Revenue Service (Bartlett, 2011; 2012).

This pattern of mobilization and demobilization illustrates how dependent the U.S. polity is on immediate plebiscitary sentiment. During emergencies, depressions, or disasters, popular support for government action can quickly escalate—as it does in the event of major weather events such as hurricanes and floods—only to wane and vanish once the disaster subsides from the front pages and TV. These cycles of public sentiment produce moments of state building. Later retrenchment often occurs as popular enthusiasm declines or sours on these innovations. The 1930s was one such "collective moment" when state building escalated because of popular sentiment. But this effort ultimately lapsed. Building an effective state was later abandoned as prosperity returned in the 1950s (see Chapter 7). This pattern stymies efforts to build a state that is both competent and transparent. But it does make for a polity that is highly responsive to articulated public demand.

CYCLES OF CRISIS

One other feature of the political system also distinguishes the United States from many of its European counterparts. Huntington (1981) and Linz (1978; 1993) have both pointed out that legitimacy crises are a regular feature of American politics. Linz (1993) noted that this is inherent in the design of the American state. It is a system prone to legitimacy crises and gridlock (see Yglesias, 2015). This occurs because of the extreme diffusion of authority in the system. Since the people elect both Congress and the president, these officials can consistently claim to speak for the people, often fostering a gridlock that cannot be resolved within the governmental system. When serious disagreement occurs, "there is no democratic principle on the basis of which it can be resolved," according to Linz (quoted in Yglesias, 2015). The Constitution offers no help in these cases because the solutions it offers are too complicated and legalistic to capture the support of the electorate. The only solutions to this impasse are chronic gridlock, political realignment in the wider society, or civil war.

Parliamentary systems solve this problem more readily by calling for new elections when the current government fails to prevail against a no-confidence vote. Parliamentary parties can also discipline individual politicians for political deviance. If extreme disagreement surfaces, new parties or coalitions can form to contest elections. Some become dominant. This is harder to achieve in the United States because local and state rules make it difficult to organize new parties.[10] Third parties have not fared well in American politics (Rosenstone et al., 1996).

The result of this inability to avoid legitimacy crises is that gridlock in American politics is common. This occurs at both the federal and state level (Fiorina, 1996). Given public distrust of the state, the American voting public often prefers this kind of stalemate. As polarization between the two political parties has increased, the inability to act has increased.

These characteristics indicate how exceptional the U.S. state is from others. The classic liberal distrust of a strong state has evolved into a working blueprint of government. Authority is purposely diffused, creating many points at which veto power can nullify action. Suspicion of government led to a design intended to hobble the state. This persists, even with big government.

There is, however, one period in recent American history when alternative conceptions of government emerged and more collectivist, though nonsocialist, alternatives gained legitimacy. The next chapter examines the collectivist moment and the conditions that gave rise to it.

CHAPTER 4

The Collectivist Moment

AS LIPSET (1963, 1996) ARGUED, there has been a good deal of continuity in the civil religion of American society. The American creed has persisted but not without challenges. Huntington (1981) has shown that American society has gone through many upheavals in which dissident groups contested the fundamental tenets of the nation-state. A critical one occurred in the 1930s when alternative narratives became plausible and led to social developments that have been at the center of political conflict ever since.

Democratization in the United States up to the 1930s had primarily involved the slow extension of citizenship. This involved the extension of legal equality and political rights to more groups in the population over time, such as white males with no property, slaves, and women (see D. King et al., 2009; Marshall, 1963). Furthermore, the federal government left the implementation of these rights to local authorities, so many states did not implement them. Authoritarian regimes persisted in many parts of the country, particularly where there were large minorities of nonwhites, such as blacks, Hispanics, and Native Americans.

Unlike in Europe, there were few social welfare rights for citizens until the 1930s. Dealing with social welfare issues was a prerogative of states, municipalities, and private philanthropy. There were a few exceptions like Civil War pensions, but the federal government lacked the mandate and funds to establish such rights. The federal income tax, for example, did not become law until 1916. Many groups contested this transfer of authority to the federal government, even though a war in Europe was unfolding that might affect the United States. Acceptance required a Supreme Court ruling that it was constitutional.

In a society under the sway of a hegemonic business class, unwanted government intervention in the economy was unthinkable (Lindblom, 1977). During the Great Depression, the business class fought New Deal efforts to get people back to work via government programs like the Civilian Conservation Corps.

During the Progressive Era when outrage at the economic excesses of the gilded age became public and political, the solutions were regulatory and legal (Novak, 2010). Commissions were set up to regulate public utilities, oil fields, and railroads, and the national government enacted federal laws like the Interstate Commerce Act. In many cases reforms established at the local level, like municipal civil services, diffused because Progressives believed that they were good antidotes to the corruption and inefficiency of political patronage regimes (Tolbert and Zucker, 1983). But the idea that the federal government had any responsibility for alleviating poverty among the poor or elderly or developing standards for industry was foreign to the major political parties. In the critical election of 1896, for example, even the vote in heavily immigrant (and poor) counties went for the Republican Party, which was solidly pro-business (Thomas, 1989). While other traditions existed, like those that underpinned Midwestern cooperatives or "social gospel" missions, they were in the minority. Few wanted the federal government to interfere in the private affairs of the citizenry or in the local politics of states and towns.

The Great Depression changed this political culture. Describing the emergence of and legitimation of collectivist solutions to the problems of capitalism in American society is the purpose of this chapter. It is a critical period because it inaugurated an adaptation of the American creed. Government became a legitimate actor in society, once it became clear that capitalist elites could not resolve the crisis brought on by the Great Depression. The success of government action during this period introduced a new, and controversial, element to American political ideology. It has since become one of the major axes of political conflict.

In the Progressive Era, reformers had enacted an avalanche of legal controls to give the national state authority to regulate interstate commerce and monopolistic practices in the economy (Novak, 2010). It was also an era in which professional civil service expanded at the state and municipal level.[1] It became what historian Ira Katznelson (2013) calls a "procedural state." State control was indirect through legal rules and regulations. The courts became important players in this form of regulation. While the Progressive Era strengthened the authority of the state, it did not change its design and turn it into a European-style state. Progressives augmented the state's legal controls, but its authority remained fragmented and decentralized. While the Progressives expanded government controls, it was a government that took a distinctively American form (Pierson, 2007; Steinmo, 2010; Prasad, 2006; Mann, 2013; Crouch, 2004).[2] One way of characterizing this development is that the state expanded in the United States without producing a more statist society (Nettl, 1968). Changes in government occurred without a corresponding cultural shift legitimating the state, either nationally or locally, as an independent actor.

THE GREAT DEPRESSION: A MOVE TOWARD MORE COLLECTIVIST SOLUTIONS

The Great Depression of 1929 initiated a more collectivist period—though many contested the policies of the New Deal and resisted them throughout. In response to crisis, the United States "turned left" (Mann, 2012). The result for a short a time was a far more active and prominent state—and a period of greater legitimacy for government activity. The 1930s were a period of social experimentation that led to an incipient social welfare state.

The federal government under Franklin D. Roosevelt did not plan the innovations of this era. They emerged in response to an international crisis of historic proportions, followed by World War II. What resulted were experiments, some of which failed, that had widespread popular backing. Business and their conservative allies, however, bitterly contested these experiments launched by the federal government. The irony is that the main project of the New Deal was to save capitalism from itself.

This was also a period in which external events heightened nationalism, despite the efforts of President Woodrow Wilson and others to build an international social order after World War I. Given the weakness of the global framework, every nation was on its own. There was no international community that could offer international support and solutions. Mann (2012: 222) argues that this condition produced a "caged" form of nationalism that magnified the search for separate solutions to the crisis. "Nationalism worked, diminishing globalization," according to Mann. Nationalist solutions were in vogue because they were the only available ones during this era.

In the United States, the sheer scale of the crisis overwhelmed traditional responses to economic depressions. Nothing seemed to work. Classic policies of cutting taxes and downsizing government had no effect in reviving the economy. Furthermore, the Great Depression of 1929 created a public climate of enormous fear and panic (Katznelson, 2013: 27–96). Elites and the public at large were frightened by the scale of the debacle. In addition, it appeared that democracy was undergoing a global failure. Europe was under stress and struggling. At the same time the available evidence suggested that authoritarian regimes in Russia, Germany, and Italy were succeeding economically. The trains were running on time in Germany and Italy, while the American economy was devastated. The prospects for democracy looked grim.

The sheer unprecedented magnitude of the economic catastrophe created conditions that temporarily undermined the classic American creed. Capitalism was in crisis and the public was open to other solutions. Union membership soared, as did popular support for the presidential candidate Norman Thomas and the socialist party. The Great Depression was a unique historical moment that led to the suspension of normal cultural narratives.

One significant consequence of the crisis was that it promoted imagery of an integrated nation with a common fate. "Cognitive nationalization" emerged. This changed consciousness heightened sympathy for the poor, unemployed, and dispossessed, *and* for labor (Abrams, 2006; Mann, 2012). With a quarter of the population unemployed, it was clear to everyone that this was not a problem of individual failure to work and thrive. Something seemed wrong with the system. Furthermore, the available evidence suggested that failure was not universal. Parts of Europe were recovering faster than those that were relying on unregulated capitalist institutions to govern the economy. For example, the countries that abandoned the gold standard and then reflated emerged most quickly from the Great Depression.

The Great Depression also radicalized America. The direness of the situation created space for novel cultural experiments. Roosevelt's own rhetoric of "relief, recovery, and reform" also widened this window of opportunity by suggesting that government and the public had to entertain unusual methods to salvage the democratic experiment and to save capitalism from itself (Katznelson, 2013). Circumstances and politicians at the center challenged the cultural hegemony of the myth of American exceptionalism. While Roosevelt and his advisors did not have a plan for recovery, their rhetoric that government could devise successful measures for relief added legitimacy to the idea that collectivist solutions might work. The Great Depression created this opening by casting doubt on the legitimacy of classic American myths and narratives of appropriate solutions. Incipient collectivist approaches to policy emerged, though they quickly collapsed in favor of pragmatic, limited ones (Rubin, 1996).

The failure of traditional alternatives also supported policy innovation. The fledgling efforts to revive capitalism through classic budgetary measures failed in the early part of the New Deal. This fact emboldened the Roosevelt administration to try more radical alternatives. It soon became clear that attempts to balance budgets or to cut them did not work. Raising taxes was an unthinkable option, as Table 4.1 shows. The Roosevelt administration did not try this option, and taxation remained stable. Democratic politicians realized that public support would wane if more dramatic responses weren't attempted. The Roosevelt administration, and perhaps democracy itself, might not survive.

This was also a period in which new economic policy solutions were becoming available. John Maynard Keynes had just reinvented economics and offered novel policy solutions for lack of liquidity and economic crisis. In his view capitalism created regular crises. One role of government was to intervene to save it—and democracy—from self-destruction. American students of Keynes became government officials who were ready to try his remedies. For example, Harvard professor Alvin Hansen and his students (Karabel, 2014) became key government advisors. In addition, elites in Europe were experimenting with a variety of quasi-statist and collectivist experiments with apparent success. Some alternative models suggested solutions that before the crisis had been "outside the box" dictated by American political culture.

It was also clear to Roosevelt and his advisors at the time that electoral success, and the democratic experiment itself, depended on finding pragmatic solutions to unemployment and lack of liquidity in the economy (Katznelson, 2013: 27ff). Politicians recognized that they had to save capitalism if the American experiment was to endure. The Roosevelt administration dedicated itself to this project. They were fortunate to have a Democratic majority in each house to work with. And it was clear to congressional Democratic politicians that reform experiments were necessary to save them from electoral defeat.

Political support also existed at the time for innovative solutions. A liberal-labor alliance emerged that normalized the American state in the direction of European welfare states (Mann, 2012). The Depression had strengthened public sympathy for the unemployed and for organized labor. Unions flourished, and membership grew. Indigenous radical movements and support for Norman Thomas's Socialist Party also grew. It was clear that any programs that put people back to work and helped the economy would have public support.

These conditions created room for collectivist solutions and what became the New Deal. It became permissible to imagine that government might be part of the solution to the biggest economic crisis the country had faced. The alternatives were not working.

While traditional business groups, the conservative South, and the Supreme Court contested and resisted the new policies, they proved popular

TABLE 4.1   The Historical Levels of Taxation per Capita and Public
Indebtedness per Capita

Year	Taxation Levels per Capita	Indebtedness per Capita
1902	$18	$41
1913	24	58
1927	80	281
1936	83	416
1940	108	479
1944	389	1,644
1950	364	1,861
1955	537	1,939
1960	709	1,979
1965	860	2,151

Source: Mitchell and Mitchell, 1968: 273, Table 1.

with the public. A sense of urgency required that government had to do
something to put people back to work.

As a result, this era saw the birth of an activist state. One form that
state activism took was a Keynesian approach—borrowing money to
fund public investment. The 1930s begins a trend of much higher public
indebtedness per capita than occurred in earlier periods (Mitchell and
Mitchell, 1968: 273, table 1). Table 4.1 shows that public indebtedness
during the 1930s almost doubled in size and then continued to climb
through the 1940s, 1950s, and 1960s.

THE NEW DEAL REGIME

The pragmatic collectivism of the New Deal became plausible because the
Great Depression had served as a radicalizing experience for the citizenry.
Such policies temporarily discredited conservatism, so that antigovernment
sentiment and individualism were temporarily suppressed (Lipset, 1996).
Furthermore, a normal liberal-labor welfare regime emerged as labor's
strength surged (Mann, 2012: 241).

The New Deal produced a surge of social welfare legislation, federal
spending, and federal regulation that represented a permanent break with
the past (Mann, 2012: 249). Keynesian economic planning also emphasized federal rather than state administration of projects. This action

strengthened the center and the role of federal officials and experts who controlled these bureaucracies at the center.

Given the power of the South, a strange alliance grew up between northern liberals and Southern Democrats. The latter were supportive of federal spending because of the money it poured into the South—the poorest region in the country. States and regions were also grateful for federal funding and requested them for locally approved programs. One result was that states and local governments became more dependent on the federal government, and this enhanced the symbolic importance of the center as well. However, the power of Southern Democrats prevented a fully bureaucratic state or universal welfare system from emerging (Amenta, 1998). Their opposition signaled that there were clear political limits to this new development.

Katznelson (2013) points out that one of these limits was the idea that government's management of the economy should focus on taxation and spending rather than economic planning. Lemann (2013: 90) points out that the politics of the era prevented agencies that could have established a larger part for central government in the economy from doing so. Politicians from the South pushed for more *local* control for racial reasons. For example, their efforts led to the removal of the U.S. Employment Service from the Labor Department and put under local control, a move that Southern legislators favored. The overall result of the New Deal was that the United States became a pluralist, *procedural state* in domestic affairs. In military affairs it became a far more expansive and less democratic state. In this sphere it was committed to corporatist planning in the national interest.

The political bargain that created the procedural state came about because it was clear to Democrats that they could not win politically without the South. Lemann (2013) also suggests that the emerging business groups in the "new South" would have resisted a regime in which the federal government engaged in more central planning.

WORLD WAR II AND THE POSTWAR PERIOD

While the liberal-labor alliance ran out of steam after 1939, the collective experiments of the 1930s intensified as the United States entered into World War II. International political elites won the battle for entry into World War II, largely because of the Japanese attack on Pearl Harbor. During the war, regulated capitalisms emerged everywhere. The United States was no exception (Luttwak, 1999; Reich, 1994; Mann, 2012; 2013; Judt and Snyder, 2012). This was a period of enormous world economic collectivism. Government controls over the economy and society ratcheted up. The U.S. government instituted rationing, price controls, public employment, and workforce planning, all as part of the war effort (e.g., Galbraith, 1971).

One consequence of wartime practices was to legitimate postwar ideas of the necessity of elite coordination of the economy. The internationalists of each party believed that in a threatening postwar environment, elite management, planning, and social control were necessary for America's success (Bell, 1973). In addition, they pushed for postwar reconstruction efforts abroad under international elite coordination. These efforts lent support to the idea of an activist state. The success of the Marshall Plan, the European Coal and Steel Community and other developments in Europe, and even the achievements of Soviet collectivism showcased the usefulness of state planning and elite management of the economy.

The result was that the postwar period was one of expanded government activity. In addition, support for state expansion grew in the late 1950s. This hinged on a bipartisan consensus that had emerged between Republicans and Democrats as a response to the Cold War (Gourevitch, 2002). The isolationist wings of each party were in retreat. They and their allies in the antigovernment ideological bloc suffered temporary defeats. This development, however, was contingent on electoral politics and the long Democratic Party incumbency. That began in 1932 and lasted to 1952. However, elite reactions to the Soviet Union and its expansionist ambitions continued the support for government action during the Cold War.

One result of this temporary political stasis is that a whole generation of Americans moved in a more collectivist—though not socialist—direction. The irony is that "the greatest generation" is the most collectivist one. Mann (2013), for example, refers to the "GI welfare state" (see also Putnam, 2000; Janowitz, 1983). This generation witnessed a variety of experiments that are now part of mainstream political culture, such as the creation of Social Security and old-age pensions; the legalization of labor unions; federal direct support for higher education; the creation of the Veterans Administration; war and postwar government planning; government efforts to halt racism, first in the military and later in civil society; and the creation of a national security state.

International developments also heightened the legitimacy of government action. As Soviet expansionist ambitions became apparent in the late 1940s, this threat reintroduced fear along with the real possibility of nuclear war (Gaddis, 2005; Friedberg, 2000). These tensions heightened nationalism and supported the image of an imagined homogeneity of public consciousness. As a result, scholars branded this period as one in which a national civic culture prevailed. Patriotism was high, trust in fellow citizens swelled, and confidence in governmental and other social institutions was at an all-time high (Almond and Verba, 1963; Fischer and Hout, 2006). Both fear and optimism prevailed. The prospect of nuclear war stoked the former, while the return of prosperity at home and international hegemony honed the latter.

The other side of the coin is that this was also an era in which national security collectivism prevailed along with virulent xenophobia. This period also witnessed a retreat from democracy and the strengthening of the corporatist military-industrial sector. Elites successfully defined the budgets of these agencies and their work as in the national interest. As a result, xenophobia was common. One response was the requirement of loyalty oaths for employees at all levels of government, such as federal employees and local schoolteachers (Sniderman, 1981). Witch hunts for enemies of society also took off. Anti-communism led to "red baiting" and scapegoating of suspected "fellow travelers." Public hysteria about enemies within the U.S. government and society was rampant. Opportunistic politicians like Senator Joseph McCarthy stoked this fear. Populism was the force behind much of this activity, but political elites at the center and their media allies were eventually able to crowd out and control such groups.

THE POSTWAR POLITY: CHECKS ON POPULISM

Features of the political system that had endured as the United States emerged out of the war sustained governmental activism during this period. A main one was that opinion making was still in the hands of elites who had links to local grassroots groups through party organizations and media control. There were still strong local parties capable of mobilizing the public on issues. And local influentials still dominated and controlled public opinion. An elite-dominated national media gave elites opinion space and their views widespread diffusion (Janowitz, 1978).

Furthermore, the national government remained accessible to local groups because it was weakly integrated. There were many points of access for local interest groups (James Wilson, 1981). And the network of national political and economic elites was weakly integrated and therefore less influential at the national level.

It was an era when structural conditions made it less plausible for groups to develop ideologies of out-of-touch politicians at the center versus the grass roots at home. Politics was local in this era. Networks of local institutions connected politicians with local elites and the local media. TV was in its infancy and the primary media of communication were local radio broadcasts and locally controlled newspapers.

Under these conditions, political parties held populism in check. They gave the grassroots channels of access and influence and they gave elites at the center influence over local elites.

These conditions generated a politics that still embedded political elites and political parties in the social controls of local community elites (e.g., Janowitz, 1978, 1983). This facilitated both a measure of elite control and the integration of the public into the national political system. It also sustained a series of associated mythologies that were part of the U.S. image as an "imagined community" (Anderson, 1983). The fact that elites at the center and local influentials functioned as corresponding parts of an integrated political system supported popular perceptions of the nation as a community. Voluntarism was its ethos, and belief in the American way was its civil religion. A dense set of local institutions networked with regional and national ones supported this civic culture (Almond and Verba, 1963; Schudson, 1998b; Bright and Harding, 1984).

Another development of the period was more problematic for democratization. In the postwar period a national security state developed that gave further legitimation to state action. It also prompted the emergence of a military-industrial complex. America became a "garrison state" (Friedberg, 2000). Government secrecy grew during this period, as did peacetime military expenditures. Public preoccupation with the "red scare" also fueled a wave of xenophobia that dampened political dissent. Anti-communism became the watchword, and those who dared to criticize the Federal Bureau of Investigation (FBI) or other agencies of the national security state fell under government and public suspicion as internal enemies of America and freedom. This was particularly true in high-profile institutions like academia (Lazarsfeld and Thielens, 1958). Dissent from mainstream political views also engendered public suspicion and scapegoating. Anyone visible to the public was vulnerable, such as public schoolteachers, news media personnel, Hollywood celebrities, and labor union activists.

In addition, as the national security state became permanent, military speech and metaphors spread.[3] The language of politics became militarized. Solving social problems now required "wars," not experiments to test the most workable policies. The metaphor of war changed tactics as well as strategy. Politicians taught the public to favor short-term attacks or assaults on problems. They also demanded quick results, in part because a change in administrations could mean the defunding of given policies and programs.

This strategy may have been the price politicians had to pay to mobilize public support for government in a society that was by design skeptical and distrustful of state interference in society. Nevertheless, it led the public to believe that there were quick solutions to entrenched problems. One result has been that the failure of many such efforts has cast doubt on the efficacy of collective solutions and government action itself, such as the war on drugs.

The growing use of the language of war has also had another regrettable side effect. Once political elites declare war on a problem, such as crime or drugs, one is either for it or against it. The middle ground of skeptical but interested concern narrows. Instead of solving problems, showing support for the "war" becomes the issue. Policy prescriptions become politicized, as do measures of success. Just as the "body count" became the measure of victory in Vietnam, similar stunted, and easily manipulated, metrics emerge in other areas to show-case success for policies that politicians or parties favor, e.g., arrest rates as a sign of success in crime control.

One consequence of the twin development of an activist state and a national security state was that for a brief period a political consensus developed that allowed the American state to become more engaged in re-constructing society. The next chapter turns to examine this development and the resulting consequences.

CHAPTER 5

The Liberal Activist Society

ONE OF THE ANOMALIES of the postwar era is the continuous expansion of government and the emergence of a supportive ideology. This was in part due to the rise of the national security state as the military response to the Cold War (Friedberg, 2000). It was also a result of American hegemony in the world and government efforts to use key institutions to maintain this superiority. This led to generous federal funding of science, universities, and the military-industrial complex. The concept of the "knowledge society" emerged as the key ideological support for this development.

American hegemony and optimism during this period had another effect. It supported the reemergence of the American creed (Lipset, 1996; Martinelli, 2008). It lent renewed support for two basic tenets. First, it legitimated the classic libertarian push for expanding civil rights and legal equality in society. American society in this period became a hothouse for liberal reform movements. But second, it also stoked demand among conservatives and the business community for a return to unregulated capitalism. Deregulation of the economy became their war cry. During this period these two latent tensions flared up and destroyed the consensus that had prevailed in the 1950s. This chapter and the next describe how these conflicts developed and destroyed the "civic culture" of the postwar period.

RATIONALIZING SOCIETY AND
EXPANSION OF THE PUBLIC AGENDA

Liberal political elites in the postwar period continued the wartime drive for mobilizing and rationalizing society in pursuit of "progress" and national security. This occurred in a context of postwar European reconstruction, optimism about the future, and Cold War competition. Elite support for a national security state was high and tax rates were also high enough to pay for it. President Dwight Eisenhower, for example, was a self-proclaimed progressive for most of his life and saw the dangers of both Soviet expansionism and internal strife.

The period was one of a continuously expanding agenda of public responsibilities (of perceived problems and opportunities), government growth, and the associated explosion of reform "movements" pushing for social justice on behalf of an array of constituencies.

As the public agenda grew, so did government. Jones and Williams (2008: 102ff, fig. 5.5) chart four periods of governmental expansion from the 1940s, using the yearly median percentage change in total budgetary authority of the government as the measure of growth. The first period extends from 1948 to 1956. Jones and Williams (2008) call it the "era of experimentation." Budgetary expansion was small—less than 1 percent a year. The next period, the era of big government liberalism, extends from 1956 to 1978, when the yearly median change in budgetary authority reached 6 percent. The third period of budgetary restraint lasted from 1977 to 2000, with median budgetary increases averaging 2 percent. In 2000 with the election of President George W. Bush, the "era of big government conservatism" begins again with budgetary authority expanding to a median of 5 percent per year. Expansion of the military, subsequent wars and tax cuts for the wealthy propelled Bush's budgets and deficits. In hindsight, the 1950s to the 1970s are the crucial years of government expansion.

Important ideological changes accompanied these upward shifts in government spending. Narratives concerning society, the role of government, and societal elites changed. An important aspect of this period was the emergence out of World War II of a picture of the nation as a *collective project* with broad goals. Society became an object for rationalization and social engineering.

GLOBALIZATION AND NEW MODELS OF SOCIETY

There were many drivers of this process. One was the postwar transition and rebuilding of Europe together with the Cold War. In the United States the internationalist elites of both parties thought they could best handle these challenges through elite coordination internationally. This process, they argued, would lead to a successful search for realistic solutions and best practices in achieving them. To be successful they would have to co-ordinate many institutions, whose expertise would be necessary for success. This included business, science, the military, and higher education.

Similarly, the strategy they developed to enhance national security during the Cold War also required such coordination. Liberal political elites argued that the federal government was the only agency that had the resources, personnel, and vision to accomplish this objective. The American strategy for doing this was to devolve authority to private corporations and universities to accomplish these tasks with oversight from the Department of Defense and other agencies (Friedberg, 2000). Thus, corporations rather than government got authority to run shipyards; build fighter planes, bombers, and drones; and to run the armament factories that would produce equipment for this effort.

This led to the birth of the military-industrial complex and another set of allied institutions, the science and technological complex. In his farewell address, under his newfound guise as a conservative, President Eisenhower inveighed against the dangers of this twin development. In his view it gave corporate America and the government too much power. They were becoming too big to fail and hence a permanent feature of the political landscape. Corporate elites and their conservative allies later used this criticism to argue against giving *government* too much power (Pierson and Skocpol, 2007; Micklethwait and Wooldridge, 2004).

Both the Cold War and incipient globalization drove this development. International competition among nations grew. This went beyond simple military and economic competition. It included pursuit of political and cultural hegemony as well. The question raised was: what is the best model of society for producing prosperity, equality, and well-being? The American response in 1956 to Sputnik, a successful Soviet space rocket launch, indicates the depth of this competition. It led American educators and politicians to question the effectiveness of the *entire* U.S. educational system. And it inspired grossly exaggerated and imagined successes of the Soviet Union (and later Europe) in science and other arenas. International competition was particularly intense with respect to technological and economic success. But it also spilled over into many other areas: the arts, intellectual achievement, sports, science, students' international standing on achievement tests, and so on.

Globalization fueled other international cultural movements as well. This was particularly the case for ideas of human rights and equality that began to emerge. It was a continuation of ideologies that democracies had used in World War II as the rationale for fighting the war. These ideas spread with the proliferation of nationalist and decolonization movements. This process led over time to an international consolidation of human rights into a global ideology (Cole, 2012a).

In this context racism became an important problem for the United States (Mann, 2013; McAdam, 1982). Gunnar Myrdal's book *An American Dilemma* (1944) had a wide audience at home and abroad. Many in the United States and elsewhere found Myrdal's critique compelling. Other governments, particularly the USSR, also used it for propaganda purposes. American government officials became sensitive to the charge of racism, along with critiques about elevated levels of poverty and unemployment among minorities. These criticisms were effective and forced the government to respond. One response was to provide legal support for desegregation cases brought before the Supreme Court by the National Association for the Advancement of Colored People (NAACP). In one case in 1952, the U.S. Attorney General intervened, to the surprise of the NAACP. In that case the Justice Department argued that racial discrimination "furnishes grist for the Communist propaganda mills and raises doubt even among friendly nations as to the intensity of our devotion to the democratic faith" (quoted in McAdam, 1982: 83).

Other government agencies also responded to this challenge. In 1954 in the case of *Brown v. Board of Education*, the Supreme Court in a unanimous decision nullified the legality of the "separate but equal" doctrine that the South had used to support segregated schools. Desegregation of public facilities became the law of the land but not necessarily the reality. Chief Justice Earl Warren convinced his fellow justices that this was such a weighty decision that it must be a unanimous one or the country would not accept it. All nine justices agreed, despite reservations.

As part of Cold War competition, critiques of the most powerful nations extended to many other areas. Poverty and inequality within countries became highlighted issues. The response of the United States, amid postwar optimism and its newfound status as a superpower, was to develop a new ideology of national reform. Liberal elites believed that a wealthy, technological society could turn to science for answers about how to solve problems that domestic and foreign critics had raised. Racism was one, but there were many others, such as poverty, lack of access to medical care, and unequal educational opportunities that violated the egalitarian tenets of the American creed. There was much optimism then that American society could find consensual solutions to these issues. The country had weathered the Great Depression, was a victor in World War II, and was now the foremost economic and military power in the world.

THE KNOWLEDGE SOCIETY

Academics and liberal political elites developed a new social/folk epistemology during the 1950s and 1960s. The idea they advocated emerged out of the experience of World War II when collaboration between government, the military, and scientists produced technical innovations that helped secure victory. The idea was that truly modern societies must be knowledge societies (Lane, 1999; Kerr, 1963). This was the era of the "multiversity," which was to be a major source of solutions for social problems in many spheres. Big science had helped win World War II through its application to warfare, for example, radar and the atomic bomb (Jungk, 1958). Given this history, it seemed reasonable to many liberals to use science to develop policy in peacetime. The idea of a government-coordinated economic policy was a key plank of liberalism.

The worldwide emergence of the social sciences and their rapid growth rate in university curricula during this period expanded this optimism to include domains outside technology and science (Frank and Gabler, 2006). All societal domains were now subject to the application of secular knowledge in pursuit of progress.

The institutionalization of social science and the policy sciences brought about another important change that became important as interstate competition intensified: the emerging significance of social indicators.

Elites believed that reconstructing Europe and producing economic and social development in the third world required policies based on the best practices available. There was now a strong international lobby of experts and officials demanding quantitative empirical evidence on the performance and conduct of nation-states. They succeeded in spreading the idea that if social science was to achieve its purpose of understanding and improving societies, its practitioners had to have access to comparative empirical data to determine the best policies for developing prosperous and open societies.

Political elites accepted this idea, and one of the goals of the newly founded institutions after World War II like the World Bank and the International Monetary Fund was to collect statistics on nations' economic performance, health status, and educational outcomes. While individual nations had had such agencies since the Domesday Book of England of 1086 surveyed national wealth, no agency had the charter to collect such data internationally on a wide variety of social indicators over time (see Karabel, 2014). That was one of the purposes associated with the World Bank. Founded in 1950, the newly established World Bank began publishing data comparing countries on a wide variety of health, education, and economic outcomes. In 1951 it published its first volume of international statistics. These institutions had now quantified the pursuit of justice and equality for all to see. Comparisons between the United States, Europe, and the Soviet bloc were inevitable and highly politically charged. The age of social indicators had gone global.

In the optimism of this period, it was an article of liberal faith that science would be a source of modern technology, economic competitiveness, and national security. The availability of social indicators would only enhance this possibility by giving society empirical benchmarks of progress. The hope was that a knowledge society would also be a more just and egalitarian one.

The work of these postwar agencies added a new ingredient to the burgeoning Cold War and intensified international competition. The rising availability and use of social indicators meant that policy makers could now compare nations' achievements in many areas. These reified pictures of national well-being became part of both international political competition and the internal politics of national societies.

Use of comparative indicators of social welfare began to be an important part of international competition. In the 1950s and 1960s these comparisons intensified. The results of these international comparisons played their part in the propaganda wars of the period. One could now benchmark which societies had the best record of offering good life chances for their citizens.

SCIENCE, UNIVERSITIES, AND IDEOLOGICAL SATURATION

A key feature of knowledge societies is that journalists, economists, politicians, intellectuals, scientists, academics, and others saturate them with ideological doctrines of how to reform society. These often have only the loosest connection with the knowledge base of experts. The idea that low tax rates always produce higher economic growth is one such example (see Bartlett, 2012). Another example is the general belief that more and better education will solve a wide range of social problems—from inequality to crime. My colleague Ronald Jepperson coined the term *imagined knowledge* for this phenomenon. It is endemic in modern society and is one result of the millennial optimism Americans associate with education.

The explosion of knowledge fills society with competing theories (or rational mythologies) of how to organize institutions to achieve national purposes. None are exempt from the march of knowledge and its policy prescriptions for success. This includes the economy, organizations, workplaces, schools, families, and intimate relations, to name a few of the domains contemporary science now covers. In sum, the knowledge society is one filled with myths of rationality and the resulting "recipes" to achieve more individual happiness and societal prosperity. This is not new. The American Constitution, for example, used this slogan to promote its blueprint of government. But the idea of the knowledge society enhanced the social commitment to education and science as a secular source of worldly salvation (Shils, 1971).

One result is that schemes for reform invaded many formerly private spaces. Corporate hiring practices, for example, have become part of the public and as such a political issue (e.g., Kanter, 1978). A wide variety of other areas also became politicized. Schudson (1998a: 264–275) details some of the areas that have become political and hence the proper subjects of a federalized national consciousness: schools, the workplace, higher education, the home, the professions, environmental protection, and the political process itself. For example, the current drive for campaign finance reform is one such reform movement that is gaining traction. Schemes for reform in all these areas were, and still are, constantly debated in the polity.

Universities are critical sites in this process. They are the carriers of rationality and a main source of rational narratives of how society should work. They are also the producers of the secular knowledge to achieve societal goals (Meyer, 1977; Bell, 1973). University curricula generate authoritative knowledge. The disciplinary training they give to students legitimates their status as professionals and experts (Collins, 1979). Universities train cadres of practitioners who will carry out efforts to reform society. Higher education also credentials the commentators and think tank professionals who generate publicity and credibility for given reform agendas. Neoliberalism, for example, owes much of its plausibility to the work and legitimacy of economists (Fourcade, 2006; Fourcade-Gourinchas and Babb, 2002). Similarly, globalized free trade pacts between countries or groups of countries gain legitimacy from economic doctrines and their carriers, whether they are technical specialists in developing countries or business groups in developed countries that have internalized such knowledge within their organizational structures.

Science becomes prominent as a credible source of progress and societal revitalization. Credentialing becomes a major source of authority and privilege within society (Collins, 1979). In a society whose creed emphasizes individualism and anti-elitism, the idea of a population trained in science and technology as the basis for progress is appealing. Human capital theory turns this idea into an important strand of economic theory and a general ideology of how society achieves progress (Becker, 1994). This ideology helped promote the idea that a successful society must be one with widespread schooling (Baker, 2014).

Given the widespread credibility of this ideology across nations, expanded international political competition in the 1950s fueled the expansion of universities and science (Riddle, 1990, 1993). With few exceptions like England, Riddle's research shows that political competition has historically been one of the main drivers promoting the establishment and diffusion of universities. Universities have been important sources of national identity and national culture(s). University-trained scholars, artists, scientists, and writers have been instrumental in creating the languages, history, science, and art of imagined (national) societies, thereby constructing nations out of empires (Anderson, 1983). Much of the legitimacy of nationalism results from the cultural constructions that such groups create. This includes revitalized religions that often become part of the nationalist fabric in many countries.

In this era, expanding higher education in the United States had widespread popular support. Federal tax rates were high during the Eisenhower era of the 1950s, and public confidence in government was high as well (Almond and Verba, 1963). Political elites endowed higher educational institutions with massive public support to expand and modernize. States, communities, and many private actors financed many new institutions (see Table 5.2). Older ones became bigger as many colleges morphed into universities.

This was the beginning of the era of big science, funded by the federal government. The expansion of supply produced a surge in enrollments that dwarfed the earlier expansion that followed the return of GIs after World War II under the GI Bill (Schofer and Meyer, 2005; Geiger, 2009). This change was the result in part of a conscious effort to increase the numbers of highly trained personnel for industry and government and to ensure their appropriate indoctrination in democratic forms of citizenship. This was the precise intent of the National Defense Education Act of 1958—passed over a year after the Soviet Union launched the first successful space rocket, Sputnik. The act included government subsidies to expand university faculties and fellowships to help students finance graduate and undergraduate education.

From the standpoint of Cold War liberal political elites, scientific knowledge was an important weapon both for reforming American society and for showing the effectiveness of the democratic path to societal revitalization to emerging nations and the Soviet bloc. Part of the liberal vision behind the knowledge society was that science could be a source of policy that would help regulate the economy and other institutions to make them more effective and just (Bell, 1973; Gauchat, 2012).

This development has led to the production of a wide array of scientized doctrines and ideologies for societal reform. They are compelling because they invoke law, science, and social science, however tangentially. As such, they became part of public discourse. Elites on both the right and the left used them to justify the public policy solutions they offered.

SOCIETY AS A SOCIAL PROBLEMS MACHINE

In a knowledge society, science and social science create streams of solutions that address a flow of social problems in society. Increasing spheres of society become problematized by this process. This idea suggests that one can usefully characterize modern universities as "garbage cans" of solutions awaiting problems to resolve (M. Cohen et al., 1972). This metaphor catches both the messiness of the process and its institutionalization. The policy sciences expanded to offer a variety of solutions to fix societal problems across society, such as poverty. Academics and their political allies used this knowledge to generate reform proposals and the latter rapidly politicized such attempted solutions. They then became the subject of national debate, for example, "welfare" versus "workfare," the "war on poverty."

A second consequence of the development of an activist knowledge society is to intensify the public discussion of social problems. One can aptly characterize modern societies as social problem machines. They discover both problems and imagined solutions. An activist state allied with science and universities builds into society a new dynamic that *expands* the public agenda and public policy in many spheres. This is both a top-down and a bottom-up process.

As a result, the vastly expanded problematic features of society become known to the public and are the subject of expert analysis and political debate. Drug abuse, drunk driving, violence in families, low achievement in school, gender gaps in achievement, and income inequality are all examples of areas that have been problematized and turned into social problems. The result has been an enormous expansion of the public agenda and of issues and groups that are now part of the organized polity (Dahl, 1994).

INTERSTATE COMPETITION AND
GOVERNMENT GROWTH

During the height of the Cold War in the late 1950s, global interstate competition both became more intense and occurred in more domains across societies. With many new nations emerging from former colonies, the quest for the most just and effective models of society took on new urgency. As the new world leader, the United States had a prominent stake in this debate. It was the leader of the group of modern democracies whose leadership and models of society faced challenges from the Soviet bloc. It had a stake in showing that progress toward justice and equality were compatible with capitalism and democratic political institutions.

At the time, liberal political and corporate elites felt that the United States had a strong stake in performing well in these comparisons because its model of social organization was under challenge. They envisioned that there would be important international consequences if the United States lagged in these competitions. In this context the "discovery" of social problems in the United States like widespread elder poverty and the plight of minorities ceased to be primarily internal problems. They tainted the United States' presentation of itself to the world and undermined its claim to moral leadership.

Liberal elites argued that national government had to attack and resolve these problems. Others, particularly in the South, thought that they could suppress them from public view through control of media access and censorship. Both in fact happened. In 1964 President Lyndon Johnson declared a war on poverty. During this period, the South and much of the national media ignored the issue of racism and the civil rights movement until it erupted with the "freedom rides" in 1961. TV was now a major news medium and burning buses and attacks on unarmed black civilians was hard to ignore. Since it involved interstate commerce, these conflicts forced the federal government to get involved.

To the internationalists in both parties it was clear that the United States had a strong stake in arguing that these issues were historical aberrations from the main trends of U.S. history and that government at all levels was resolving them.

One result of these pressures was the growth of U.S. government. It became a massive new presence as a funder of programs in science, technology, education, and state and local governments. Outside the national security state, however, this did not involve *central planning* and direct control of funds. Instead, the federal government continued its role as funder and depended on administrative rules and oversight for accountability. Local governments controlled the allocation of funds and the methods to resolve these issues. The federal government continued its role as a *"procedural state"* (Katznelson, 2013). There was little federal effort to examine the results of programs or compare regions or states on outcomes. In the case of the National Assessment of Academic Performance, for example, Congress weighed in and made it *illegal,* and technically impossible, for academics and educators to make such comparisons. They wanted to avoid the invidious comparisons between states and whole regions that such studies would inevitably produce and the political furor this would cause.

This effort produced a massive growth of federal and state support for science and higher education. It had become clear to political elites that the United States was not just in a military competition with the Soviet Union. It was in a much broader race to show which model of society offered the best prospects for its citizens on many counts. Liberal elites looked to the federal government to steer and fund these endeavors. With the loss of the South to Republicans over civil rights and the rising power of corporate conservatives, this outlook became increasingly controversial in the 1960s.

THE GOLDEN DECADES OF SUPPORT FOR SCIENCE

The liberal effort to reform society was not the only source of support for expanding universities and science. The militarization of U.S. foreign policy also gave an enormous boost to science and the universities that housed it.

There was political consensus among elites that technological prowess was critical to military strength and superiority. The United States could not outcompete countries like China in the size of its military and workforce.

In the uncertain world of the 1950s, military prowess was a critical concern of American elites (Gaddis, 2005). Many believed that if the United States was not a preeminent military power, its international influence would fade and its major competitor, the Soviet Union, would win the support of the emerging third world as well as influence in a weakened Europe that was in the process of reconstruction.

Given these elite views, the Cold War played an important part in persuading political elites to expand education and science. Internal competition among states and cities for funding, faculty, and students then kicked into gear as well. All levels of the federal system joined this effort. Much of the funding for student grants/loans and for university construction came from the federal government. The national government subsidized the expansion of higher education through the National Defense Education Act of 1958 and other agencies like the Departments of Defense and Agriculture. The states themselves provided substantial funding as well.

Table 5.1 shows the extraordinary expansion of the college-educated population in this period. Between 1950 and 1980, the proportion of the population age twenty-five to twenty-nine with college or graduate degrees almost tripled. Since then growth has slowed to 4 percent per decade. Wyatt and Hecker (2006) show that this trend tracks closely with the enormous expansion of managerial and professional jobs in the economy, also shown in Table 5.1. In a knowledge society, education invades the workplace so that businesspeople and corporate officials believe that managerial and professional jobs require increasing educational credentials (see also Baker, 2014: 125–156).

The same wave of competition and aspiration also produced support for the expansion of science and graduate education. Table 5.2 shows the pattern of accentuating support for science. First, the *number* of colleges and universities grew by a third between 1950 and 1970 (column 2). Both the federal government and states facilitated this expansion by providing funds directly to colleges and by funding grants and scholarships like the GI Bill and the National Defense Education Act in 1958.

THE LIBERAL ACTIVIST SOCIETY

TABLE 5.1 The Percentage of the Population Age 25–29 with a Four-Year College Degree or More and the Percentage of Technical and Professional Workers in the Economy

Decade	Four Year College Degree	Tech./Prof. Workers
1910	2.7%	5%
1920	2.3	5
1930	3.9	6
1940	4.6	7
1950	6.2	10
1960	7.7	12
1970	11.0	15
1980	17.0	18
1990	21.3	21
2000	25.6	25
2010	29.9	–

Sources: NCES, *Digest of Education Statistics*, 2010, Washington, DC: U.S. Government Printing Office, April 2011; Wyatt and Hecker, 2006: 38, chart 2.

Doctoral programs also expanded. The National Science Foundation (NSF) report on doctoral education concludes that "the greatest growth in doctoral programs at U.S. institutions of higher education was in the 1960s and 1970s, after the Soviet Union launched the satellite *Sputnik*." After 1957, new policies emerged that focused on increasing the number of research universities. "The number of doctorate-granting institutions grew by 73 in the 1960s and by another 87 in the 1970s. By the mid-1960s, institutions with doctoral programs were in all 50 U.S. states, the District of Columbia, and Puerto Rico." (Thurgood et al., 2006: 5). During this period science became a *nationwide* institution, moving from its original base in the northeast westward to the West Coast as more institutions competed for federal largesse to fund their programs.

As graduate education in science expanded, so did support for graduate students in these fields. The expansion of doctoral programs prompted a buildup of graduate education in the United States through a variety of programs, including graduate fellowships funded under the National Defense Education Act of 1958 and fellowship and traineeship programs of the NSF, the National Institutes of Health, and the Public Health Service (Thurgood et al., 2006: 6).

Table 5.2 (column 3) shows that federal overall spending on science research and development tripled during this period, 1950–1972. The NSF

TABLE 5.2 Indicators of the Expansion of Science, 1940–2008

Year	Number of Four-Year Institutions	Total Federal R&D Funding	Federal Academic R&D Research Funding	Federal Basic Research funding to Universities	Number of Scientists and Engineers
1940	1,252	(millions)	(millions)	(millions)	
1942	1,308				
1944	1,237				
1946	1,304				
1948	1,316				
1950	1,345				557,000
1952	1,380				686
1954	1,344	15,957	846	85	784
1956	1,388	24,342	1,018	116	874
1958	1,404	32,228	1,294	159	1,001,000
1960	1,451	20,352	2,039	215	1,104
1962	1,479	44,583	3,019	293	1,210
1964	1,495	54,688	4,263	402	1,327
1966	1,608	57,910	5,458	494	1,418
1968	1,588	34,249	6,030	621	1,525
1970	1,639	51,563	5,800	748	1,595,000
1972		50.406	5,940		
1974		47.206	5,898	1,125,103***	
1976		47,971	6,191	1,320,736	
1978		50,732	6,901	1,738,104	
1980	1,957	52,656	7,599	2,291,264	
1982		56,200	7,364	2,693,269	
1984		65,188	8,045	3,490,727	
1986	2,029	72,648	9,331	4,088,365	
1988		75,028	10,712	4,829,815	
1990		71,285	11,485	5,470,029	
1992		66,336	12,548	6,230,381	
1994		63,316	13,525	6,947,337	
1996		63,392	14,067	7,417,978	
1998		64,743	15,103	7,907,976	2,650,800*
2000				10,022,175	
2008					5,800,000**

Source: *Historical Statistics of the U.S., Colonial Times to 1970*, 1975, U.S. Department of Commerce, Bureau of the Census: Table Series H, 689–699: 382, Part I; U.S. Census, Historical Statistics; Part II: W 168–180: 967; *U.S. Doctorates in the 20th Century*, 2006, Table 2-2: 8.
* National Science Foundation, Scientists, Engineers and Technicians in the U.S., 1998, March 2002.
** http://www.nsf.gov/statistics/inbrief/nsf10315/.
*** Source: National Science Foundation, *Federal Funds for Research and Development: Fiscal Years 1973–2003*, July 2004.

report (Thurgood et al., 2006: 6–8) notes that "national expenditures for research and development (R&D), both federal and nonfederal, increased at an annual rate of about 8 percent in real terms between 1953 and 1969."

Federal funds for basic research also increased during this period. Funding went up by a factor of seven (Table 5.3, column 5). Since basic research was a complete monopoly of university scientists, most of this research money went directly to universities (Science Progress, 2011). These expenditures dramatically increased the size of the scientific labor force. Government grants and contracts supported many graduate students as research assistants.

The NSF report (Thurgood et al., 2006: 6–8) notes that "the annual number of doctorates awarded rose from 8,611 in 1957 to 33,755 in 1973, an increase of nearly 9 percent per year." In addition, the total number of scientists and engineers in the United States tripled from about half a million to one and a half million (column 6, table 3.1).

A similar picture emerges when the subject is the number of doctorates awarded in science and engineering. Table 5.3 shows the extraordinary expansion of these fields between 1950 and 1969. Table 5.4 shows that 18 percent of the PhDs ever awarded in the United States were awarded during the period 1950–1969.

While science and higher education exploded during this period, so did the social sciences and the professions (Frank and Gabler, 2006). The "credential society" was quickly coming into being (Collins, 1979). Think tanks, scientized management, and the rationalization of organizations were also trends inspired by the vision of a knowledge society (Lane, 1999). These trends represent the aspiration for a "scientized polity" (Habermas, 1991; Foucault, 1991; Bell, 1973). Politically this often meant the dream of a more egalitarian, meritocratic society (Young, 1958).

THE GROWTH OF GOVERNMENT EFFORTS
TO COORDINATE SCIENCE PROGRAMS

Another aspect of the knowledge society was an emphasis on the public accountability of science. Since the national government was committed to developing and funding science, it sought to develop ways to coordinate scientific efforts and ensure accountability for the funds received. This

TABLE 5.3 Doctorates Awarded in Engineering and Science, 1920–1999

Period	No. of Science/Engineering PhDs	% of Total PhDs
1920–1924	2,724	64.9
1925–1929	4,907	63.4
1930–1934	7,455	62.2
1935–1939	8,487	62.0
1940–1944	9,267	62.9
1945–1949	10,014	63.0
1950–1954	25,277	65.4
1955–1959	28,308	64.3
1960–1964	38,267	65.2
1965–1969	66,183	64.0
1970–1974	94,862	58.8
1975–1979	90,804	56.8
1980–1984	91,690	58.7
1985–1989	100,930	61.8
1990–1994	123,214	63.7
1995–1999	134,271	63.8
All Periods	835,221	61.6

Source: Thurgood et al., 2006, table 3-2: 13.

TABLE 5.4 Number and Distribution of Doctoral Awards by Decade

Period	No. of PhDs	% of Total PhDs
All decades	1,364,069	100.0%
1900–09	3,654	0.3
1910–19	5,542	0.4
1920–29	11,935	0.9
1930–39	25,674	1.9
1940–49	30,629	2.2
1950–59	82,689	6.1
1960–69	162,071	11.9
1970–79	320,936	23.5
1980–89	319,501	23.4
1990–99	403,861	29.6

Source: Thurgood et al., 2006, 9.

mission led to the creation of departments within the federal government that would explicitly fund and coordinate scientific efforts for societal mobilization. These agencies would of course also be helpful in securing funding from Congress by ensuring accountability. Such a strategy was part of the liberal dream—an "activist society" that could achieve progress by harnessing science and public policy to developmental goals (Gauchat, 2012).

Table 5.5 shows the main federal agencies concerned with science and their founding dates. Of the twenty-one agencies concerned with science or data analysis, fourteen had their origin in the years 1947 to 1979. Government established only four new agencies in this area after 1980. One of them, the Department of Education, was not a new entity at all. Administrators separated it into its own agency, apart from health and welfare. The period after the 1950s–1970s saw the creation of the majority of all the formal agencies concerned with science and public policy within the federal government.

Another notable development during this period was the creation by Congress in 1976 of the Office of Science and Technology Policy. The purpose was to establish an office in the White House that would advise the president on science policy and coordinate national science and technology activities among the federal agencies. This office has been especially important in giving presidents scientific advice during important crises like

TABLE 5.5   Date of Establishment of Key Government Departments and Agencies in Science

Department or Agency	Date of Founding:
Bureau of Labor Statistics	1884
Bureau of the Census	1903
National Institutes of Health	1933
Centers for Disease Control and Prevention	1942
National Institute of Mental Health	1949
National Science Foundation	1950
Department of Health, Education, and Welfare (HEW)	1953
National Aeronautics and Space Administration	1958
National Communicable Disease Center	1967
National Institute for Occupational Safety and Health	1970
Bureau of Economic Analysis	1972
Defense Manpower Data Center	1974
Nuclear Regulatory Commission	1975
Department of Energy	1977
U.S. Energy Information Administration.	1977
HUD USER: Information on Housing Center	1978
Department of Education (formerly HEW)	1980
Bureau of Transportation Statistics	1992
President's Council of Advisors on Science and Technology	2001
Research and Innovative Technology Administration	2005

Hurricane Katrina; the nuclear meltdown at the reactor in Fukushima, Japan; and the anthrax attacks in late 2001. Only recently has a disdain for science become normal. Under President Donald Trump there was a long period when the office was left vacant.[1]

While agencies dealing with science expanded during this period, little attention was paid to their coordination. We have seen this pattern before (Pierson, 2007): the growth of a vast network of regulatory agencies with low levels of rationalization and coordination between them. In the case of science, the president does this job with the advice of the lone, distinguished scientist who heads of the Office of Science and Technology Policy and a small staff in the White House. The president is free to accept or reject this advice and decides whether or not to have a science advisor.

STATE EXPANSION AND THE EXPLOSION OF REFORM

State expansion helped produce a wave of reform movements in this period. A wide array of citizens' groups also emerged (Barry, 1999). The expansion of government created niches for such movements, and the optimism of the era gave many hopes that such efforts would succeed (e.g., McAdam, 1982, 1988; McCarthy and Zald, 1973).

The conflicts ignited in the 1960s focused on two key issues in American society (Schudson, 1998a; Abrams, 2006). The first is civil libertarianism. It involved the extension of civil and legal rights in society to groups that had been historically marginalized. This debate also raised the contentious issue of the national government's responsibility for ensuring such rights in localities where historic practices and community cultures favored various forms of discrimination.

Political liberals supported the extension of civil and political rights. Many conservatives did not. Conservative elites also thought that these conflicts were undermining national solidarity in the face of the Cold War and were threats to national security (Zolberg, 2002).

The second major issue concerned the role of government in regulating the economy to achieve full employment, economic growth, and higher wages. Conservatives maintained the view that it was time to resurrect classic laissez-faire capitalism in the United States. With mutual nuclear deterrence between the United States and the Soviet Union; the reconstruction of Europe and Japan; and a new, stable international order (Gaddis, 2005), the time for government regulation was over.

Liberals continued to pursue Keynesian arguments that government had a significant role to play in managing the economy to soften the effects of the business cycle and maintain liquidity in the economy. But as their political losses mounted in the 1960s and 1970s, these views became problematic (Petrocik, 1981).

These two issues created the cultural context in which reform played out. These developments helped frame the narratives that movements of the 1960s and 1970s developed. They also shaped the responses of government and other actors to these demands.

THE BIRTH OF REFORM MOVEMENTS

One of the consequences of these conflicts was that during the period from the 1950s to the 1980s societal reform and re-vitalization became a narrative around which many groups mobilized. Many of the major liberal reform movements were born or came to life during this period. Civil rights and equality became leading issues in the courts and on the streets.

Tables 5.6 and 5.7 below show the rapid rise of both gender and ethnic advocacy groups between 1955 and the 1980s (Skocpol and Fiorina, 1999; see also M. Katzenstein and Mueller, 1987; Berkovitch, 1999). Sixty-eight percent of women's advocacy groups were created in the years 1975 to 1980.

TABLE 5.6 Founding Dates of Gender/Ethnic Associations, 1955–1980s

Type	1955	1960	1965	1970	1975	1980s	Total Number
Women	6%	6%	7.2%	12%	26.5%	42.2%	830
Blacks	5.9%	5.9%	11.1%	25.2%	25.2%	26.6%	675
Hispanics	2.2%	2.2%	8.7%	21.7%	30.4%	34.8%	230

Source: Skocpol, 1999: 470; Skocpol and Fiorina 1999 fig. 13.2.

TABLE 5.7 Founding of Women's and Ethnic Advocacy Groups, 1960–1980

	1960	1965	1970	1975	1980
% of Total ($n = 595$)	4.2%	5.0%	15.1%	33.6%	42.0%

Source: Skocpol, 1999: 471; Skocpol and Fiorina, 1999: fig. 13.3.

Hispanics also founded most of their advocacy associations during the same period—the 1970s and 1980s. Almost two thirds of Hispanic associations were born in this era. Blacks had mobilized earlier (McAdam, 1982). Still, over half of black advocacy organizations emerged during this period.

Similarly, women and minority groups formed over 75 percent of their advocacy groups between 1975 and 1980 (see Table 5.7).

This was an era of reform as well as one of burgeoning reaction (see Chapter 7).

SOURCES OF SOCIAL MOBILIZATION

Two points are important in accounting for such rapid mobilization during this period. First, rapid government expansion from the 1950s to the 1970s helped create new markets and niches in society for such movements (Pierson and Skocpol, 2007). This is a common observation among resource mobilization theorists (e.g., McAdam, 1982, 1988; Skocpol, 2003; McAdam and Scott, 2002). This feature of the activist society supported reform movements in many ways.

One change initiated by activist government was to create new sources of funding for movements. For example, the anti-poverty programs of the period often had mandates for public participation along with money to fund local groups (Taub et al., 1984; Fainstein and Fainstein, 1976).

The federal government also initiated programs that created clients and constituencies for reform (J. Wilson, "The Rise," 2006: 362–363). As Wilson notes, one of the purposes of many programs was to create local constituencies for program agendas. Such clients then become important constituencies of support for federal programs and for supportive members of Congress.

Government action also created large constituencies in civil society for reform and expansion of civil liberties. As Senator Daniel Moynihan pointed out at the time, the expansion of universities themselves created ready-made constituencies for reform movements. Many students saw career opportunities in fields expanded by government action, such as science, education, local government, law and law enforcement, defense, social welfare programs, and the military-industrial sector. Furthermore, a decline in discriminatory rules concerning gender, race, religion, and so on was for many an important source of occupational success.

The expanded authority of federal courts also facilitated mobilization. The evolution of the courts as policy-making bodies created space for social movements to act in, and supportive legal decisions and doctrines (Glazer, 1975; Lieberman, 1981; Friedman, 2004). The spate of civil rights legislation created the possibility of legal mobilization among reform groups (Pierson, 2007). This became a major strategy for reform because it allowed groups to circumvent legislative arenas.

The courts' support for civil rights also generated new legal doctrines that gave many such groups standing as litigants. Legal doctrines like that of "disparate effects" made it easier to prove discrimination without having to prove intent on the part of legislators. The Supreme Court's decision against the doctrine "separate but equal" in *Brown v. Board of Education* also facilitated litigation against segregation by nullifying one of its previous key legal supports. This created more possibilities for lawsuits focusing on collective grievances of oppressed groups.

Legal and political success of various civil rights groups generated optimism about the future. Rising hope facilitated more organized mobilization (e.g., McAdam, 1982). As a result, many reform groups thrived in this period, buoyed by the ideological support they found for a more inclusive and egalitarian society.

Second, an activist government institutionalized the narrative of the activist society during this period. Government programs, federal activity, and changes in law all helped signal this regime change. Government action and programs during the period highlighted the fact that the activist society was a functioning regime. President Eisenhower's decision to send federal troops to Little Rock to enforce the Supreme Court's desegregation decision is one instance. President Johnson's "war on poverty" also invoked the imagery of a nation mobilizing to resolve a long-standing problem. Federal funding of universities and science was based on the same narrative. So was the civil rights legislation of 1965 and President Johnson's executive order banning gender discrimination in the civil service and among government contractors. Even the failed invasion of Cuba and entrance into the Vietnam War were part of this narrative. Political elites justified these actions on the grounds that they were efforts to extend democracy to other countries.

This argument is not meant to slight the role that organizational factors, leadership, and other conditions played in the emergence of social movements during this period. The point is simply that the macro conditions of an expanded government that was determined to be activist in society and the economy created a powerful narrative, opportunity structure, and incentive for social movement groups to form and succeed. It also led to conservative countermobilization.

RIGHTS AND LIBERATION LOGICS
BEHIND THE MOVEMENTS

The movements pictured in Tables 5.6 and 5.7 grew out of two institutional logics that had become highly legitimate during this period. One was a logic that extolled personal liberty and freedoms. Government propaganda during World War II and afterward was one of the sources of this ideology that extolled personal liberty (Abrams, 2006; Mann, 2013). Contemporary propaganda had depicted the struggle for such liberty as one of the main reasons for World War II.

This logic produced movements for equality in the United States among a wide variety of groups. The "rights revolution" exemplified one of the institutional logics that emerged to support such movements. While these movements were hotly contested, much in the liberal tradition supported their claims (Schudson, 1998a). Both the narratives of individualism and equality supported these movements. In this view the women's movement and the civil rights movement were all efforts to extend traditional rights to women and blacks. The American polity tends to be open to rights claims against discrimination and arbitrary cultural distinctions. The difficulty arises over what governmental bodies have authority to enforce these claims and determine whether violations have in fact occurred.

A second institutional logic underlying some of these movements was and is more contentious. This logic involves substantive rights claims that go beyond freedom from discrimination and involve substantial purposive action by government. The claims of blacks for reparations for decades of slavery or of women for paid family leave fall under this category. These claims encounter difficulties in a liberal polity. It is hard to justify substantive rights in a polity that focuses on individual rights and responsibilities. These claims invoke the logic of *group* rights and the authority of the state to act as an arbiter. Neither finds much legitimation in the tradition of U.S. liberalism and its institutional structure.

AREAS OF CONSENSUS AND GROWING DISSENSUS

An enduring part of the liberal agenda has been the promotion of individual rights in a variety of spheres. There is an increasing consensus across the political spectrum on the importance of individual freedom from state or social oppression. Equality and populism are prominent parts of American political culture. This legitimates social movements for individual rights, even if this means destroying established social order. For example, the trade-off involved in supporting women's and children's rights is dilution of the traditional authority structure of the family. For conservatives, this element of populism has been problematic.

Another part of the liberal agenda was support for state action in breaking down legal barriers that supported discrimination. This part of the liberal view of social order is still intact, though contested. Many corporate neoliberals also find this compelling because it frees markets from artificial constraints and expands opportunity for individual creativity to surface.

Consensus has vanished, however, concerning the role of the state. This plank of liberalism collapsed. The idea of an activist society and state has been under successful attack since the 1960s under the successful reign of neoliberalism. As the narratives of individualism and populism have thrived, the idea of an activist state has come under assault. Developing human capital has become the new main narrative of how to improve society. Experts and politicians who support this view define problems like inequality as the result of inadequate skill sets and motivation among segments of the population. The proper solution, they offer, is more and better education, including copying the German model of apprenticeship and vocational education.

It has become contentious to suggest that the state should directly attack these problems through tax policy or redistributive efforts. Under neoliberalism all the benefits of state social policies have become defined as *individual* ones. As a result, many kinds of purposive activity by the federal government have become contentious, except national defense and anti-terrorism measures.

This view of government activity has percolated down through society, so that many, particularly young voters, think that government is "usually inefficient and wasteful." Polls show that roughly 65 percent of youth under age 30 hold this view (*The Economist*, October 18–24, 2014: 30–31).

STRATEGIES FOR CHANGE AND NEW IDEOLOGICAL FAULT LINES

This process of development created two main societal strategies for pursuing progress. These have now become major fault lines of conflict. The traditional American strategy of development relied on mobilizing the populace and communities behind common social goals. The role of the state was to support these efforts with resources and support. Education and literacy have always featured heavily in this narrative. Individual striving and social mobility were also part of the recipe for the success of such projects.

The postwar expansion of higher education added a new dimension to this narrative. Building human capital through credentialing and professionalization became part of the recipe for social mobilization. Human capital theory in economics provided intellectual justification for these efforts (Schultz, 1961; Becker, 1994). The result was massive societal support for college attendance and for public financing of higher education during this period.

Liberal theory offered a new modification of this approach. It argued that government had a key role to play in achieving modernization. Social planning and coordination of societal activities by the state were important components of this ideology. In this view science would be critical for achieving success. Expanded education was also crucial. Much of the funding for science and education was to come from government sources. Government would also have the task of developing industrial policies and strategies to harness these resources. This required an implicit industrial policy. Research and development of the military-industrial complex, in association with universities and Congress, was to aid this process (Mann, 2013). Government would coordinate and regulate the implementation of these policies.

The conflicts unleashed in the 1960s shattered any such consensus underlying the liberal activist society. Conservatives rallied around an earlier vision of individual and community mobilization as sources of "progress" enhanced by expanded public education. The role of government became controversial.

These distinctive approaches then became highly politicized as separate narratives of how to achieve progress. These disparate views separated distinctive factions of the American public and elites. With the demise of consensus on the activist society, support for government efforts to regulate the economy and provide safety nets for the disadvantaged diminished.

As external threats diminished and interstate competition became more regulated, liberal society reverted to its classic institutional culture. The next chapter shows how individualism reemerged in the 1960s in a more intensified form. Ironically, this development provided support for neoliberal views of government and the new conservative movement. The emergence of an enhanced version of individualism, helped conservatives frame the state as an enemy of personal liberty and creativity.

CHAPTER 6

The Intensification of Individualism and the Displacement of Citizenship

IN 1912 ÉMILE DURKHEIM identified the "cult of the individual" as a new civil religion that was emerging in Europe and America as traditional sources of authority collapsed. This chapter argues that a century later this civil religion has intensified in the United States to the point where it has eclipsed citizenship as a meaningful social role (Jepperson and Meyer, 2011; Lipset, 1996; Crouch, 2004).

Under the shadow of the Cold War, individualism had been suppressed. The emergence of a global political and economic order helped normalize intercountry relations. This change made space for the emergence of an enhanced form of individualism that has diminished the significance of citizenship as well as a primordial base of community, such as race, ethnicity, and religion (see Jepperson and Meyer, 2011; W. Wilson, 1978; Hout, 1988). This development raises the question of whether there is any basis for a common political ethic and a durable political community in the United States (see Bell, 1973).

Other factors discussed more widely in the social science literature have also contributed to this political change. These include the well-noted arguments about the growth of big money and lobbying in politics (Crenson and Ginsberg, 2004; Mayer, 2011; Alexander, 1980); the decline of local organizations as sources of mobilization (Skocpol and Fiorina, 1999; Janowitz, 1978); the increasing role of national media and the growth of politics as a spectator sport (Fallows, 1996; McChesney, 2004); and the rise of social media as the link between individuals and the political system (Norris and Inglehart, 2009).

The intensified cult of the individual is another important but less noted phenomenon, connected to the eclipse of citizenship. This chapter discusses how it has contributed to changes in the meaning of citizenship. These include declines in civic participation and civic consciousness and the decline of patriotism (Putnam, 2000; Janowitz, 1983). As we discuss in Chapter 9, it has also paved the way for the emergence of very radical forms of populism.

"THE INDIVIDUAL" AS THE NEW SOCIAL REALITY

As a central narrative and myth, individualism has now become the transcendent story of how American society works and why it is exceptional (see Chapter 2). The individual has now displaced society or prominent subgroups, such as status groups like ethnic groups, social classes, and aristocracies, as the new social reality (Ramirez, 2006a). With this narrative now dominant, socialization becomes the modern theme of how society works (Meyer, 1986; Jepperson and Meyer, 2007; Meyer and Jepperson, 2000).

This view of reality increasingly penetrates all social spheres, as modernization breaks down older forms of community and versions of social reality (Berger and Luckmann, 1967; Berger, 1967; Douglas and Tipton, 1982). Parenting changes, for example, as both fathers and mothers no longer play scripted roles. Men as well as women are free to enact their own versions of parenting and family organization.

This changing perspective of social reality places the individual as the central agent of action. British prime minister Margaret Thatcher once famously quipped: "There is no such thing as society. There are only individuals and families." Families have disappeared as primordial units of social reality in American society. Now there is only the individual. In this new social reality, charisma is transferred to people and drained from many other institutions (Shils, 1958). The public no longer regards them as primordial and rooted in nature the way individuals are. This change empowers individual actors and leads to a vast expansion of abilities and capacities attributed to them. Economists, for example, now view society as a vast aggregate of human capital. The highly socialized individual is one of its primary drivers (Becker, 1994).

This changed social reality has altered many institutions in fundamental ways. Take the case of marriage. Many changes occur if the public learns to see it *not* as a set of organized social roles that individuals play but rather an institution built on a contract between freely consenting adults that is meant to secure their individual happiness and health. Modern American marriage takes on much of the character of a voluntary association under these conditions (see Varenne, 1977). Laws now make it easy to contract and easy to dissolve. Divorce becomes more readily imaginable if the parties believe that marriage is not fulfilling their hopes. The stigmas and sense of failure connected to marital dissolution also begin to fade. Divorce rates increase and social approval for divorce also increases. Divorce is also more easily available as changes in law occur and no-fault divorce laws become common across states. Furthermore, many religions have adapted both their theology and practice in accepting divorced people into their communities.

The definition of what constitutes a marriage also changes under this new reality. If two people love each other, the idea that they should be able to marry gains ground, even if they are of the same sex. Same-sex marriage is now legal in the United States and is fast becoming accepted as a social reality. Many religious groups condone it and social approval of this quest has been rising, particularly among younger generations (Putnam and Campbell, 2010: 56off).

Marital roles also become more fluid as individuals acquire the right to organize marriage to fit their individual personalities and needs. Childbearing, for example, becomes an option, not a socially defined purpose of marriage. Partly because of this change, couples are freer to make decisions about whether to have children and when to have them. Birth rates decline, and many couples opt not to have children or to have them much later in the life cycle.

Single-parent families have also become a viable and socially approved form. Having children is also a choice many see as independent of marriage. Fifty percent of births to women under age thirty are now to women who are unmarried. An unknown number of these cases result from carefully planned choice by the mother. There is growing social approval for such behavior. In a reanalysis of the 2005–2007 World Values Surveys, I found that 50.9 percent of the U.S. sample ($N = 1,219$) approved of the following statement: "If a woman wants to have a child as a single parent but she doesn't want a stable relationship with a man, do you approve or disapprove?" Among women, 54.9 percent approved compared to 46.9 percent of men. This sea change heralds the emergence of a new and legitimate family form consisting of a mother and children. This level of approval seems vastly different from the 1950s, when such behavior was highly stigmatized and was often hidden when it did occur.

Sexuality also becomes divorced from marriage. Sexual freedom increases and becomes defined by many young adults as independent of courtship and marriage (see Abrams, 2006, historical survey; F. Allen, 1931). Sex for mutual pleasure is now widely condoned if it is consensual. Sexual activity among young, nonmarried adults increases and the stigma once associated with it for women declines.

Society is also becoming increasingly tolerant of a variety of types of sexuality. Sexual identity and behavior become viewed as a matter of *personal* choice. Homosexuality ceases to be a criminal offense. Much of the public accepts the view that it is biologically based and therefore not a choice people make (Walters, 2001). Adultery also loses its legal stigma. As a result, both adultery and homosexuality no longer face criminal sanction in many countries (Frank, Camp, and Boutcher, 2010).

As choice expands, the public airwaves and media become saturated with news and advice about sexuality. For heterosexuals, worldwide websites are filled clips and photos demonstrating a variety of erotic practices that viewers may try out for their pleasure. Manuals, advice columns, and websites proliferate to accommodate the concerns, interests, and anxieties that the public shares concerning their own sexuality. The counseling professions also proliferate in response to these demands and concerns (Frank, Meyer, and Miyahara, 1995).

At the same time, many kinds of behavior that were previously acceptable within marriage become taboo. Violence is one of them. It becomes inconceivable that women would freely consent to beatings or other abusive behavior. The crime of rape within marriage is now legally and socially imaginable and punishable in the criminal law. So is spousal abuse.

Where people live as adults also undergoes a change as the cult of the individual intensifies. Adults no longer expect their children to live with them as parts of families or to establish families of their own as soon as they leave school and get jobs. Instead there is a growing trend of people choosing to live alone during their early adult years—often for prolonged periods of time. In 1950, 9 percent of households consisted of single adults. In 2010, 28 percent of American households were occupied by one inhabitant. For the brief period 1996–2006, the growth of single occupant households is up 33 percent (Klinenberg, 2012a: 5ff; 2012b). And in many large and cosmopolitan cities like New York and Atlanta, 40 to 50 percent of the households are composed of single adults. This trend coincides with another that Marsden and Srivastava (2012) document. Young adults report spending much of their social time in public spaces like bars and restaurants with friends, who are neither relatives nor near neighbors. Families are no longer the basis for much of the sociability that young adults act out.

With the decline of community and the stable order of social roles that entails, the public increasingly ascribes action and order in society to the behavior of properly motivated people. Socialization becomes the main narrative of how society achieves and maintains a viable social order. In this perspective, such phenomena as dropping out of high school or college and low achievement levels in schools become major social problems (Baker, 2014). They signify not just individual failure but the inadequacies of families, schooling, communities, and perhaps the nation itself. For example, a major policy report on education in the 1980s was titled *A Nation at Risk*. Low international achievement scores were the source of this risk.

The new individual in this narrative is not, however, an id with wild, anarchic impulses. He or she is a highly disciplined person whose self is oriented to collective purposes (Frank and Meyer, 2002). There are many sources of this new standardized self: education, the professions, science, the media/mass communications, social media, and so on. This development has created a fluid society but not a rootless one in which men and women have no permanent social bonds. This does not create a society built on "liquid modernity" (Bauman, 2013). Nor is this a society organized around selves that are built on personal narcissism (Lasch, 1979; Twenge, 2006). The "cult of the individual" instead refers to highly constructed selves that many believe are now prominent sources of all kinds of social value: human capital, cultural capital, social capital, and the various other capitals that social scientists have discovered to signify the various values that individuals create.

These changes involve the reorganization and rationalization of all sorts of roles. This process involves widespread efforts to reorganize social institutions so that they produce the appropriate kinds of personalities for modern societies (Inkeles and Smith, 1974). Education, for example, becomes more student-centered in national ideologies (Ramirez, 2006a; Bromley et al., 2011). Models of parenting also focus on the child and her specific needs and less on behavioral conformity. And in the workplace, employers are urged to respect the dignity of all employees and are legally bound not to create hostile work environments or discriminatory patterns of supervision.

THE BREAKDOWN OF PUBLIC/
PRIVATE DISTINCTIONS
"Be who you are"—Brooklyn, New York, graffiti, June 2014

The new individualism has also changed society in one other important way. It has reduced, if not obliterated, the distinction between public and private spheres. Under these changed conditions the presentation of self that Goffman (1961: 85ff) analyzed so brilliantly may be less of a central issue that individuals must deal with. As public and private spheres become less distinct, there is no "back stage" and "front stage" for individuals to manage. The public sphere of the self becomes vastly enlarged.

Two major cultural changes signal this shift: identity politics is one, and the rise of new forms of religion is another. Both involve a search for authenticity and personal meaning in each sphere (Boli and Elliot, 2008). And both quests are linked to broad collective goals such as the search for justice, equality, and progress, broadly conceived. Identity politics indicates that politics and citizen roles are changing, and the new religious movements signal that traditional religion is in decline (Putnam and Campbell, 2010). The public no longer believes that voting or church attendance is a *civic duty*. It is voluntary and becomes a personal choice.

The effort to redefine social role(s) so that they fit one's self identity suggests that there is broad awareness of this change. The personal has now become public and vice versa. The fact that this is happening in many institutional sectors strengthens the argument that a major cultural shift is occurring. The shift has, for example, taken place in the world of work among younger generations. In trying to explain why science is a less attractive occupational choice in industrial countries than in the developing world, Charles and Bradley (2009) show that young people expect work to be a source of *intrinsic* satisfaction in advanced industrial societies. Jobs are not just sources of income, status, and security. Youth are sorting out occupations and choosing those that fit their own personal narratives of achievement and meaning. As a result, the search for careers that are satisfying often involves extensive trial and error, characterized by job changes and surges into and out of advanced education.

Mass communication is another sphere that exemplifies this cultural shift. I refer to the use of the new social media. Millennials often post incredibly personal or intimate photos, videos, and text concerning themselves or their friends on a media that is in fact public. The fact that *sexting* has now become a well-established word signifies this fact. As sophisticated users, young adults know that such communications are in fact public. Many unauthorized parties have access to such communications, including government, corporations, and educational institutions. Yet they continue to do it. This suggests either that they are naïve about the consequences, which implies a naïveté that is not credible, or that they do not care. The latter seems a more viable explanation. In a culture that extensively empowers individuals, the millennials may be right—not caring is indeed appropriate. Public/private distinctions have faded to the extent that employers, schools, colleges, and so on may be enjoined or self-censor themselves from using this information as evidence of a person's fitness for work, education, or trust. Demography is also on the millennials' side, since their employers are increasingly likely to be like themselves—people who share their outlook and understand that these communications are meant to be personal and irrelevant to occupational or corporate considerations.

A related trend is the increasing use of body art (tattoos) by millennials. The Pew surveys report that up to 30 percent of this age group has tattoos, compared to 5 to 10 percent of older generations (Pew Research Center, 2010). Older generations often acquired tattoos during military service. They were often a sign of social solidarity with comrades doing similar duty. The notion that one's body is one's own, and not a public matter, also legitimates other forms of privacy such as patients' rights and the importance of informed consent in many other relationships.

The decline of the distinction between public and private spheres is a cultural shift that is associated with the eclipse of citizenship. This and other public roles rely on a civic consciousness that is separate from private concerns and moralities. This distinction is collapsing, and with it goes lip service to many forms of public morality. Patriotic nationalism and the idea of "my country right or wrong" decline as individuals align their public attitudes with their private sentiments and interests (Putnam, 2000; Janowitz, 1983). This change also undermines one of the core myths of nationalism: that the nation is constructed of people who share a common culture (Anderson, 1983). The rise and acceptance of multiculturalism signifies such a change (see Mirel, 2010). People and entire communities now celebrate ethnic and other identities and valorize them. They are no longer suppressed in a common public melting pot. People also view them as voluntarily chosen identities, not necessarily rooted in ethnic or other communities.

This change legitimates widespread variations in the way people enact *citizen* roles. And it also sanctions the alignment of citizen roles with other identities people assume. A dramatic illustration of this change concerns the way wars have been presented in American high school textbooks (Lachmann and Mitchell, 2014). Between 1945 and 1970 the authors found an unusual consensus in textbook presentations. The emphasis was on patriotism, national sacrifice, and military service. After 1970, there was a shift toward emphasizing individual soldiers' experiences and the suffering that war entailed. This represents a major shift from emphasizing the *nation* to focusing on the *individual*. The film *Saving Private Ryan* represents this trend well.

These changes have affected notions of citizens' responsibilities. Military service, for example, has now become voluntary. Unlike the period of World War I and World War II, many young adults will not volunteer to fight in wars they think are unjust or unnecessary (think Vietnam). Volunteering and formal religiosity are two examples of behavior that much of the public no longer considers civic duties. They are now options and choices people may decide to make or reject.

In the process, personhood eclipses other social identities, such as race, religion, and social class. Ideologies justifying the latter are on the defensive, while those legitimating the person as the main social agent are dominant (Hout, 1988; Frank and Meyer, 2002). This statement does not mean that there is no conflict over race and other ascribed sources of privilege. The point is that personhood is the likely winning trend among both conservative and liberal elites and much of the population at large.

THE ECLIPSE OF CITIZENSHIP: POLITICS WITHOUT CITIZENS

With intensified individualism, traditional citizenship loses cultural centrality. It becomes voluntary action (like military service). The more dutiful "civic culture" and its rituals (including voting and voluntarism) are displaced, moving quickly into romanticism and archaism (the so-called eclipse of citizenship, "post-citizenship" [Crouch, 2004; Putnam, 2000). Accordingly, voting rates decline to a degree, and memberships in traditional community organizations decline (Brody, 1978; Burnham, 1984; Skocpol and Fiorina, 1999). Both are forms that have fewer carriers and plausibility structures in the new polity (e.g., Shienbaum, 1984). Patriotism also declines along with ideals of community service among younger age cohorts (Putnam, 2000; Janowitz, 1983).

The remaining citizenship role also changes, as the modern political system evolves. As the administrative state grows and politics is more media-oriented and funded by large donors, the remaining citizen role changes. The citizen is more an entitled and empowered claimant than the more dutiful and participating citizen of the civic culture. Behavior changes as well. Political and civic participation become more episodic and idiosyncratic. Voting declines while populist forms of political action become common and widespread, for example, boycotts, protests, and actions (Kamens, 2009).[1]

At the same time, other bases of traditional citizenship are weakening (Mitchell and Mitchell, 1968; W. Miller and Niemi, 2002). Local, generalist voluntary associations that used to link citizens to the polity have declined, as have locally based political organizations (Skocpol and Fiorina, 1999). Single-issue organizations have taken their place, and these are often centralized organizations that are staff-driven in terms of the selection of issues to pursue. Political campaigns are now organized around candidates and are more like social movements than stable local political organizations (Agronoff, 1978). These are typically funded from nonlocal sources and are staffed by professionals, who are often drawn from outside the community. Candidate and other campaign advertising is also controlled by sources outside the community, and often designed by paid professional campaign staff. Polling becomes more important (Herbst, 1993). And urban TV and radio networks dominate media coverage. Some, like Fox and MSNBC, have their own political agendas. As small-town newspapers decline, the media treat viewers to news that represents events and stories of major urban centers. Local news declines.

In addition, traditional citizen action is crowded out by a variety of new sources of political action (McCleskey, 1981). Political parties have become massive national fund-raising organizations and expert at assessing which electoral candidates to support based on rational calculations of their chances of winning. This involves the use of paid professionals and reliance on both "big" money and "dark" money that is untraceable (Mayer, 2011). These crowd out and displace traditional sources of citizen action (Crouch, 2004; Ginsberg and Shefter, 1999). Even social movements now rely on crowdsourcing and social media for their support rather than on local community organizations. They too use paid organizers and staffs to develop agendas and disseminate them to candidates, news media, and the public. The "local" of *local* communities and political parties disappears in this process.

These changes encourage passivity on the part of citizens. But they also create in many a sense of connectedness by participating in the virtual reality that media, social media, and campaigns create.

THE INCREASING POWER OF PUBLIC OPINION

While these processes undermine traditional citizenship, people have gained legitimated roles as opiners in the new politics. Citizens are certainly empowered, but more as actors and personalities than as citizens. As a result, public opinion has become a powerful force and has displaced the role that local influentials and party bosses used to play in the political system. Southern evangelicals' suspicions about science, for example, become key factors in determining conservative Republican agenda regarding support for scientific research (Gauchat, 2012). Climate science and modern biology thereby become taboo as subjects or as legitimate objects of research in important political circles. The Environmental Protection Agency, for example, appears to be banning support for proposals dealing with climate change (*New York Times*, September 6, 2017: A1).[2]

The imagined public in this scenario is credited with a wide range of competencies, due in part to increasing education levels (Menand, 2007). One result is that the public role of experts in all fields declines. The result is an extraordinary expansion of the power of public opinion, despite research showing that a majority of the public has scant knowledge on many of the issues on which they are asked to opine, such as science, global warming, sexuality, politics, foreign policy, etc.

The sheer plausibility of public opinion as an agent opens the way for a wide array of irrationalities to emerge and to be taken seriously by the public and elites. Creationism can masquerade as science, and global warming can appear to be a hoax among much of the public at large—particularly, conservatives (Gauchat, 2012). With intensified individualism, there are no important gatekeepers who can determine what views have enough plausibility to be on the public agenda and which ones do not.

Similarly, as the power of public opinion grows, the possibilities for unfiltered populist politics increases. Elites are no longer in charge of the public agenda under such circumstances. The public is free to choose its own issue agendas, based on its own uncensored opinions, and empowered to choose leaders whose attitudes and sentiments they admire and identify with. Unconventional leaders on both the right and left like Bernie Sanders and Donald Trump can thrive under these circumstances. They are media creations fueled by public opinion.

These changes have displaced traditional citizenship. From this viewpoint, the mass public is now wired into a changed polity—but not in the ways celebrated by civics-text political theory. The empowered individual displaces the earlier citizen accounting for the changes in mass civic engagement and political participation in the post–World War II period.

INSTITUTIONAL IMPACTS OF INTENSIFIED INDIVIDUALISM

This change in culture has had a major effect in liberating individuals from the constraints of *local* communities and families. *Loss of community* is part of the process of building a society around the cult of the individual. One can see the consequences of this change empirically in a variety of areas.

Decline of Political Parties as Mobilizing Agents: Kevin Baker, a political analyst, puts the issue this way: "the long- term problem is how to maintain a coherent, mass political party when so many individuals are empowered as never before, to redirect it to their own personal ends" (Kevin Baker, "The Outsourced Party," *New York Times*, March 25, 2012, SR 5). Chrystia Freeland, a Canadian journalist and politician, notes that one consequence of this decline is that the ranks of populists are growing despite the rising wealth of plutocrats in both the Republican and Democratic parties. In her view, "the populists, the wilder the better, are taking over" (http://www.nytimes.com/2013/11/03/opinion/Sunday/plutocrats -vs-populists.html).

Politics in many rich democracies has therefore become more plebiscitary, forcing politicians to appeal directly to the electorate as an aggregate of independent individuals freed from many of the restraints of ideology and party.

Politics in turn has become individualized in all advanced industrial democracies. Class and group-based voting has declined in all these societies. Citizen orientations have become anchored to other bases (Dalton and Wattenberg, 1993; Norris, 1999; Dalton, 2002a; 2002b; 2007). One result is that studies of voting show declining patterns of participation (Dalton, 2007; Wilensky, 2002); Burnham, 1984, 1995; Lowi and Ginsberg, 1996; Elkin and Soltan, 1999; Jennings et al., 1989; Kleppner, 1982).).

Politics also becomes more exclusionary and polarized. Education is at the leading edge of this change (Dalton and Wattenberg, 1993; Flanagan and Dalton, 1984; Dalton, 2002a; 2007). It has become a central part of people's social identity and therefore a major boundary of social solidarity. For individuals, voting is primarily an enactment of solidarity (Shienbaum, 1984).

One result is that education's significance for participation has *increased* over time for all groups, including minorities (Brody, 1978; Nie et al., 1996; Kamens, 2009; Stanley, 1987). In the United States as national levels of education increase, voting participation has decreased (Brody, 1978). The result is a rising gap in participation between the most educated and other segments of the society (Nie et al., 1996). These findings strongly suggest that new rules of inclusion/exclusion have developed in American society. As higher education has become more prevalent, the less educated have become economically and socially marginalized and have withdrawn their participation from politics and other public spheres (see Wuthnow, 2002).[3]

There has also been a prolonged decline in local civic associations that were once the foundation of local communities. Membership in the Elks, the American Legion, Rotary International, Kiwanis, the Moose, and other voluntary associations has declined (Skocpol and Fiorina, 1999). People now are more likely to become members of special interest groups, such as sports clubs, and single-interest groups or coalitions, such as the Sierra Club or Common Cause. These groups are now parts of national organizations, whose staffs determine their agendas.

One result of these changes is that politics has become more tribal as individuals have been released from parties and other social constraints. Single-issue movements thrive in this context. Similarly, extremism on controversial issues prevails, given the single-minded commitments of participants. In addition, as polarized positions on issues develop, the parties themselves become pushed to extremes by the most active of their leaders and members. The space for, and interest in, compromise similarly declines.

Decline of Ethnicity and Religious Communities: As personhood becomes the dominant cultural reality, ethnicity and religion lose their force as boundary markers too. Ideologies that justify such solidarity, such as racism and other forms of bigotry, are in decline and on the defensive. As a result, ethnic and religious boundaries are declining. For example, many Americans are choosing to marry across religious and ethnic lines. Putnam and Campbell (2010: 144ff, fig. 5.3, and 151, fig. 5.4) estimate that between one third and one half of all marriages in the United States are between faiths. Ethnic intermarriage is a dominant trend in society.

Surprising numbers of people also change their faith. About one third of Americans have switched religions (Putnam and Campbell, 2010: 144ff). And there is a rising trend of people saying that they belong to no organized religion along with declining rates of participation in conventional religion. This is particularly strong among younger generations (Pew Research Center, 2018).

New forms of religiosity have also been invented and tried by increasing numbers of people (Wuthnow, 1988). These tend to emphasize personal spirituality, growth, and the search for authenticity. Both private prayer and diffuse spirituality, for example, are forms of religion and ritual that are becoming more common in the United States (and Europe), while biblical literalism and church attendance have declined (Wuthnow, 1988, 2002; Chaves and Anderson, 2012: 221ff; Baker, 2014). Private religiosity and spirituality both derive from formal religion, but they are now often detached from attendance at collective rituals.

Organized religion used to be a pillar of civic responsibility. But once the grip of mainstream religions declines, it too becomes a personal option. In the post-1960s era, voting, military service, volunteering, and church attendance are no longer civic duties but become civic options.

A parallel symptom of declining community in religious circles is the decreasing popular confidence in religious elites. Along with this waning confidence is increasing public disapproval of efforts to introduce religion into politics (Chaves and Anderson, 2012: 222–223). These trends suggest that increasingly religion has become a private, personal matter removed from politics and from conceptions of nationhood.

Socializing and Associations: There is also much more freedom to organize relationships around individual preferences in American society. Younger cohorts of Americans tend to socialize more in bars with friends who are non-neighbors *and* are not family members (Marsden and Srivastava, 2012: 246ff).

The upshot of these changes is a general decline in emphasis on people's *embeddedness* in (and obligations to) family and community—the so-called sociological release from traditional embeddedness (Lane, 1999; Crouch, 2004). Instead, the individual has many choices of affiliation, from local and regional networks to national and even transnational ones of every sort. In this environment, the idea of global citizenship complete with a global language and cognitive culture has become a plausible reality (Kamens, 2012; Meyer, Boli, et al., 1997). Similarly, with the development of the European Union (EU), a sense of pan-European citizenship is now viable and real (Fligstein, 2008), especially among the young and well-educated citizens of Europe and Eastern Europe.

PUBLIC DISCONNECTION FROM POLITICS

While the link between voters and politicians has weakened with the decline of locally based parties, it is also clear from research that voters know what the public agenda is from watching TV, and now by participating in social media (Iyengar and Kinder, 1988; Iyengar, 1992; Norris and Inglehart, 2009). As spectators, they are aware of the agenda that politicians create and TV/media publicizes. When agendas change, their reporting of this objective reality also shifts.

Like natives everywhere the informed public are good observers of what the authorities think are critical issues. But this does not mean that the public agenda, as reported by them, is an agenda that is attentive to issues that they are concerned with. This is particularly true for working-class citizens who correctly believe that the political system is tilted against them. The result is that we are living in a polity where much of the public is disconnected from politics (Crenson and Ginsberg, 2004). And the natives know it.

There is also some evidence that citizens recognize their new role as spectators and have adapted accordingly. Putnam (2000; Janowitz, 1983) finds that older generations, especially the pre–World War II one, exhibit more patriotism than younger ones. They volunteer more, vote more, and take community service more seriously as an ideal. Their attitude is that "we're all in the same boat"—an ideology that was characteristic of the 1930s when people recognized that individuals were helpless in the face of a mass depression (Mann, 2013).

With the reemergence of prosperity and ideologies like neoliberalism, this attitude has changed and with it civic practices and attitudes. For example, many researchers have found that trust in fellow citizens has declined since the 1950s (Putnam, 2000; Paxton, 1999; Lane, 1999; Steuerle et al., 1998). This was a hallmark of political culture in the 1950s (Almond and Verba, 1963). And many observers believe that it is an important feature of effectively functioning democracies.[4]

The perception of society as a community and as an unfinished project has also changed. Society has become privatized and individualized. Many perceive that there are few collective benefits of institutions and personal action, and hence believe that they have few individual responsibilities to society. Obligations to fellow citizens thus fade in people's conscience under this ideological regime (Judt and Snyder, 2012: 383). Volunteering, political participation, and local organizational participation decline as does participation in other rituals of national solidarity. If people do not believe that "we're all in the same boat," all these activities lose meaning. Individuals become free to pursue their own agendas and manage their schedules with few collective responsibilities in this scenario.

THE EMERGENCE OF IDENTITY POLITICS

Identity politics are another consequence of post-1960s changes in the polity. The new individualism leads people to pursue personal goals in the search for valid social identities instead of feeling integrated into a larger cultural community. Modern individuals are encouraged to work to create their own social identities that link them to meaningful purposes. Some have argued that it is based on a cult of authenticity (Boli and Elliot, 2008). These efforts create a new and different kind of society.

Instead of a melting pot that was often a product of socially coerced assimilation (Anderson, 1983), the new society is more like a mosaic (see Lipset, 1987). However, unlike classic mosaic societies, such as Canada, this emerging version is much more fluid. Social boundaries are not clear and stable. Such a system seems more authentic to younger generations because it has relatively fluid social identities people may assume.

This fluidity creates a good deal of space for the emergence of new social movements and other forms of nontraditional politics. Just as the urban economy has created spaces for pop-up stores and restaurants, similar phenomena are now visible in the political system. Novel issues surface and new movements arise and often quickly die once their moment has passed. The new polity is awash with many forms of politics outside the electoral arena (McGrath, 2010; McCleskey, 1981).

SOLUTION TO A CLASSIC PUZZLE

This view of the polity helps resolve one of the central puzzles of American politics—the fact that participation rates are declining despite rising education levels. Recognition of how the new American polity has evolved, and attention to the new individualism that is a part of it, removes the putative "puzzles of participation" that have long perplexed political science (Brody, 1978). Talk about lack of mass civic engagement (Putnam, 2000) misdescribes the situation. Instead, the system is different, the individual is different, and the role of the individual within the new system is different. Over time, the activity repertoires taken up by people have evolved within the changing political system—and behaviors over time have accordingly changed. People enact these new distinct roles, producing new behaviors that seem anomalous to commentators who have reified the civics texts' pictures of the 1950s.

One consequence of the changes described in this chapter is that politics has become individualized and the role of political parties has changed (Dalton, 2007). They are no longer mobilizing agencies or carriers of plausible political agendas. That role is now played by individual politicians and the social movements they organize for campaigns (Agranoff, 1978). Social media also are important intermediaries between citizens and the political system. These wire citizens into politics as a virtual reality but not as a practical system for accomplishing collective ends. One result is that the less educated have much less representation in the political system and participate less as politics has become less grounded in the local community. Instead it is anchored to a media dominated national community (Teixeira, 1987; Teixeira and Rogers, 2000; Rosenstone and Hansen, 1993; Gitlin, 2012).

One result of these changes is that the institutional links between citizens and the political system have weakened. This is happening in Europe as well, but for a variety of reasons it is not as intense or as highly developed a process there. Nevertheless, one consequence in both regions is the emergence of populism as a major element of the new politics. When parties fail in voters' eyes, populist and third-party movements can seize the spaces and resources abandoned by major parties and become successful (Rosenstone et al., 1996).

SOURCES OF CHANGE

Numerous forces have propelled the individual to center stage as the most important agent of social progress. The world educational revolution, and especially the move toward mass higher education, is one major source (Schofer and Meyer, 2005; Meyer, Ramirez, and Soysal, 1992). In their classic study of eleven countries, Inkeles and Smith (1974) showed that even modest levels of education transformed individuals from pre-modern to modern persons. This included having personal goals; believing in rational planning to attain them; believing that hard work, education, and planning are the roads to achievement rather than luck or connections; and being optimistic about the future instead of fatalistic. Furthermore, education was by far the most key factor in this transformation (Baker, 2014). Participation in the modern economy, that is, factory work, mattered but much less than primary and secondary education.

The expansion and popularization of the social and psychological sciences and their models of agency has also contributed to the dominance of this paradigm of society (Jepperson and Meyer, 2011). The emphasis on human capital is one important example, whose influence is world-wide given the stature of economics and economists (e.g., Becker, 1994; see Fourcade, 2006). Education and human development are now major themes in national plans for development and strongly linked to major societal goals (Fiala, 2006; Rosenmund, 2006). Once the idea of a stable occupational structure with a fixed number of positions became obsolete, national plans envision education as the main source of trained, flexible people who can both create and move comfortably into new occupational positions.

The decline of community that economic modernization fosters is an-other source that fosters the rise of individualism as the prominent social myth of society. As individuals experience "sociological release" from communities, there is declining emphasis on communal and corporate identities. These changes, for example, have propelled the rationalization and reorganization of American religious doctrines and church organi-zation. Many now emphasize individual purposefulness and autonomy. This in turn has contributed to the intensification of individualism in religious communities in the United States (Wuthnow, 1988; Froese and Bader, 2010; Putnam and Campbell, 2010).

Similarly, while racial, ethnic, and other identities have become valo-rized, they too have at the same time been individualized and stripped of the communal relationships they once symbolized. One can, for example, prize one's Italian identity without being involved in an Italian commu-nity. Such identities become personal adornments rather than symbols of primordial ties. This change, paradoxically, has helped the emergence of identity politics. People are freer to choose identities and issues that are on the margins of traditional parties and political arrangements. And such movements, even those involving race or ethnic issues, can gain support from many who are not members of these communities. The gay movement and Black Lives Matter movement, for example, have legions of partisans who are not gay or black.

The liberation and rights movements of the 1960s have also contrib-uted to dismantling older ideologies and identities (Abrams, 2006). The women's movement, like the civil rights movement, has put older ideolo-gies and stereotypes of race and gender on the defensive. The culturally dominant social and legal view is that members of such groups are people with their own distinctive histories and abilities. These constructs have widespread public support so that violating them is widely condemned and in many cases legally sanctioned, for example, sexual harassment and racism as hate crimes.

This view of society has gained broad international support, as evidenced by the expanding international human rights movement. Human rights have become a civil religion for society (Cole, 2012a). The international expansion of human rights treaties illustrates this change. The number has grown rapidly. In 1975 there were only 52 such treaties globally, compared to 100 in 1990 and 147 in 2005 (Beck, Drori, and Meyer, 2012: 491). Thus the twenty-first century has seen a shift in focus from the rights of citizens of nation-states to human rights.[5]

These forces have all contributed to the intensification of historic American individualism. Durkheim's ([1912] 1969) "cult of the individual" has been achieved and intensified in a way that would surprise him and other early observers and commentators. As a result, there has been an extraordinary expansion of the imagined capabilities, potentials, personality features, and multifaceted "identities" of the individual person (Bell, 1973; Meyer, 1986; Lasch, 1979). The educated individual joins governments, communities and formal organizations as the cultures' main empowered actor—and reigns as ultimate sovereign and totem (Jepperson and Meyer, 2011).

This process appears to be diffusing to other parts of the world as cultural modernization occurs. Empirically, individualism has expanded both across institutional realms and across geographical regions. It is a cultural construction that has been widely accepted across societies as the narrative of how societies make progress. For example, in a study of forty-three countries in 2007, I found that 73 percent of university graduates across these countries strongly agree or agree with the following statement: "I see myself as an autonomous person" (Kamens, 2012: 56ff). This does not mean that such individuals disavow nationalism and globalism. The identity of "global citizen" and "national citizen" are positively correlated with individualism. In global culture, these identities are all quite compatible.

NEW RITUALS OF SOLIDARITY, NEW MODELS OF NATIONHOOD

An important consequence of the growth of intensified individualism is that it undermines national solidarity. Under this new cultural regime, traditional rituals of solidarity that reaffirm an older notion of the nation as a melting pot decline. At the same time, it creates new sources of social identity and solidarity based on new models of nationhood. Younger generations have new, more fluid social identities that intensified individualism has helped to create. Multicultural models of nationhood have gained traction and support. Human rights rapidly have become a new civil religion of modern society (Cole, 2012a).

These developments create a society based on the premise that individuals are free to invent and develop their own communities. In this narrative society has become defined as a loosely organized mosaic of people and groups with distinctive identities. These are fluid and do not necessarily mean that their users are active members of the communities these identities signify. For example, using a hyphenated ethnic identity, such as Irish-American, does not necessarily mean that an individual is rooted in that ethnic community and committed to its traditions and customs. It is more a matter of personal identity and expression. To many it represents a freedom of choice that is now more available and valued in society.

New rituals of solidarity emerge to symbolize and valorize this new model of society with its much more fluid and shifting social identities. This change has reconstructed society. For example, the salience of denominational religious identities is declining, as is denominational religious attendance. At the same time, however, new forms of religiosity have emerged. One involves the rise of megachurches that are multidenominational in recruitment (see Baker, 2014; Putnam and Campbell, 2010). They are successful because they have attracted adults who are wary of traditional, denominational religion. They are searching for more inclusive identities. While traditional in theology, megachurches cater to the secular interests of parishioners as well as their spiritual concerns. With dozens of groups covering a wide variety of interests and tastes, such as Bible study or business and community building, they appeal to their members' various secular and spiritual interests. They are also distinctly modern in their music and religious performances, using TV and the media for easy access. Their most important feature, however, is that they offer parishioners individualized choices of how to achieve a sense of authentic personal spirituality.

The withering of religious and ethnic boundaries frees individuals to cross such boundaries. Intermarriage rates increase across religious-ethnic lines, as do friendships and other relationships (Putnam and Campbell, 2010: 212ff). At the societal level such change increases tolerance for individual choice in many domains. New rituals of solidarity develop in response to this change. Younger generations, for example, spend less time socializing with family members and neighbors and more time in public places with friends they have chosen (Marsden and Srivastava, 2012). They are also more likely than older generations to tell pollsters that they have no religion. They do not identify as atheists. They are using their freedom from traditional social roles to experiment in the search for more authentic lifestyles (Boli and Elliot, 2008).

These experiments in finding valid selves occur across society. Efforts to develop a plausible culture that integrates distinctive ethnic and other groups occur in many settings in society. Recent laws, for example, enjoin corporations and their executives *not* to create discriminatory or hostile work environments for employees. Under the pressure of public norms for ethnic, gender, and racial inclusivity, businesses and other organizations have invented structures that symbolize this commitment. Human resource departments are one instance. Corporate elites created them to manage diversity and celebrate it as a company value. Rituals like sensitivity training for employees are enactments of this commitment. These innovations have spread quickly and become accepted, even though evidence suggests that they do little to reduce racial and other forms of prejudice and discrimination (see Dobbin and Kelly, 2007).

In politics, while voting has suffered a decline, participation in more populist forms of politics has risen (Kamens, 2009; Barry, 1999; McGrath, 2010; Andrain and Apter, 1995). People are choosing movements rather than established parties to express their political identities because they offer a wider choice for unsanctioned viewpoints. Anti-immigrant parties and movements, for example, have become popular in the United States and Europe. Participation in protest and social movement politics has been growing. Many commentators see the United States and other societies as being transformed not through electoral politics but through social movement politics (e.g., Judis, 2016; McAdam and Scott, 2002; Meyer and Tarrow, 1998; Boggs, 1986; Klandermans et al., 1988; McCarthy and Zald, 1973).

How these changes will affect national levels of solidarity are hard to predict. Their virtue is that they promote positive images of a population trying to develop identities that are appropriate to changed national circumstances. The danger is that they become sources of intense friction and enduring conflict. White nationalists and older Americans, for example, find it hard to accept the diversity these choices point to. They also do not accept multiculturalism as an appropriate image of American society.

Yet social libertarianism has great legitimacy as part of the American creed. The emergence of enhanced individualism as the main social construct of society has strengthened this movement. There is therefore a good deal of support for more pluralistic models of nationhood.

The next chapter focuses on the conservative reaction to state expansion and the rise of enhanced individualism. It makes the common point that government growth politicizes society and expands the polity (Pierson and Skocpol, 2007). But it makes the less common point that the rise of resurgent individualism supported conservative attacks on the state by helping to frame it as the enemy of individual liberty and freedom. At the same time, to the chagrin of many conservatives, it added support to liberals' push for more democratization and the extension of citizen rights across society—also in the name of individual freedom. In this way it helped polarize society. This development destroyed the image of the United States as a society united around common goals and values.

CHAPTER 7

The Growth of Big Government and the Conservative Counterattack

"The biggest obstacle (to political reform), I think, is the general public's
reflexive, unreasoning hostility to politicians and the process of politics.
Neurotic hatred of the political class is the country's last universally
acceptable form of bigotry. Because that problem is mental, not mechanical,
it is really hard to remedy. . . . Our most pressing problem today is that
the country abandoned the establishment, not the other way around."

—JONATHAN RAUCH, "What's Ailing American Politics?"
The Atlantic 318, no. 1 (July–August)1: 63

THIS CHAPTER DESCRIBES THE GROWTH OF THE STATE, the external context that made this possible, and the unfolding counterattack
against government and the political class (Hacker and Pierson, 2005;
Hacker, 2006). The resulting revolt against liberalism and the welfare
state produced one of the two major enduring fault lines in American
politics. This development helped pave the way for anti-party politics
and the resurgence of populism (Shafer, 1981).

THE COLD WAR, MILITARIZATION
AND WORLD CULTURE

Initially the "military ascendancy" and associated "national security
state" were at the core of initial governmental expansion (Abrams, 2006;
Friedberg, 2000; Mann, 2013). This resulted from a consensus among the
international wings of each political party that continuation of the development initiated by World War II and then the Cold War was important
to maintain. This included the regulated capitalism that came out of this
era. It had involved detailed regulation of business, as well as an industrial policy associated with the military-industrial-big-science-university
complex (Steinmo, 2010; Prasad, 2006; Friedberg, 2000).

In the United States these developments gave government unprecedented authority to reorganize society (Lowery and Berry, 1981). The state expanded rapidly between 1955 and 1974 (Pierson, 2007). Political leaders accomplished much of the expansion of the state during this period. This transition expanded social welfare expenditures, increased military expenditures, expanded the social and legal regulation of industry, and accentuated the expansion of civil rights. Both the federal courts and Congress were busy creating a large body of positive law regarding citizens' rights and claims on society (Orren and Skowronek, 2004: 181ff; Friedman, 2004; Glazer, 1975).

The form this expansion took was also peculiarly American. Instead of instituting direct government control over sectors of the economy and other areas by expanding its administrative capacity and building a competent civil service, the United States resorted to regulatory law.

CONTROL THROUGH REGULATION

Pierson (2007: 24–25) observes that much of government growth reflected a vast expansion of *regulations*. They were at the heart of an expanded state. This was the biggest expansion of legal regulation of the economy since the Progressive Era (Novak, 2010). It did not entail changes in government to facilitate direct control of education, health care, or industry. No national health care system, for example, emerged from government expansion, nor did a national curriculum in education. It also did not reduce the fragmented system of authority within government itself.

While government became more centralized, the expansion of departments and regulatory staff meant that while it became larger, its fragmentation only increased. More statutes, more agencies, more staff, and bigger budgets accelerated this drift. Another way of putting this point is that American society now has more bureaucracy, more administrative activity, more law, and more law-related judicial activity. And of course, it has more lawyers per capita than it did—and more than most other countries.

America is a litigious society, but the availability of more administrative rules and law creates more opportunities for litigation and negotiation (Lieberman, 1981; Friedman, 2004). This development has increased the work for lawyers, who both help draft legislation and later litigate it, and lobbyists who help frame the issues that later become law. The increasing salience of government has caused a growth spurt in the numbers of both lawyers and lobbyists. Washington, D.C., for example, has between 68,839 and 89,427 practicing lawyers (as estimated by the U.S. Census and the Washington Bar Association; *Washington Magazine*, December 2009). The number of registered lobbyists has grown from 10,405 in 1998 to 11,518 in 2015. And the annual spending of lobbyists has increased from $1.45 billion in 1998 to $3.22 billion in 2015 (Center for Responsive Politics, 2016: http://www.opensecrets.org/lobby). These estimates suggest that 20 percent of Washington's population (of about 500,000 people) are involved in either the practice of law or lobbying.

In addition, more government bureaucracies generate more law like policies and rules. One way to characterize this trend is that it entails a shift away from legislative to judicial, bureaucratic/administrative, and executive decision making (see Orren and Skowronek, 2004).

Pierson notes that from 1965 to 1977 the federal government adopted thirty-four major regulatory laws—almost double the total legislation passed in the other four decades combined (Pierson, 2007: 25). Furthermore, real spending on regulatory services also grew during this period. Federal regulatory staffing levels increased during the 1970s. In the case of environmental protection, it experienced the largest and most sustained increases in staffing. Employment almost quadrupled in the 1970s and has grown by more than 50 percent between 1980 and 2004 (Pierson, 2007: 26).

This regulatory blitz covered a wide variety of areas: consumer protection, workplace health and safety, and the environment. The Traffic Safety Act of 1961, the Clean Air Act of 1970, the Occupational Safety and Health Act of 1970, the Clean Water Act of 1972, and the Consumer Product Safety Act of 1972 were all passed during this era (1969–1974).

One result was the movement of authority from Congress to regulatory agencies and to the courts (Silberman, 1985; Glazer, 1975). Administrative law grows and so does litigation. This is particularly true in the case of civil rights. One result of sweeping civil rights–based legislation (1969–1978) was that all branches of the federal government grew more open to rights-based claims. The "rights revolution" in turn produced a huge amount of litigation in the federal courts (Schudson, 1998b; Friedman, 1973; 2004). For example, in 1933 the Supreme Court's agenda devoted to civil rights and liberties was just 9 percent of its case load. In the 1971 term the topic was 65 percent of its agenda (Pierson, 2007: 28).

One way of describing this change is that no major structural reform of American government occurred, other than a haphazard evolution in the direction of a more centralized federalism (Scott and Meyer, 1983; Laumann and Knoke, 1987, 1988). In comparative perspective, the American state remained fragmented and porous. It had not developed cadres of long-tenure policy and management professionals staffing the bureaucracies. And—crucially—it was without a political elite that carried a distinct political culture or knowledge base, with pretensions of steering and guardianship (e.g., Heclo, 1977; Sachs, 2012; Dahl, 1971, 1984; Putnam, 2002b; Putnam, Leonardi, and Nanetti 1993; Badie and Birnbaum, 1983; Finer, 1970; Judt, 2012).

GOVERNMENT AS ACTOR

However, government did become a more central and independent actor. One of the unique features of government expansion in the 1960s was the changing way in which the purposes of federal aid were determined. Before that period most grants were for purposes initially defined by *states*, such as highway and airport construction. Starting in the 1960s the *federal government* increasingly acted to define the purposes of these grants, often without any initiative from the states. Furthermore, many of these purposes had no well-defined or organized constituency until federal laws were passed. Unlike earlier periods Congress increasingly allocated money in ways that created such clients (J. Wilson, "The Rise," 2006: 362–363). That was one of the objects of the Great Society programs—to create such constituencies. In this endeavor, they succeeded. And once government creates clients in the name of the common good, bureaucratic clientelism becomes self-perpetuating.

THE SLOW DECLINE OF THE LIBERAL STATE

President Bill Clinton announced in 1996 that "the era of big government is over." This was in fact a funeral oration for a death that had occurred much earlier. The conservative onslaught, beginning in the 1960s, had managed to kill off the idea of an activist society led by government. It did reemerge later under President George W. Bush but under an entirely different guise. It was part of a more militarized foreign policy.

Government expansion and the idea of an activist state created a backlash (Hacker and Pierson, 2005). The liberal dream did not go uncontested. There were plenty of groups who had reason to contest the political consensus behind the liberal, activist state. Conservatives had many reasons to find expanded government troubling. For business groups the very idea of an activist society led by government was a contradiction of fundamental principles of liberal society (Lindblom, 1977; Thomas, 1989; Hartz, 1955, 1964). They took for granted the fact that the hegemony of business was normal in American society. An activist state was therefore by definition an attack on their prerogatives and hegemony.

To moral conservatives, big government and big corporations threatened citizen freedom and invited tyranny. They argued that as government agencies grew and claimed more resources, they would become "too big to fail" and thus permanent features of the landscape. This was a fundamental violation of the American creed and of American-style capitalism. Even President Eisenhower, who had always called himself a progressive, took on the mantle of conservative to rail against the military-industrial complex and the technological and scientific complex that supported it.

Others found an activist state threatening on economic and social grounds. For white workers, equal rights for women and minorities meant more competition for good jobs. For business owners and corporate executives, an activist government meant more regulation and higher business taxes to support more redistributive programs.

For religious conservatives and evangelicals, the deregulation of morals that many movements demanded meant the decline of community morality and the irony of government support for a variety of forms of "immorality" in their view. This reaction produced countermovements in support of government regulation of morality, such as anti-abortion groups, anti–gay rights movements, and the League of Decency (for censorship and against pornography).

Still others found the idea of a multicultural/multiracial society threatening. As a result, nativist groups and white supremacists emerged and joined the conflict against an activist state pursuing social libertarian goals.

THE RETURN TO NORMALCY: THE BIRTH OF CONSERVATIVE COUNTER ORGANIZATIONS

Given these reactions, conservative business groups found many allies. Most important, they were able to join common cause during this period with evangelical, religious groups, particularly in the south (Fitzgerald, 2007; J. Glaser, 1986). Both groups argued for a return to normalcy once the crises that fueled state growth had passed. In the late 1970s evangelical Christians became allied with conservative political groups. Conservative foundations like the Heritage Foundation and religious TV programs helped get the message out to evangelical Christians (Lapham, 2004: 37). This created a huge constituency for the conservative message. And it also created a large grassroots funding base for conservative campaigns and candidates.

This alliance also produced a wave of conservative countermovements and interest groups. This development intensified the proliferation of groups in the polity. It also created a revolt against government by harnessing populist suspicion of government to conservative business interests and ideology.

Conservatives mobilized against the activist society. One sign was the founding and funding of significant numbers of interest groups during this period. Walker's (1991) data in Table 7.1 shows that 50 percent of all interest groups in the United States were founded between 1960 and 1980. Many of these represented conservative interests and are part of the countermobilization of conservatives against their liberal opponents.

Schlozman and Tierney's (1983, 1984, 1986) studies of lobbying organizations in this period show that they had a distinctly upper-class bias.

TABLE 7.1 Founding Dates of Interest Groups in the United States, 1950–1991

	1940s–1950s	1960s–1970s	1980s
% of Total (N = 808)	25%	25%	50%

Source: Walker, 1991: 63.

Not all were conservative, but the best-funded ones tended to be. Their robust funding also facilitated the development of tight networks among conservative groups and the think tanks that gave them ideological support and analysis (see Choi, 2011).

Conservatives also founded their own think tanks during this period to spread their views. Table 7.2 shows that 89 percent of these advocacy organizations were born between 1970 and 1990, when the conservative movement was rapidly gaining momentum and resources. The table includes only those think tanks directly connected and funded by the conservative movement, so it may understate the number of pro-conservative centers.

The number of conservative think tanks multiplied enormously over the decades. According to the National Committee for Responsible Philanthropy (NCRP), 79 conservative foundations made more than $252 million in grants to roughly 342 nonprofit policy organizations between 1999–2001 (NCRP, March 3, 2004. The median grant was $102,000. The largest grant was $28,569,700 to the Heritage Foundation and the smallest was $225 to the Free Enterprise Defense Fund.

Unlike others, conservative foundations made grants primarily to non-profits that would be *active* in politics. It gave money to those that would lobby lawmakers, challenge laws and regulations in the courts, and broadcast conservative ideas and ideologies (Schulman, 1995). The focus of such grant making was to sustain a small group of grantees over the long haul by making long-term core operating grants. These tended to be multi-issue think tanks as well. Such organizations received 46 percent of the grants.

BIG BUSINESS MOBILIZES TO TILT THE REGULATORY SYSTEM

Big business also mobilized during this period against the regulatory state (Alexander, 1980; Epstein, 1979; Handler and Mulkern, 1982). Political

TABLE 7.2 Founding Dates of Conservative Think Tanks in the United States

	1945	1950s	1960s	1970s	1980s	1990s
% of Total (N = 105):	0.001%	2.8%	5.7%	25.7%	44.7%	20%

Source: National Center for Responsive Philanthropy, July 1997, *Moving a Public Policy Agenda*, 42–43. Washington, D.C.: NCPR.

action committees (PACs) grew at an astounding pace after 1970. In 1970 there were six hundred PACs and by 2010 there were ten thousand. Before 1970, PACs had not been significant actors on behalf of corporations. Traditionally, corporate executives got together and bankrolled candidates of their choice with little pressure or need to disclose the recipients of their largesse (Andres, 1985). The advent of corporate PACs introduced a fundamental shift in the way business funneled money into electoral politics.

The growing importance of corporate-state relations also affected the *size* of PACs. Boies (1989) found that the biggest PACs established by Fortune 500 corporations in 1976 and 1980 were formed by the following kinds of corporations: (1) those with the richest history of interaction with the state, (2) top defense contractors, (3) corporations that were major acquirers of other businesses, and (4) those that had been prosecuted for criminal acts. In short, a larger, more activist government had pushed the largest U.S. corporations to rationalize their campaign contributions and to increase their political contributions. The reward for doing so had suddenly gotten much bigger.

As political polarization increased in the system after the late 1980s, another trend in giving emerged: the decline of bipartisan giving by large donors and corporations (Heerwig, 2018). This trend coincided with the decline of funding for political moderates. Donors who gave to both parties tended to support more moderate incumbents. They also tended to be more frequent donors, suggesting that they had longer-term interests in the political system and were ideologically less extreme. This changed pattern of funding supported the growing polarization between parties.

During this period corporations were also able to influence legal doctrines that reduced the restrictions on corporate campaign contributions. This campaign culminated in the 2010 *Citizens United* Supreme Court decision. The decision gave corporations the right to give unlimited money to campaigns but not to parties. Candidates now had access to extraordinary funding if they pleased corporate donors and had a real chance of winning. "Dark money" is now flowing through the political system (Mayer, 2011; Ginsberg, 1984). A donor class has arisen that is very vocal about the policies and candidates that they will support. The net result is that candidates have lavish funding while parties often struggle to get donor dollars. Parties, as a result, have lost control over the selection of candidates. Donors can now shape this process to their advantage.

RENEWED POPULIST ATTACKS ON GOVERNMENT

Populism also reemerged during this period as a force in politics. It too was spurred by the growth of national government. World War II, its aftermath and the Cold War, and its attendant fears kept support for an active government alive (Gaddis, 2005). But when these fears subsided, so did support for big government as an agent of society (Pierson and Skocpol, 2007; Petrocik, 1981, 1982; Hacker and Pierson, 2005). Support for government and a national political class simultaneously withered. The conservative counterattack that began in the 1960s with Barry Goldwater's defeat in 1964 railed against big government with success. The unraveling of support for government began during this period (Ginberg, 1984; Hadensius, 1985, Lane, 1966, 1999).

Results of this effort were a continuing cycle to delegitimize political elites and the rise of radical populist movements on all sides. The center was under attack. The "imperial presidency" that analysts in the 1960s and 1970s noted (Lowi, 1985) was disappearing. In Daniel Moynihan's famous phrase, the office of the president had been "miniaturized." No new big societal projects were possible and even incrementalism was problematic. Political analyst Adam Gopnick (*New Yorker*, May 23, 2016: 23) argues that the presidency for Americans is now akin to the medieval papacy: not a powerful office but one that is expected to produce an "epoch of spiritual leadership": "We expect our Presidents to shape the meaning of their times." Rather than dull policy makers, brokers, and important functionaries, the public expects political leaders to be societal cheerleaders, speaking in a language everyone can understand. This was the beginning of a new era of "operatic nationalism" that highlights "exceptionalism" and exclusivity (Hobsbawm and Ranger, 1983).

Congress was also losing popular support. Starting in 1964 its approval ratings began to sink (Steuerle et al., 1998). They have continued to slide. While individual members of Congress found support among their constituents, the public began to see the institution as part of "big government" that was unresponsive to ordinary people.

POLITICAL-FINANCIAL CONSEQUENCES
OF THE ATTACK ON GOVERNMENT

Given the success of the conservative attack on liberalism and the social welfare state, a general unwillingness to support it emerged (Hadensius, 1985; Judt, 2012). This trend crested during the Reagan presidency. Tax rates had steadily declined starting in the 1950s (Jones and Williams, 2008). Under Reagan, deficit financing became the main tool for financing tax cuts and the military. This has continued (Krippner, 2011). One result is that many parts of the government are not funded adequately to carry out their missions, such as the post office, the Internal Revenue Service, and Amtrak. Conservatives have used this tactic as a deliberate effort to downsize government. It is part of conservative strategy to undermine the ability of regulatory agencies and other parts of government to function effectively.

Developments since the 1980s have intensified these effects (Edsall, 1984; Edsall and Edsall, 1991; Shefter and Ginsberg, 1985). Politicians are now in a real bind. Neoliberalism and the "no new taxes" mantra of conservatives constrain them from raising taxes to pay for infrastructure and other necessary investments that citizens demand. Economic moralism about government spending also prevents them from borrowing to pay for these investments, even at historically low interest rates. Conservatives have successfully argued that this would raise the national debt, reduce growth and employment, and lead to higher taxes. That the evidence for such claims is slight appears not to matter.

The result of this moral position is that technical fixes for many problems in public finance are not available, such as fixing Social Security. Public finance has therefore had to rely on short-term tricks and opacity to hide the fact that politicians are borrowing money to pay bills and satisfy their most important constituencies. Many expenditures, for example, are "off the books," such as current wars and prescription drug costs for the elderly under President George W. Bush. Once Congress dropped "pay as you go" as a rule, and covert deficit financing was adopted in the 1980s, public finance lost both market discipline and political self-restraint (Krippner, 2011).

CHANGES IN THE RELATIONSHIP BETWEEN STATE AND SOCIETY: THE RISING IMPORTANCE OF THE CENTER AND THE DECLINE OF LOCALISM

The growth of national power, framed as a response to foreign threat, has ensured that the national state has become the sovereign symbolic center of the polity (e.g., Zelinsky, 1988; Friedberg, 2000; Lunch, 1988). For a brief time, this process helped produce a political culture in which society itself seemed like a unified, collective project (Lunch, 1988). The growing charisma of national leaders has drained the localism out of the system (e.g., Mann, 1990). What happens at the center matters more and the natives know it.

As the center expanded its influence, it also accentuated the trend toward plebiscitary relations between the public and their institutional leaders. This development heightens the importance of public opinion and the media. Opinion polling became more important, and more prominent in the media. It is also more consequential for politicians (Herbst, 1993; Brehm, 1989; Beniger and Herbst, 1990). Media itself became a more significant part of the new political system (e.g., Ranney, 1983; Katz and Dayan, 1985; Baumgartner and Morris, 2006). As politics become national, nationwide media events dominate the news, for example, Congressional hearings, presidential debates, and news reports of poll results. This development helps turn politics into a spectator sport. Citizens lose their status as participants but become wired into the system as opiners and editors. The emergence of social media has heightened this effect.

This trend toward plebiscitary politics also drains leadership out of the political system and invests it in a national political class with few connections to the grass roots (Ron Jepperson, personal communication). The founders saw leadership as a solution to the problem of factionalism and division in the new republic. James Madison (*The Federalist*, no. 10) argued that the elected representatives will "*refine and enlarge the public views by passing them through* a chosen body of citizens whose wisdom, patriotism and love of justice will help them determine the true interest of the country" (italics mine). Plebiscitary politics becomes a media-driven enterprise built around the cult of celebrity and media exposure.

Similarly, crowdsourced opinion drives out knowledge, expertise, and the wisdom of experienced leaders. It elevates the power of social media and a national donor class. It even enhances the political role of late-night comedians. As reporter Hank Stuever of the *Washington Post* put it: "lacking leaders we look to class clowns to guide us" (see also Baumgartner and Morris, 2006).[1] Instead of acting like leaders, politicians frequently become followers of public opinion and popular trends within their respective parties. One consequence is to ratchet up divisive conflicts. Leaders who feed on frenzy and divisiveness gain the upper hand, pushing out those pursuing strategies that bridge divides. The current politics of divide-and-conquer exemplifies the declining reservoir of leadership available.

Lacking stable parties as a basis of support, leadership is based on personal charisma. The result is that those who do become leaders find that they cannot readily use this support to help other politicians in their party. Public perceptions of charisma and authenticity are not easily transferable to others. It is doubtful, for example, that Bernie Sanders has coattails that will help other candidates win their elections. As Max Weber noted, charisma is a very unstable basis of authority in political systems.

INCREASING POLITICIZATION OF PUBLIC LIFE

The expansion of government blurs the distinction between private and public sectors in society. Formerly private spheres of behavior become public as government authority expands, for example, drunk driving, workplace behavior, and parenting. Citizens find that more of their private lives become subject to public norms. For example, the meaning of children's grade school test scores changes under these new conditions. They no longer merely index a child's progress. They also help determine if she has an ineffective teacher and may be used to determine if she is in a failing school that should be closed. Public norms now emerge in many spheres that were formerly defined as private domains.

INCREASING SPACE FOR POPULISM

The move toward a national plebiscitary politics also opens ecological space to emerging revitalization movements on both the left and the right.

It gives a national platform to reformers and opportunists. At the same time, it undermines the significance and influence of local political institutions, parties, and elites. American political parties, for example, have lost many traditional functions and instead have become giant financial enterprises. Candidate-based movements and donors now vet potential political candidates (Grodzins, 1960; Burnham, 1984; Reichley, 1985; Kayden and Mahe, 1985; Jackson and Hitlin, 1981; Ginsberg, 1984, Ginsberg and Shefter, 1999; Gourevitch, 1986). This change opens the path for charismatic politics, based on candidates' ability to manipulate the media and to appeal directly to audiences via mass media, social media, and aggressive, negative campaigns (Agranoff, 1978; Geer, 2006).

CENTRALIZATION OF RESOURCES AND AGENDA SETTING

Federal budgets and agencies have also grown over time under both Democratic and Republican administrations, though none of these trends are at Western European levels (Laumann and Knoke, 1988; Rose, 1984, 1985b). This gives national government enormous leverage over state and local decisions. Increasing central transfers and new regulatory mandates tie subcentral governments more closely to the center (Lowi, 1969, 1996; Gourevitch, 1986). Republicans as well as Democratic politicians have supported this development. Efforts at devolution mainly involve giving states more autonomy in how they spend their allocation of federal resources.

So-called preemptive laws have also been important in this shift. The center has greatly augmented its authority to dispense social resources, establishing entitlements for individuals and groups, leaving implementation and financing arrangements at local and state levels. Observers have depicted the Great Society programs, to take one set of examples, as a concerted attack upon entrenched municipal bureaucracies and interest alignments (Shefter, 1977; Lowery and Berry, 1981).

Leadership and agenda setting in many policy areas have also passed decidedly to the center in the postwar period. In one depiction, the United States has moved from a federal to a decentralized national system (Seidman and Gilmour, 1986). In some instances, one finds increasing localism tied to broader central grants, and thus some devolution—but note that this localism is understood as a devolution from the (symbolically sovereign) center.[2]

These changes remove much public decision making out of democratic processes. Much *policy initiative*, for example, comes from organized publics operating through bureaucratic channels. Agencies rather than Congress become sources of policy specification. These actors incorporate public interest concerns into administrative processes (Shefter, 1977; Orren and Skowronek, 2004). Some scholars argue that the bureaucracy offers more representation than legislative processes to those who have access (Woll, 2006).

The growth of the center has also increased the delegation of public functions to private organizations and actors (e.g., Friedberg, 2000). McDonald's and other companies provide schoolchildren with publicly subsidized lunches, operate prisons and refugee centers, provide subsidized care to the elderly via Medicare and Medicaid, and develop and build fighter jets and other hardware for the military. Charter schools compete with public schools, and for-profit colleges benefit from government subsidies and loan programs.

Such developments *reduce* the differentiation between public and private sectors. Private bodies become more public in funding and purpose but *less subject* to democratic control. Still, the symbolic center is the national state. It is the agent that has the authority to devolve control and resources to local states and private bodies to perform public functions. And it often takes the blame when these organizations fail.

THE INCREASING IMPORTANCE OF LEADERSHIP

It is arguable that the growth of government has increased the discursive importance attached to "leadership" and management. As government and private bodies use public funds to expand or enhance services in many sectors, (e.g., education, medicine, science, military procurement), calls for public accountability mount. This pressure forces all client organizations to develop centralized controls and leadership. Even universities are expected to act collectively as rational actors.

These pressures change organizations but do not necessarily make them more effective. One predictable result is that recipients of government largesse assemble structures that comply with these demands. The following are instances of ways organizations have developed to comply with these concerns: the growth of quality assessment in schools and colleges, human resource departments to ensure fairness in hiring and promotion in industry, and efforts to develop cost controls in military procurement. These units, once founded, develop protocols and best practices for dealing with particular issues, and these tend to spread across organizations. Student evaluations of faculty, for example, are common in American universities and are often mandatory.

Given the decoupling between rules, processes, and results in American government, the development of indirect controls over agencies that receive federal funds leads to a good deal of symbolic action and hypocrisy. Sensitivity training, for example, is often mandated to deal with racism and sexism, even though good research shows that it is largely ineffective (Dobbin and Kelly, 2007). Similarly, the practice of student evaluations of faculty is widespread but is also known to be heavily affected by the grade distributions individual faculty members produce. A whole industry has grown up to help organizations meet federal mandates on safety, worker health, and so on. In the military, recent congressional reports indicate that there is little evidence that the Pentagon really knows how federal money is spent, despite having an accounting bureaucracy.

In lieu of clear operational goals of success, having such programs with appropriate staffs, protocols and budgets is often the main criterion to show that states, communities, companies and universities are complying with federal requirements (Meyer and Rowan, 1977). One major job of the leadership of organizations receiving public money is to sustain the image that there is accountability and to deal with fallout when evidence surfaces that this is not the case.

ORGANIZATIONAL-LEVEL CHANGES: MORE ACTORS, MORE ISSUES, AND MORE MOBILIZATION IN THE POLITY

Under an expanded state, interest group liberalism as a system of representation has gone through a remarkable growth surge since the 1960s (see (Lowi, 1967, 1969; Walker, 1991; Dahl, 1994). More organized actors have become involved in the polity, and more issues have become part of the public agenda. The result is a greatly expanded number of legitimated interests and actors in any given domain.[3] Civil society has become more politicized and organized at the state and national level.

The increasing salience of the central government, as representative of public authority, has also produced more political action—and counteraction—at these levels (see Skocpol, 2003; Skocpol and Fiorina, 1999; Ginsberg and Shefter, 1999). Much of this action is collective. For instance, the availability of federal welfare and urban programs stimulated the formation of local political growth coalitions between Republican businesspeople and Democratic mayors, organized around the restructuring of urban land use (Mollenkopf, 1983). And there is evidence that a wide variety of local community and neighborhood political organizations were formed or resuscitated in response to federal legal mandates associated with urban redevelopment programs (Fainstein and Fainstein, 1976; Taub et al., 1984).

Federal support of aerospace, electronics, and energy industries also occasioned the massive sectoral shifts represented by the economic and political rise of the Sun Belt (see esp. Mollenkopf, 1983). As Skocpol (1999) has pointed out, expanding states create markets that encourage the formation of a variety of new organizations.

SHIFTING MOBILIZATION SITES

An expanding center also impacts the points at which effective entry into the national political system occurs. One development is that mobilization sites have shifted upward. Similarly, the scale of resources required to achieve voice has increased (Ginsberg, 1984; Skocpol, 2003; Verba et al., 1995; Schlozman and Tierney, 1986; Skocpol, 2003). Parties too have become national organizations that control vast sums of money to allocate to candidates across the country, based on rational calculations of their chances of success (Grodzins, 1960; Burnham, 1984; Reichley, 1985; Kayden and Mahe, 1985; Jackson and Hitlin, 1981). Elections are now sites for national mobilization and consequently have become more expensive. The 2008 presidential election, for example, was the first billion-dollar election in history.

INCREASING CLIENTELISM AND
DEPENDENCE ON THE STATE

This change has linked communities, states, and individual citizens to the national state as *clients*. Increasing portions of state budgets now depend on federal largesse. Over 40 percent of the budget of states for higher education, for example, now depends on federal support. Citizens often now see themselves as *clients* and less as participants in the process of governing (Crenson and Ginsberg, 2004).

Some of this change involves direct transfers of resources to citizens or other entities, such as Social Security checks. But even indirect federal policy instruments have the effect of expanding the importance of the governmental center.[4] In these schemes the federal government gives states the right to experiment with reforms under federal guidelines. They then reward the most successful efforts. Federal guidelines encourage copying successful efforts, and the national government backs this with promises of additional federal money for those who are compliant. President Barack Obama's Race to the Top program for schools had this character. It rewarded schools that successfully adopted the Common Core curriculum and other reforms. They received additional federal resources. These policy instruments all have a clientelistic character, tying private actors or local officials to the governmental center.

A good deal of corporate welfare also depends on clientlike ties with the center. The military-industrial complex that President Eisenhower spoke of is entirely a result of the militarization of foreign policy. The financial industry also benefits from such ties in many ways. The federal government guarantees student loans issued by private banks, for example. Private banks profit while government takes the risks of default by students who can't repay these loans.[5]

Similar clientlike ties have become prominent between communities, states, and the federal government. Between 1960 and 2004, federal grants as a percentage of state and local expenditures almost doubled, going from 14.8 percent to 25.0 percent (Stanley and Niemi, 2006: 328, table 8-12). Given the weak finances of many states, the pressure for more federal funding is likely to increase. Keeping the physical infrastructure intact and supporting public agencies like schools, police, and fire departments will depend increasingly on the federal government. That is where the money is.

The citizenry at large also has become increasingly dependent on the national state for a variety of benefits. There is no doubt that these ties of dependency have grown. For example, according to the Congressional Budget Office, 48 percent of all American households in 1994 received some form of federal entitlement check—unemployment compensation, Medicare, Social Security, food stamps, pension, veteran's benefits, or welfare unemployment (Lauter, 1995: 92). And many of these were high-income families.[6] This dependency will undoubtedly grow as older age groups increase in size.

This dependency has steadily increased, as shown by Table 7.3. Social spending as a percentage of GDP has almost tripled since 1950 (Wilensky, 2002: 213, table 5.1). In 1960 U.S. total social transfers amounted to 7.26 percent of GDP, while the OECD median was 10.41 percent. By 1995 the United States was spending 13.67 percent on social transfers.[7]

Expenditures on social welfare are also growing. Table 7.3 shows that between 1950 and 2009 the United States went from spending 4.6 percent of GDP on social spending to 16 percent—even considering the

TABLE 7.3 Social Welfare and Defense Spending as a Percentage of GDP in the United States, 1950–2015*

	Social Welfare Spending		Defense Spending	
	U.S.	Sweden	U.S.	Sweden
1950	4.6%		5%	
1966	7.9%		9%	
1971	11.7%		9%	
1980	14.6%		5%	
1986	12.5%		7%	
1990	11.7%		6%	2.4%
1995	13.7%		3.6%	2.2%
2009	16%	29%	3.8%	1.1%
2011–2015			3.5%	1.1%

Sources: Wilensky, 2002: 213; Lindert, 2004: 13; Friedberg, 2000: 84; Kensworthy, 2014: 125; World Bank Tables, 2016.
* These figures probably *understate* the degree of clientelism that exists between citizens, communities, corporations, and the state. Citizens, for example, receive huge tax benefits via mortgage and charitable deductions. Religious organizations, education, and charities receive large federal subsidies through the tax code. They are tax exempt and contributions to them are deductible from individual and corporate taxes.

2 percent drop in social spending during the Reagan years (Kensworthy, 2014: 125). Such spending is still far behind OECD levels, even considering America's enormous military expenditures in 2009—3.8 percent of GDP versus Sweden's 1.1 percent (Friedberg, 2000: 84; World Bank Tables on defense spending, online, https://data.worldbank.org/indicator/ MS.MIL.XPND.GD.ZS). Sweden's welfare expenditures in 2009 were 29 percent of GDP.

Two points are noteworthy about these U.S. expenditures. First, they are tilted toward older Americans and the military. Medicare, Social Security, and military spending make up the bulk of federal entitlements and expenditures.

Secondly, few of them are universalistic. Many have eligibility requirements, such as age, income, or work requirements. Grants to students, for example, are tied to family income. And public housing is legally able to exclude people on illegal drugs, those who are not working, and those with criminal records. Since the Clinton-era reforms, public welfare also has a "workfare" requirement. As a result, single mothers with small children are required to work to be eligible for benefits.

INDIVIDUAL LEVEL INFLUENCES: ELECTORAL INCENTIVES

With the weakening of parties, more voters are untethered to the political system (King et al., 2009; Ladd 1978, 1999; Ladd and Bowman, 1998; Lane, 1966). Conventional politics declines. Together with the rising significance of social media, this change makes it easier for the public to view politicians and the "Washington establishment" as out of touch with ordinary citizens. Citizens become clients of government and spectators rather than participants.

These changes alter the distribution of incentives in the system (e.g., Crenson and Ginsberg, 2004; Ginsberg and Shefter, 1999). The incentives to vote decline as these processes increase the distance between politicians at the center and voters (Shienbaum, 1984). Solidarity and a sense of national unity also decline as such ties weaken. In these circumstances it is also more plausible for the public to imagine that significant, unbridgeable conflicts exist in the political system and that politics is a zero-sum game (see Chapter 9; Judt and Snyder, 2012). This change encourages the development of polarized views of the political system.

Changes in scale also have altered the strategies that groups use to influence the political process. Voting, while important, becomes more a political and symbolic ritual of solidarity. Much of the activity of determining who gets what in politics is based on organizational mobilization and media strategies (March and Olsen, 1989; King, 1990; Reichley, 1985; Jackson and Hitlin, 1981; Ginsberg, 1986; Gitlin, 1980). Legal and other strategies also become more important in developing recognition as a legitimate agent (e.g., Offe, 1981; Zemans, 1983; Orren and Skowronek, 2004). Lubell (1970) noted in the early 1970s that voters were becoming aware of this change in the political system and were turning away from conventional politics. He called the change the "politics of visibility."

Political Polarization: The growth of state power is a double-edged sword in American politics. While it has allowed the national state to attack problems that are too big for individual states, such as interstate highways, its growing power has also fueled ideological attacks on it (see Pierson and Skocpol, 2007; Lane, 1966; 1999). Both government and the national political class that emerged are under assault as elitist. To many, the state has become an un-American institution and a symbol of what went wrong in American society. Attacks on political elites have become common (Ladd and Bowman, 1998).

The tradition of a strong antigovernment ideology among the public has meant that state growth has produced an enormous politicization of the public sphere and polarization over its benefits (Hacker and Pierson, 2005; Hacker, 2006). While initially the public itself was not polarized, the whole polity has become politicized over the issue of the power of the state and the distribution of benefits (see Chapters 6 and 9; DiMaggio et al., 1996; Baldassarri and Gelman, 2008; Fischer and Mattson, 2009; Pew Research Center, 2014). Many people feel that they are paying for benefits that other people get (Bartlett, 2011, 2012). And this widespread feeling is the source of much public anger at political elites and the system itself.

Cognitive Nationalization: Despite this polarization, cognitive nationalization has also occurred. Whether they approve or disapprove of government, Americans are aware that Washington is now the center and source of the public agenda, as well as the source of much government funding. Public evidence of this trend is abundant. News reports have become more national in content, and there is a national media corps that is huge and focuses exclusively on the activity of the president, Congress and the courts (Pew Report, 2009, online; Fallows, 1996; Fan, Wyatt, and Keltner, 2001).[8]

TV and media coverage also make it clear that much of the national agenda is set by the action of Washington politicians and officials. News of it appears in daily (and hourly) media reports (see Iyengar, 1992). Whatever people think of this agenda, they know that it will dominate the forums of public discourse. In this sense, they are part of a "captive (national) public" (Ginsberg, 1986). And they know it.

The public has two other clues that alert them to the importance of the center. First, their federal tax bill is typically the largest of all their tax obligations, even though the rates have been going down (Jones and Williams, 2008). And second, many are aware of the federal presence in local and state budgets.

The changes detailed here have reconstructed the polity in important ways. Despite its structural weakness, the reorganized American state has become a central actor in the polity. But challenges to its legitimacy often make it inert in responding to well-known problems, such as infrastructure repair.

The next chapter turns to the major splits that developed in society with the rise of intensified individualism and the growth of an expanded state. Two conflicting narratives emerged from these developments. An expanded educational system helped intensify classic American individualism. Americans were told, and many believed, that they were endowed with extraordinary abilities and powers as educated *individuals* living in the most powerful country in the world. The expanding state simultaneously led citizens to feel that they were *clients* of big government, not participating citizens. In addition, many felt that they were involved in a zero-sum game with other groups of clients and that there would be, and already were, clear winners and losers (Hacker, 2005). These conflicting narratives undermined Americans' sense of citizenship and social solidarity. Society and the polity fractured.

Conservatives rallied around antigovernment sentiment that individualism promoted, while liberals found support for social libertarianism from the same development (Hacker and Pierson, 2005). Fear of the state, supplied by intensified individualism and the sense of being a client of a big and remote government, became strong ideological pillars of support both for a society with vastly expanded civil and political liberties/rights for all and also for one distrustful of government and willing to tolerate elevated levels of economic inequality. The result has been a complete breakdown of the old postwar order. The next chapter describes this development and the conflicting political cultures that emerged from it.

CHAPTER 8

The Breakup of the Postwar Order

ONE CONSEQUENCE OF THE BREAKUP of the postwar social order was the freeing of dissent. In the shadow of the Cold War and the garrison state, political elites stifled nonconformity in the late 1940s and 1950s. The South took serious steps to suppress black voting as the civil rights movement grew (McAdam, 1982). Patriotic populism held political nonconformity in check as well. The public and special agencies hounded people and groups deemed un-American in many ways. For example, as the militarization of foreign policy proceeded, loyalty oaths became common for politicians and others in public office (Sniderman, 1981). Expressions of patriotism became important markers of loyalty. In this spirit, labor unions became solidly anti-communist and along with the business community attacked those with "un-American" ideas and ideologies. Conservatives found much of the New Deal to be "un-American," particularly the provisions that enhanced the strength of unions. Efforts to dismantle parts of the New Deal thrived under this cover. Witch hunts for communists and "fellow travelers" grew. This included people in sensitive government posts like the State Department, universities, and New York City school teachers. The FBI, the House Un-American Activities Committee, and the media did their part by exposing "radicals" in Hollywood, universities, science, and other domains for public vilification and job loss (e.g., Lazarsfeld and Thielens, 1958).

With the stabilization of Europe and success in containing the geographical expansion of the Soviet Union in the 1960s, political space for dissent reemerged. The successful negotiated settlement of the Cuban missile crisis also aided this process of normalization by demonstrating that nuclear war was not inevitable between the great powers. One consequence of these developments was that suppressed points of conflict in the United States became public again.

As pointed out in Chapter 6, the increasing authority of individuals in the reconstructed political system powered growing nonconformity. This change increased the charisma and authority of the individual and diminished that of the state and other social institutions. This change happened dramatically and suddenly in the 1960s as higher education was expanding. One result was that this new political ecology energized both liberals and conservatives. Both mobilized as conflict increased in the post-1960s to contest what direction society should take in terms of regulating morality and the economy. With the breakdown of the postwar consensus, charting the future was now an open contest for all parties.

In this chapter, I examine the growing splits that arose in American society over the issues of government regulation of the economy and public morality. These conflicts helped break up the postwar social order. I distinguish the four political cultures that these two major fractures produced and their consequences for the political system.

BACKGROUND

Elites and later the general public rallied around different sides on two major fault lines that emerged in American society: (a) economic libertarianism, the traditional ideology of a hegemonic American business class, and (b) cultural libertarianism, a classic part of the American creed. These cleavages produced new alignments in society that fractured both political parties.

These cultural and social cleavages intensified conflict in society by producing contradictory popular impulses vis-à-vis government. Support for extending political and legal equality to many groups grew during this period. Rights groups flourished and achieved significant victories. Public sentiment grew in favor of government intervention in extending *individual* rights in society.

Neoliberals successfully challenged government regulatory programs in the post-1960s. The reemergence of conservatism fueled growing public opposition to "big government." This trend counterbalanced the victory of liberalism on civil rights and liberties. Both parties came to favor curtailing government by reducing federal revenue through tax cuts and dismantling the rules and agencies that the New Deal and the postwar governments had established for regulating commerce and the economy (Gourevitch, 2002).

These two main fault lines of conflict have polarized both elites and increasingly the population at large (Abrams, 2006; Fischer and Hout, 2006; Pew Report, 2014). On the one hand, the intensification of civil libertarianism in the 1960s produced a chasm between liberals and cultural conservatives on a wide variety of social issues, such as sexuality, abortion, sexism, gay marriage, and the death penalty. On this front, evangelicals and their allies contested the demands for more individual freedoms. They saw them as increasing immorality and undermining traditional authority structures like the family. Civil libertarians, on the other hand, supported these claims as extensions of the basic freedoms guaranteed to individuals by the Constitution.

On the issue of the economy, conflict centered on the expansion of the welfare state and on government regulation of the economy. With the rising political power of the conservative right, the attack on government and its intervention in the economy intensified. Neoliberalism arose and became dominant as the prevailing orthodoxy. The left wing of the Democratic Party contested this development as inequality in the economy increased and successful attacks on unions intensified. But alternative positions that are popularly acceptable did not emerge.

Movements formed on each of these axes of cleavage. They have produced serious unconventional splits and realignments on the issue of civil liberties and economic liberalism.

THE DEVELOPMENT OF A CULTURAL FAULT LINE

The chasms produced by Vietnam and the civil rights movements have led to an ongoing intensification and broadening of the culturally libertarian thrust of the 1960s social movements. These now extend into a wide variety of social spheres: sexuality, disabilities/physical limitations, environmentalism, worker rights, equality for women, human rights for immigrants, animal protection/movements against speciesism, and so on (Abrams, 2006).

Neotraditional countermovements have reacted to these liberal tendencies. Religious communities and a reconstituted "conservative" movement were the main carriers of such counter ideologies. They have successfully fused libertarian, militarist, and religious themes in a would-be revitalization movement (Wuthnow, 1980, 1987a, 1987b). These movements are reactions to the real and apparent decline of deference, canons of etiquette, civility, privacy, and hierarchies of authority in society. The imagery conservatives used took the view that liberalism was fueling anarchy and tribalism in society. Their reaction included critiques of universities and science in general as culturally deviant, subversive, and profane institutions (Gauchat, 2012). They also chastised big government for fostering individualism, the decline of local communities, and a general decline in traditional religion and morality.

As a result, a major cultural-ideological fault line emerged in American society: cultural libertarianism versus cultural neotraditionalism (in effect, the 1960s versus anti-1960s). On this issue, the political responses to the 1960s have produced a politically polarized society among elites that is rapidly percolating down to the mass of citizenry.

A POLITICO-ECONOMIC FAULT LINE

The other fault line is an economic one. Here the conflict centers on neoliberal laissez-faire views of the economy versus Keynesian economics that favors government regulation of the economy to counter the economic disruption produced by booms and busts and recent challenges that have raised the issue of rising inequality and wage stagnation as central political themes.

Neoliberalism benefited from the economic failures of the late 1960s and 1970s and the "stagflation" of the 1970s, together with globalizing trends in finance and banking. Both provided an opening for the resurgence of a conservative, pro-business anti-collectivism—an attack on the

U.S. form of postwar coordinated/regulated capitalism (e.g., Luttwak, 1999; Reich, 2007; Prasad, 2006).

The success of neoliberalism and the Republican Party led to a rapid shift in the direction of deregulation, marketization, and privatization in the economy. In the 1980s, President Ronald Reagan's retreat from government intensified this shift. These changes in macro policy occurred within a context of broader ideological attacks on government (Ginsberg and Shefter, 1985).

The policies that the Reagan regime enacted spelled the end of the collectivist moment. Neoliberalism became the dominant macroeconomic policy and philosophy of government. President Reagan filled the government with managers who took his rhetoric seriously and put the brakes on a variety of oversight bodies—the Securities and Exchange Commission (SEC); the Federal Communications Commission (FCC); the Federal Trade Commission (FTC); and others—that were designed to monitor their respective industries. New doctrines emphasizing deregulation in favor of markets gained the upper hand in both theory and practice (Ginsberg and Shefter, 1985, 1999).

Along with it came a rapid collapse of alternative politico-economic pictures (i.e., neo-Keynesian, managerial/corporatist, liberal-labor progressivist). With this ideological collapse, the Democratic Party lost any distinctive economic theory. In the wake of this creative destruction came the consolidation of neoliberalism and its rapid rise to ideological hegemony (Prasad, 2006; Fourcade-Gourinchas and Babb, 2002). This represented a resurgence of a classic part of the American creed.

After the "Reagan revolution" in the 1980s, there was a general decline in support for collectivist policies among elites and much of the public (Ginsberg and Shefter, 1985). The military was the only securely legitimated collectivist project—and later, even it underwent partial privatization (Friedberg, 2000). Over time, all goods have been reimagined as individual ones. Conservative elites and large segments of the public have come to view public institutions of all kinds, such as education, as having few collective benefits (Judt and Snyder, 2012; Judt, 2005). The result was the devaluation of public goods and services.

There are ideological variants of this theme that also invoke nativism and racism. The campaigns of presidential candidates Ronald Reagan and George H. W. Bush invoked racial fears and stigmatized welfare recipients as lazy and disreputable. Reagan chastised "welfare queens" living off public funds, and Bush's campaign dramatized a black convicted rapist named Willie Horton, whom Michael Dukakis, then governor of Massachusetts, had paroled but who later went on to commit a murder.

The Perot splinter movement of the 1990s inveighed against ineffective government and its lack of technical expertise. Much later, in early 2007, the Tea Party movement took a dim view of the welfare state in general. For them the welfare state and its entitlement programs were valid expressions of democratic liberalism, as long as they were reserved for "reputable" elements of society. This included citizens who have had a long work history and who were reputable. While not overtly racist, such descriptions would exclude many blacks and low-wage white workers who experienced chronic unemployment (Skocpol and Williamson, 2012; Bernstein, 2010; McGrath, 2010).

Later in the South and in rural areas of the Midwest and West, anti-immigrant, nativist, and racist movements emerged that were often covertly welcomed by the Republican Party. Democrats had experienced similar racism in the 1960s in the urban North as well as the South. But once the South became Republican, it had to expand its base by slowly including minorities.

The Trump movement in 2016 incorporated many of these tendencies. It opened its doors to nativists with its anti-immigrant emphasis. But it hewed to Republican orthodoxy on taxes and big government, favoring massive tax cuts for the wealthy and deregulation of the economy. It also supported existing and expanded entitlement programs for *white* blue-collar workers (Nate Cohn, *New York Times*, June 30, 2016: A3). As a result, Trump's popularity among white voters without a college degree skyrocketed, compared to Hillary Clinton's standing, and even that of 2012 Republican challenger Mitt Romney.

The Trump movement also endorsed nativism and white nationalism in its appeal to white blue-collar workers. Trump excoriated free trade deals and immigration for causing unemployment and low wages. He threatened to, and did, walk away from the North American Free Trade Agreement (NAFTA) and other trade pacts and vowed to cut off immigration from Mexico and the Middle East. "Build the wall" and "ban Muslims" became two of his popular slogans. As James Surowiecki, a financial analyst, put it:

White working-class voters are willing to tolerate a handout to the rich in exchange for the rest of Trump's ideological agenda, while the Republican establishment is willing to elect an ethno-nationalist in exchange for tax cuts. If Trump's working-class supporters believe that he's with them on the issues they care most about—bringing back jobs and keeping immigrants out—no tax policy will drive them away.[1]

DIMENSIONS OF THE GROWING
IDEOLOGICAL POLARIZATION

Daniel Bell framed the problem of growing conflict in society as follows: "in the 19th and early-20th centuries we had, in America, individualism in the economy and regulation in morals; today we have regulation in the economy and individualism in morals. Politically, there may be a communal society coming into being; but is there a communal ethic? And is one possible?" (Bell, 1973: 482–483)

Now there is deregulation of the economy as well the deregulation of morality. On each of these issues there are wide divisions in society. Many find "individualism in morals" distasteful, even anarchic, and godless. Similarly, conservatives decry the remaining regulation of the economy as socialist and un-American. This is particularly the case for reforms established under President Obama, such as the Clean Air Act and legislation regulating banks and financial institutions. These divisions dim the possibility of community, as Bell so cogently argued.

The result of these two ideological developments has been the emergence of two sets of ideological conflicts during the contemporary period. The first axis concerns the freedom from regulation versus the regulation of *morality*. It is a cultural conflict that counterposes a generalized cultural libertarianism versus an initially reactive, now aggressive, neotraditional posture. Issues concerning sexuality, abortion, the death penalty, legalizing marijuana, and gay marriage have all been prominent sources of divisiveness, but they are just the beginning. Ageism, sexism, racial discrimination, animal rights, voting rights for ex-felons, and easier access to political rights such as voting have all become issues for movements operating under this banner. Human rights also fall under this category, for example, the rights of immigrants (Cole, 2012a).

A second politico-economic axis involves regulation of the economy. The contrast here is between a dominant neoliberal ideology versus an ill-defined and marginalized would-be liberal or progressive economic outlook. Here the issues concern government regulation of the economy to increase overall prosperity and to decrease inequality. The Occupy Wall Street movement, for instance, championed leftist, regulatory solutions to these issues (Gitlin, 2012). Bernie Sanders's campaign also highlighted a variety of areas for expanded government action, such as expanding higher education, increasing the federal minimum wage, protecting worker rights, implementing tighter financial regulation of banks and corporations, and increasing taxes on the rich.

By crossing the two axes of conflict, one can locate the four main contemporary American political cultures, as shown in Table 8.1. Two trends are dominant: (1) an economic "right" favoring laissez-faire vis-à-vis the economy (cells 1 and 2); and (2) a cultural "left" favoring increasing individualism and freedom concerning morality (cells 1 and 3). The upshot is that libertarianism, both cultural and economic, is ascendant. Majorities favor limiting government regulation of the economy. And majorities support the extension of rights and freedoms on many grounds to gay people, black people, women, ex-felons, and so on.

However, there are strong vocal minorities who are neo-traditionalists in morality, just as there are strong ones favoring more government regulation of the economy.

This typology is helpful in clarifying several issues in sociology and political science. It helps to account for the puzzling fact that the American public is still "untainted by ideology," in Philip Converse's famous phrase. Research still finds that much of the public have no consistent policy positions that in other political systems distinguish liberals from conservatives or the left-of-center from the right-of-center parties. These splits infect both

TABLE 8.1 Types of Political Orientations

	Civil Liberties	
Government and Economy	Egalitarian	Neotraditionalist
Laissez-faire	Free Market Libertarians Ron Paul Libertarians Young Republicans (1)	Tea Party Traditionalists Evangelicals Moral Conservatives (2)
Government Regulation	Occupy Wall Street Libertarians Labor, Blacks, and Young People Religious Liberals (3)	Religious Collectivists: Catholics; Black Evangelicals (4)

political parties so that party labels are not good guides to policy preferences among the public. Party labels primarily identify groups of people who identify with one another as peers and who imagine that they share similar political outlooks, represented by party leaders. In practice party platforms are so diffuse and unrelated to policy that they offer a big umbrella for groups with diverse preferences (Shefter, 1977). The Republican Party, for example, became dominant in much of the South by accepting into the Party of Lincoln segregationists and evangelicals who are fervently in favor of government regulation of morality and tolerate racism. Politicians grafted these groups together in common cause with Republican business circles, many of whom are social libertarians and prefer individualism in morals rather than government control (J. Glaser, 1996; Lapham, 2004). Both, however, are in favor of deregulating business from government regulations and control.

One result of this development is a division among scholars on whether the United States is a center-right country or a center-left one. Based on aggregate policy preferences, one can argue that the United States is the latter and that Bernie Sanders welfare state proposals have majority support.[2] However, looking at the growth of self-identified conservatives who vote Republican and supported Trump as president, one can read the opposite, that the United States is a center-right country. This is currently the dilemma of the Democratic Party—figuring out which route to take to make their candidates electable.

The typology also outlines the four main political cultures and argues that two trends have majoritarian support. In Table 8.1 the broad movements in favor of equal rights, exemplified by cells 1 and 3, have been big winners in terms of popular and legal support. This is particularly true among educated and younger voters (Hacker and Pierson, 2005, 2010). Wall Street and Silicon Valley, for example, are big supporters of cultural libertarianism, such as gay rights and gender equality in the workplace. On this issue traditionalists and religious conservatives are on the defensive nationally, though in some sections of the country their position is dominant. The rise of civil libertarianism has led to more tolerance for individuals, but it does *not* include support for positive efforts to equalize economic rights.

Support for neoliberal economic views grew during the 1970s and 1980s so that it is now the dominant, though contested, ideology concerning the role of government. Cells 1 and 2 represent some of the populations who are supporters of this view. This movement has strengthened anti-state views. It is dominant in part because of the lack of legitimate alternative politico-economic arguments. The liberalism concerning civil rights runs into roadblocks when the issue becomes designing policies that might bolster the opportunities of women, minorities, and other oppressed groups. Such efforts raise red flags for economic libertarians. Affirmative action, support for unions, collective efforts to raise wages have been and are highly controversial issues politically.

The rise of economic libertarianism has strengthened the hand of the free marketers, the Tea Party traditionalists, and nonreligious moralists whose idea of liberty includes limited government involvement in the economy and civil society. This view has become hegemonic so that liberal Democrats and others who favor some form of government-sponsored regulatory regime of the economy are on the defensive.

The typology in Table 8.1 also indicates lines of cleavage that are developing within political parties. The successful thrust of the movement for civil libertarianism has created conflicts within the Republican Party between the neotraditionalists and the rising number of liberals (Lowi, 1996). Free market conservatives find themselves in conflict with cultural conservatives and religious, evangelical conservatives.

Conversely, Ron Paul's brand of conservatism, which features both free markets and civil libertarianism, has wide appeal to younger and better-educated Republicans (Brian Doherty, *New York Times*, February 10, 2013: 4). This is the big business–Wall Street kind of conservatism: high on civil rights and laissez-faire in the economy (cell 1).

Such groups bitterly oppose one another on civil libertarian issues. Cultural conservatives and religious evangelicals (cell 2) represent the anti-1960s segment of the conservative movement (Fitzgerald, 2007). They favor government regulation of morality, particularly on issues involving the family, such as premarital sex, homosexuality, abortion, and the public and private roles of men and women (Frankel, 2012). However, on economic issues the Christian right is conservative and bitterly against the social welfare state. Some of them even see the hand of God in economic markets (see Somers and Block, 2005; Hicks, 2006).

As a result, their members tend to vote for conservative Republicans (Manza and Brooks, 1997; Hacker and Pierson, 2010). Their support has pushed the party in a very socially conservative direction concerning civil rights. These groups have become an important part of the Republican Party's base because they have grown both numerically and in their political sophistication and participation (Chaves and Anderson, 2012: 217; T. Smith, "Religion," 2007, "Trends," 2012).

Conservatives and evangelicals have grown powerful, particularly in the South and rural areas. They are now a dominant voice in the Republican Party. Several trends have augmented their power. The rise of megachurches, which are predominantly conservative in theology, has magnified the voice of religious conservatives in the political arena (Chaves and Anderson, 2012: 231). The size and vitality of these congregations provide important advantages politically. They are easily be mobilized through mass mailings and appeals to clergy to support and fund conservative candidates and issues. The members of megachurches are much easier to reach and organize than members of much smaller congregations. And the news media pay much more attention to the voices and views of clergy and leading members of these mega congregations.

The conservative movement also benefits from the fusion of church attendance and social and political conservatism (Chaves and Anderson,

2012: 226ff). Studies show that since the 1970s, church attendance has increasingly become linked to measures of social conservatism, such as anti-gay, anti-abortion, and anti-premarital-sex policy stances. And over time church attendance and political conservatism have also become more strongly associated. This includes both the growth of more conservative political ideology and strong Republican Party identification among evangelicals.

The upshot is that there is a divide in the Republican Party on civil libertarian issues. The problem for them is that this has become a position that large numbers of Americans are coming to support. The Democratic Party has fewer internal problems concerning civil liberties.

The Republican Party, however, holds the dominant position when it comes to economic libertarianism, and they are strongly united on this front. The Trump movement favors much of the Republican agenda but deviates on its open racism and anti-free-trade policy.

The Democratic Party has no strong counter to this position, given the hegemony of neoliberalism. It has many divisions on this issue. Older collectivist solutions to poverty and inequality still retain some support, but with the decline of labor and the liberal-labor coalition these are minority positions within the Democratic Party. Obama and Progressive Democrats now talk about the importance of education and job training. But as Thomas Geoghegan (2014), a Chicago labor lawyer, notes, this policy twist means effectively giving up on the two thirds of Americans already in the labor force who do not have a college education. Inequality and wage stagnation have become policy problems for Democrats.

The support for left-of-center movements like that of Bernie Sanders illustrates this dilemma. The party's response to this challenge has remained muted, focusing on incremental changes in governmental policy toward the economy. The two personas of Hillary Clinton exemplify this dilemma. One persona is the immediate past when as senator she was a friend of Wall Street and a promoter of markets. The other was her persona as presidential contender in 2016. Then she began arguing that the left wing economist Thomas Picketty may be right and that economic inequality had gone too far. Yet she did not enunciate any broad message on inequality as Sanders did. What policies she did offer were not up to the scale of the problem nor to the level of public anger over it. Hers is also the dilemma of the Democratic Party.

SILICON VALLEY AND THE NEW CAPITALISM

The political culture of the high-technology sector illustrates these lines of conflict. Silicon Valley, and similar areas elsewhere, pictures itself as the new frontier of capitalism. And its depiction of itself as a distinctly post-modern culture has some validity. It has, for example, been a hotbed of support for social libertarianism, though recent court cases and evidence suggest that there is some hypocrisy in practice vis-à-vis gender equality. High-tech leaders have also been overwhelmingly supportive of policies that redistribute wealth, such as higher taxes on the rich, more social services for the poor, and universal health care.

A recent study that compares technology founders with other elites, such as Democratic and Republican donors, and regular voters of each party confirms this picture.[3] Tech elites are unrepentantly liberal compared to the other elites and regular voters. They oppose restrictions on abortion, favor gay rights, support gun control, and oppose the death penalty.

Compared to Republican donors, Republican voters, and regular Democratic voters, the tech elites do not subscribe to libertarian philosophy. Tech elites are much *less* likely than other elites and ordinary voters to agree that "I would like to live in a society in which the government does nothing except provide national defense and police protection, so that people could be left alone to earn whatever they could" (24 percent tech elites versus 68 percent Republican donors, 63 percent regular Republicans, and 44 percent regular Democrats). Technology founders are even less favorable to this preference than ordinary Democratic voters (24 percent versus 44 percent).

But on economic liberalism the tech elites are profoundly conservative. They are very suspicious of the government's efforts to regulate business, especially when it comes to labor. And they hope the influence of unions in both the public and private sector will decline. Hence, the paradox: they favor wealth redistribution but not government regulation of business and the economy. When the researchers combined these choices so that high wealth redistribution and low government regulation of business are combined, 62 percent of the tech elites agreed versus 21 percent of Republican donors. Republican donors, on the other hand, are almost unanimously in favor of not redistributing wealth through taxes and of not regulating business (75 percent versus 18 percent of tech elites).

Even on the new frontier of capitalism in the United States, the old splits between civil and economic libertarianism remain. But there is a wedge in the issue of taxes and wealth redistribution. With the increasing influence of the technology industry, particularly within the Democratic Party, it is hard to see where elite support for more government regulation of the economy will come from. But taxation is a different issue and one on which the Democratic Party has some leverage and elite support.

These splits are significant in themselves as points of conflict, but they also lock in with other issues that deepen divisions in society. The next section describes these perceived threats.

PERCEIVED THREATS AND DEEPENING DIVISION

The turbulence of the 1960s and the economic stagnation of the 1970s sparked a good deal of moralizing about what had happened to American culture. A culture war broke out, essentially between the anti-1960s faction of society and the pro-1960s faction (Abrams, 2006). Much of politics since then has been a morality play around the issue of the cultural decline of the United States. The fiscal crisis that has dogged the United States since the 1970s has intensified this conflict by adding other dimensions to the feeling of loss among important segments of society.

Conflicts around these issues have deepened as the result of three types of threats, real and imagined: (1) the declining hegemony of the United States (real and perceived); (2) the threats, real and perceived, of a global village; (3) and chronic fiscal crisis. They all lock in and chronically deepen these two dimensions of division.

DECLINING HEGEMONY

Declining hegemony has hastened the growing cultural divide in the United States. The dramatic rise in oil prices in 1973 was a signal that the world had changed for Americans. It was becoming multipolar. The Soviet Union was no longer the only threat. There were now many others. Conservatives used this moment to contest the developments of the 1960s. Not only was the regulated capitalism of the period unwise in their view. It was now unaffordable and a threat to U.S. security (Zolberg, 2002; Reich, 2007; Prasad, 2006).

Conservative reactions to attacks on conventional morality, sex roles, and other forms of inequality were similar. Egalitarianism in their view was undermining the solidarity of the nation and its key institutions. U.S. conservatives took an aggressive stance on these issues and orchestrated a populist campaign against institutions and individuals, who they thought were carriers of the new immorality or were representatives of it. This included the press, universities, the media, science, and the arts. Key figures like Jane Fonda, Tom Hayden, and other radicals were also objects of their venom. Conservatives hammered the theme of U.S. exceptionalism and the importance of militant vigilance against the many enemies of the free world (Hazen, 2005). Liberal elites, they argued, were out of touch with the silent majority of Americans who constituted the moral majority of the country. They preached a righteous version of American nationalism with absolute certainty about the morality and justice of America's "incoherent empire" (Mann, 2005; Micklethwait and Wooldridge, 2004).

These populist attacks started with the Barry Goldwater movement but intensified in the first years of the Nixon presidency when the war in Vietnam escalated. Vice President Spiro Agnew became one of the leading critics and a point man for President Nixon and conservatives generally. According to David Remnick, now editor of the *New Yorker*, "In the fall of 1969, Richard Nixon surveyed his domestic enemies and appointed Spiro T. Agnew, his Vice-President, to the post of White House Torquemada. Wielding a rhetorical style that might be described as 'surrealist-alliterative,' Agnew denounced opponents of the war in Vietnam as 'an effete corps of impudent snobs'—as 'ideological eunuchs,' 'professional anarchists,' and as 'vultures who sit in trees.' Never or since has a populist attack come swathed in such purple raiment (David Remnick, "Comment: Nattering Nabobs," *New Yorker*, July 10, 2006, http://www.newyorker.com/printables/talk/060710ta_talk_remnick).

Liberals reacted with dismay to attacks on the regulatory state and the remnants of the New Deal. But with the demise of the liberal-labor coalition, alternative politico-economic pictures collapsed (see Mann, 2013; Petrocik, 1981, 1982; Petracca, 1990). Neo-Keynesianism and other such possibilities were on the defensive and marginalized. Over time the Democratic Party lost any distinctive economic theory with which to contend against neoliberalism. They too were committed to the national security state and were terrified of looking soft on defense and national security (Zolberg, 2002). As a result, a pro-business anti-collectivism prevailed.

Similarly, liberals were on the defensive concerning the rights revolution, given the working-class backlash that the civil rights movements began to encounter (Kinder and Sanders, 1996). Among blue-collar workers racial resentment was mounting in the 1970s when prosperity was eroding. The movement of large numbers of women into the workforce was another job threat to blue-collar men. Furthermore, starting in the mid-1970s, wage stagnation had begun to set in, along with increasing pay differentials for college-educated men and women versus those without a college degree (Geiger, 2009, Hacker, 2006).

THE GLOBAL VILLAGE AS THREAT

Second, many conservatives and blue-collar groups perceived the emergence of a global village as a threat. The metaphor of the global village is itself a source of conflict and drama. For conservatives, it raises the specter of a rootless society whose inhabitants are primarily attentive to the ephemera of cyberspace with little attachment to country, tradition, or local social groups (Levin, 2016).

Among liberals, this cultural shift signifies the liberation of people from local communities and allows for the growth of a more cosmopolitan culture as natives are free to participate in national and international culture. It frees citizens from the idiocies of nationalism and makes them citizens of the world, just as Marx argued that industrialization relieved workers from the idiocies of rural life.

In addition, the rise of the global village raises two other threatening specters: (1) the threat of increased immigration as people abroad learned of the opportunities in richer countries, including the United States and Europe, and (2) the imagined diminution of American nationalism and patriotism as the society becomes more multicultural (Mirel, 2010). Many working-class Democrats, for example, see immigration as a threat to their job security, fearing that corporations will always favor workers who would accept lower pay and poorer job conditions. Middle-class managers are also aware that companies are constantly lobbying Congress for more lenient immigration quotas for highly skilled jobs in engineering and information technology.

Similarly, many, especially conservatives, believe that immigration strengthens multiculturalism and undermines nationalist sentiment at a time when the United States is engaged in fierce international political and economic competition. Evangelicals, a major part of the Republican Party's base, view immigration as the source of a new demography that would also undermine the consensus that the United States is a Christian nation and civilization (Froese and Bader, 2010).

Thus the global village was threatening because conservatives perceived that trends associated with it would ensure the production of a new political order that was alien to the American tradition. This had become clear earlier when movements to ban racism and other forms of discrimination led not just to a more open society but also to a more conflicted society. It produced heightened support for multiculturalism as a model of society. Unlike individual mobility, ethnic and racial mobilization *enhances* the significance of racial and ethnic identities (W. Wilson, 1978; Hout, 1988; Enoke, 1981). This in turn strengthens the demand for acceptance of multiculturalism as the approved model of American society.

As the social and cultural demands of a variety of groups legitimated by this movement spiraled, conflicts filled the polity drowning out earlier notions of the United States as a consensual society built around a common civic culture. Politics became more tribal, as identity politics emerged and accelerated divisive rhetoric, particularly among conservatives.

THE THREAT POSED BY THE FISCAL CRISIS

The persistent fiscal crisis after the 1970s was another source of deepened conflict. This was associated with declining hegemony. But it was also a result of the growing dominance of economic libertarianism. While globalization played a part, the continued fiscal crisis of the state was in some ways self-imposed. It derived from the inability of society to support the taxation levels needed to run a modern state and society. Neoliberalism helped inspire these policies, but the roots go deeper.

Both liberal and conservative administrations have promoted the case for *lower taxes* since the 1960s (Jones and Williams, 2008). They did so, however, for different reasons. When they realized that the tax *rate* affects popular support for government programs, Democratic regimes used lower taxes to argue for more social programs. Conservatives have backed lower tax rates because they reduced the power of the state. This tension climaxed in the 1980s when "pay as you go" legislation was dropped and when the conservative case for "no new taxes" became dominant (Krippner, 2011; Peterson, 1985). Since then the Republicans have mounted an ideological campaign against taxation. In 2012 the Republican platform included the statement that "taxes by their very nature reduce a citizens' freedom" (quoted from James Surowiecki, "Trump's Other Tax Ploy," *New Yorker*, October. 17, 2016: 29).

ECONOMICS AS POLITICAL THEATER: ECONOMIC GLOBALIZATION AND THE FISCAL CRISIS

Unlike the 1930s when nations were on their own, there were now more policy options because of the intensive economic globalization that was occurring during this era. Global rather than national solutions were available as economic globalization intensified. Otherwise the pressures coming to bear on the U.S. political/economic system in 1981 would have caused a crash and a political meltdown.

These pressures resulted from two facts. First, it became apparent that President Reagan would not give up on his program of military expansion *and* tax cuts. Secondly, it was politically impossible to slash social expenditures on Medicare, Social Security, and other programs to resolve the issue on the spending side. David Stockman rightly predicted, "Deficits as far as the eye can see" (Krippner, 2011: 94; Peterson, 1985).

The solution to this problem was deficit finance. The impact of intensified global financial markets came as a surprise to U.S. policy makers. They totally underestimated the appetite that international investors, particularly the Japanese, had for U.S. debt in the form of Treasury securities. Since then others, such as China, the Saudis, and Russia, have also discovered the economic and political security of investing in U.S. debt and other securities. This discovery freed the U.S. government and Wall Street from market discipline and restraint.

Internal politics blocked other solutions to this fiscal crisis. Since the 1980s, the dominance of neoliberalism has meant that politicians cannot approach taxation as a technical or fiscal issue. It has become a *moral issue*, independent of the need for revenue to support wars or popular programs. The Reagan "revolution" helped establish the principle of "no new taxes" *independent* of budgetary requirements.

From the 1980s onward, deficit financing has become a way of life. Different political regimes have financed wars, tax cuts, and programs for seniors by *borrowing*. Both Republican and Democratic administrations totally abandoned the tradition of financing wars and other programs through tax increases in favor of deficit finance.

While the privileged position of the American dollar and the security of the United States has given the U.S. government access to foreign funds at low interest rates, neoliberals also began to view increasing government debt as a *moral crisis* (Skidelsky, 2009). Yet raising taxes was also anathema. So, any regime faced a Catch-22 situation. Raising taxes is difficult without majorities in each house. And increasingly the national debt has become a highly politicized issue and morality play with uncertain results.

As neoliberal doctrine has successfully percolated throughout society, economic elites and now major segments of the population are against raising taxes to the level necessary to support existing programs. And they have also demonized deficit finance—or government borrowing to finance the budget. Despite historically low international interest rates, deficit financing—even for investment in infrastructure—has become a sign of moral hazard. Raising taxes is also unpopular. Many see both policies as threats to the vitality of the American economy and way of life. The net result is that the fiscal crisis drags on and with it the polarized debate about what government can and should do. Given the strictures against both tax increases and government borrowing, no rational policy is possible.

THE NEW POLITICS

Both conflict over public morality and over economic policy has ushered in a new wave of politics. Gone is the solidarity of the 1950s and the kind of patriotism that such feelings produce, that is, the 1930s-era feeling that "we're all in the same boat." This change in public philosophy has widespread ramifications. First, it undermines citizens' concern and trust of other citizens. This has been a long-term trend in American society after the 1960s (Paxton, 1999; Putnam, 2000). The increased perception of real and imaginary conflicts between groups in society gives rise to distrust.

Second, this change in public philosophy undermines support for the key idea on which modern social welfare states depend. The idea that paying taxes to benefit some in many areas, such as education and health care, increases the prosperity and health of society at large is the central tenet of modern social welfare states (Judt and Snyder, 2012). When the public or elites successfully challenge it, support for a welfare state withers. Arguably, this public philosophy has collapsed in the United States.

Along with the assault on the welfare state, another trend has reemerged, reminiscent of the Roaring Twenties: the return of Social Darwinism among the upper classes and business elites. Newly enfranchised global financial elites and their corporate allies argue that because market success depends on individual talent and risk-taking skill, extreme inequality is a natural and appropriate outcome (Skocpol, 1996; Mizruchi, 2013; Page et al., 2011). This justifies not only rising economic inequality but also resistance to all government "entitlement" programs like Medicare and Social Security. Privatizing social welfare programs became the elite response to how society should deal with medical care and pensions for the elderly.

Much of the conservative political class have similar attitudes. A case in point is the debate in Congress in 2017 over the bill to overhaul the tax system. When questioned about the need to abolish the estate tax, which only multimillionaires/billionaires pay, Republican senator Chuck Grassley of Iowa told his state's leading newspaper, "I think not having the estate tax recognizes the people that are investing, as opposed to those that are just spending every darn penny they have, whether it's on booze or women or movies."

Republican senator Orrin Hatch of Utah gave a similar explanation for why the Children's Health Insurance Program was not being reauthorized. He claimed,

It's because we don't have the money anymore. I have a rough time wanting to spend billions and trillions of dollars to help people who won't help themselves—won't lift a finger—and expect the federal government to do everything.[4]

Similarly, upper-class elites see low, stagnant wages as resulting from lack of job skills, not the super market power of corporations or the outsourcing of work to the largest metropolitan areas and other countries due to globalization (Reich, 2007). Conservatives often blame workers and their class culture for lack of education and job skills. "Culture of poverty" arguments have also resurfaced, though Murray (2011; see also Ehrenreich, 2012) has also blamed the middle class for promoting this behavior and new models of immorality to working class youth.

CONSERVATIVE CRITICISMS AND COUNTERMOBILIZATION

These splits have led to the rise of populist revitalization movements in society that aim to purify society of the evils that these trends have brought with them. Political elites have not been able to contain the conflicts that changing morals and debates over economic morality have brought with them. These changes involve both emerging new moralities that lead to demands for new freedoms and to movements with demands for economic justice. These come up against conservative stances on morality and opposition to government intervention in the economy. For example, the Republican establishment has no answer to Trump, whose economic views on trade violate party economic orthodoxy and whose views on immigrants and Muslims go against the American creed and Constitution. Similarly, the Democratic establishment has no answer to Bernie Sanders's proposals for a European-style welfare state that produces more economic equality and jobs.

The growth of Washington during this period fostered two opposing trends. First, it strengthened a sense of cognitive nationalism that portrayed the United States as one nation, despite regional and other differences. But it also sparked and intensified a traditional American response to elites at the center of the nation: populism.

Populists resent the identification of nationalism with the center of the nation-state, political elites, and institutions. Neopopulism arises in opposition to this development and focuses on classic American values: individualism, small government, and civil libertarianism (Lipset, 1963, 1990, 1996; Boggs, 1986). Intensifying this brand of American ideology may be one enduring contribution of the growth of big government in the United States (Pierson and Skocpol, 2007).

It is also arguable that the growth of big government has enhanced the sense of threat among critics and dissenters (see Badie and Birnbaum, 1983; Pierson and Skocpol, 2007). If the center were weak, it would make no sense to run against it and to develop elaborate populist ideologies about the conspiracies and interlocking relationships between evil elites at the center.

One result of these developments is that U.S. governmental expansion produced an ongoing reconsolidation of aggressive anti-statist ideology. This took the form of cultural resistance and revitalization movements. There were calls for reestablishing a neotraditionalist social order, along with a call for "law and order." These countermovements emerged in the early 1960s with the Goldwater for President movement and contested not only the emergence of big government but also the social liberalism that accompanied it. Goldwater's slogan "a choice, not an echo" threw down the challenge. Conservatives were rebelling against big government and its associated evils, such as a decline of traditional morality and patriotism. For some segments of the mass public, big government was associated with social revolution (Abrams, 2006). To many conservatives the 1960s were associated with the rise of immorality, radicalism, *and* revolution.

Conservatives challenged this development on many fronts, such as on legal and intellectual grounds. For example, Philip Hamburger (2014), a conservative legal scholar, argues that much administrative law in the United States, and subsequent action, is unconstitutional. Under the Constitution, only Congress can enact law. The president executes law, and agencies implement it. In his view, the large body of administrative law that has developed usurps the authority of Congress. Americans, therefore, live under a "dual system of government, one part established by the Constitution and another circumventing it" (see the review in *The Economist*, August 9–15, 2014: 68–69).[5] Such views bolstered the legitimacy of conservative critiques of U.S. government expansion.

Others on the right criticized the growth of government on policy grounds, arguing that its policies had failed to produce desired effects. For example, Irving Kristol, a leading neoconservative thinker, gave Republicans the following advice in 1994 when President Clinton was trying to overhaul the health care system:

Passage of the Clinton health plan *in any form* [sic] would be disastrous. It would guarantee an unprecedented federal intrusion into the American economy. Its success would signal the rebirth of centralized welfare state policy now that such policy is being perceived as a failure in other areas. (Eduardo Porter, *New York Times*, October 2, 2013: B3)

Another critique of conservatives is that the expansion of governmental authority has led to the expansion of individual authority and autonomy. It displaces other sources of authority as individuals experience "sociological release" from these communities. Conservatives decried the fact that the interpersonal community and corporate-group authority of many traditional institutions died as individual freedoms expanded, for example, the authority of the extended family, parents, men (i.e., the patriarchy), church, schools and teachers, ethnic groups, and local communities (Crouch, 2004; Meyer, 1986; Caplow, 1991).

To conservatives this change has led to a pernicious decline of community at local levels. Big government in their view was both a source of elitism at the center and a destroyer of community locally. It intensified the authority of *individuals* in society at the expense of traditional sources of authority (see Chapter 6).

The emergence of both antigovernment ideologies and conflicts over civil libertarianism had major consequences for society. One of the most difficult challenges it has produced is the increasing polarization of society.

ELITE POLARIZATION

The first signs of polarization occurred among political elites and Republican activists in the 1980s (Saunders and Abramovitz, 2003). Later in the

1990s politicians like Patrick Buchanan created the imagery of "culture wars." Since then popular intellectuals, politicians, and the media have insisted that there is a cultural war and political polarization.

It is apparent that politicians and the media helped to create the idea of a culture war. There is little evidence at local levels that it exists in terms of people's attitudes toward politicians or local institutions such as schools and universities (Jennings, 1998).

The carriers of these polarized attitudes were both the political parties and the media. In its initial phase, much of this conflict occurred at national levels of the political system and among elites. It was not apparent at the local community level. In Morris Fiorina's (2004) view, political parties *and* the media drove the perception of polarization. The *parties* are polarized. Each tends to see each other as less centrist than they really are. The problem, he says, is that "we have leaders who want to divide rather than unite."

The evidence for this position is clear. Polarization between party politicians and activists began in the 1980s and intensified in the 1990s. The first signs of polarization emerged in the 1980s but it was confined to political activists. Among activists the growing differentiation mirrors that of the political system itself with Republican leaders and officials becoming the most distant in their conservatism from regular Republicans and from Democrats (Saunders and Abramovitz, 2003).

Political elites quickly became polarized during and after the 1980s. Clio Andris and colleagues (2015), for example, show that party line voting in the House intensified in the 1990s, particularly after the Republican revolution in 1994 under speaker of the house Newt Gingrich. Since then crossover voting has gotten rare. Fischer and Mattson (2009: 435) observe that political elites and activists are more demonstrably polarized in 2005 than they were in 1970. And they became even more polarized in 2014 than they were earlier (Pew Research Center, 2014). The mass public, meanwhile, did not exhibit such polarization until after 2000 (Fischer and Hout, 2006; Fischer and Mattson, 2009).

INCIPIENT POPULAR POLARIZATION

These political conflicts, waged within the national political and media system, have filtered down to the public at large. The media and political parties have both been carriers of polarized positions on civil liberties advocated by conservative groups and fights over neoliberal policies vis-à-vis the social welfare state. The result is a steadily growing set of ideological cleavages in the population at large (Fischer and Mattson, 2009; Baldassarri and Gelman, 2008; Pew Research Center, 2014).

Polarization among the public is a *new* phenomenon. Research examining public opinion data from the 1980s and 1990s found little evidence at the *individual* level of widespread and intense contention between segments of the population (Fischer and Hout, 2006; Fiorina et al., 2004; DiMaggio et al., 1996). Fiorina (1996; 2004), for example, found little support for the notion that there was a culture war visible among the population during the Republican resurgence of the early Clinton era. The blue state/red state dichotomy is a myth, he argued, when one looks closely at popular attitudes and voting across geographical areas. Paul DiMaggio and colleagues (1996) also report similar findings looking at national opinion polls in the 1970s, 1980s, and early 1990s. On most issues, except abortion and the death penalty, polarization was not evident.[6]

From 1970 to the 1990s, public attitudes remained stable. Polarization was confined to a minority of the population. Roughly a quarter to a third of the population was either consistently liberal or conservative on social issues (Fischer and Hout, 2006: 233). This evidence led Fiorina, a prominent political scientist, to conclude that Americans are much more similar than they are different. In his view, "both red states and blue states are basically centrists. Red states are a little more conservative than blue states. But people by and large see themselves in the center" (http://www.apa.org/monitor/may05/myth.aspx).

Popular polarization started to increase after the 1990s. Activists, the wealthy, the more highly educated, and the politically involved all became increasingly consistent in their attitudes and in conflict with those of the opposite political party (Fischer and Mattson, 2009; Baldassarri and Gelman, 2008). The cleavages among these groups started to become deeper. The Pew Research Center report on polarization (2014: 2), for example, found that 92 percent of Republicans are to the right of the median Democrat on issues, and 94 percent of Democrats are to the left of the median Republican. Furthermore, many saw the opposing party as a threat to the nation. Twenty-seven percent of Democrats and 36 percent of Republicans think that the opposing party poses such a threat.

Furthermore, the ideological consistency of liberals and conservatives has dramatically increased. Thirty-eight percent of active Democrats are now consistent liberals, up from 8 percent in 1994. Among Republicans, 33 percent of the politically active now express consistently conservative views, compared to 10 percent a decade ago. The most polarized groups have also become the most active in the polity. Not only has the center shrunk (from 49 percent to 39 percent), but the majority in the center is sitting on the edges of the playing field (Pew Research Center, 2014: 3).

As of 2016 the Pew Research Center found that partisan sentiment has grown stronger. Forty-five percent of Democrats and 46 percent of Republicans hold very unfavorable views of the opposing party (*New York Times*, June 16, 2017: A1, A17). There is a growing perception that the opposing party is dangerous to the nation, not just misguided about policy. This feeling now also characterizes those who are independent of affiliation with either party. Independents who leaned toward one party also feel that the opposing party is dangerous.

This distrust of opposing party members extends far beyond politics. Majorities of each party view their counterparts as more closed-minded than other Americans. Substantial numbers also think that the opposition is exceptionally immoral, lazy, and dishonest. Large numbers of each party would also be unhappy if a son or daughter married a member of the opposition.

Partisan prejudice has now become the number one cleavage in contemporary America. It even exceeds racial hostility, as measured by surveys. Shanto Iyengar, a political a scientist at Stanford, concludes that partisan animus is at an all-time high. Only in the days of the Civil War was it worse.

Politicians are primarily responsible for developing these narratives that have exaggerated the differences between groups. They have done this to build movements and to get votes. At the same time, much of the public is not personally engaged in these issue disputes. But while they may be sitting on the sidelines of public discourse, they are also aware that this polarized discourse is the *public* agenda (Iyengar, 1992). The issues it contains are the ones that political elites, Congress, and other institutions like the press attend to. Whatever their private attitudes, the public realizes that the issues that divide are the real agenda of the political system.

THE NEW, IMAGINED SOCIETY

These changes have restructured the political system. Once politicians and the media have shattered the image of society as a unified, consensual entity, rhetoric of conflict and zero-sum games replace it. Imagined differences between groups arise and intensify conflicts. Driven by vocal, radical minorities, the conflicts intensify and drag in many others. Once this happens, many citizens begin to withdraw trust from leaders and elites they disagree with. The political system itself becomes polarized around issues and ideologies that are difficult to broker.

A zero-sum game mentality develops. Every tax and expenditure debate pits one group against another in these disputes. And those who will pay for government expenditures often see themselves as people who will not benefit from them (Bartlett, 2012; Judt and Snyder, 2012). There are few cases where everyone thinks that they are beneficiaries of the welfare state.

Narratives of conflict thus have widespread effects. When elites train the population to see all government decisions as zero-sum conflicts between groups for benefits, confidence in major institutions themselves vanishes. The public no longer views them as nonpartisan. This trend may partly account for the long-term slide in public confidence in government and allied institutions (Lipset and Schneider, 1983; Kamens, 2009; Lane, 1999; Steuerle et al., 1998; T. Smith, "Trends," 2012).

The result is that a politics of bitterness and resentment prevails. In a content analysis made possible by Google Ngram Viewer, Shea and Sproveri (2012) show that the last thirty years of American politics has seen an increase in the use of the terms *mean politics, filthy politics, bitter politics*, and *hateful politics* in a wide variety of literature and commentary. They argue that incivility is a strategic weapon in politics and that it flourishes in divisive electoral contests. Their data show that the use of this kind of language spikes in every era since 1820 when there was a major realignment and critical elections.

In this polarized climate, even basic facts are in dispute. Polls by NPR (October 2014, http://www.journalism.org/2014/10/21/political-polarization-media-habits/; http://www.journalism.org/topics/political-polarization/), for example, show that 25 percent of adults do not believe *any* information published by government agencies, such as the unemployment rate, GDP growth, the size of the federal deficit, inflation, and wage growth. Among Trump supporters this level of disbelief reaches 75 percent (*New York Times*, October 25, 2016). With no agreement on facts, it is difficult to have an informed civic discourse on policy options at the federal or local level.

It is also possible in this opinion climate for candidates or party leaders to invent their own facts to coincide with their political opinions, such as climate change denials. In these circumstances, polarization can spiral, freed from any limitations imposed by empirical reality.

THE ATTACK ON HIGHER EDUCATION AND SCIENCE

A glaring example of the breakdown of consensus is the growing attacks by conservatives on higher education and science. This is an astonishing development historically. Part of the American creed has been belief in social mobility as both an individual good and a collective one (Hartz, 1955). The public has long viewed education as part of this process. Since the 1950s this emphasis has intensified. Higher education became prominently showcased as the source of many benefits, both to individuals and for society at large via human capital formation and technological innovation. Both parties supported funding for universities and science. Elites saw both as critical for national security and economic competitiveness.

This attitude began to change in the 1970s when the conservative counterrevolution and neoliberalism gained political traction. For some on the right, universities became associated with threatening changes in public morality and the decline of traditional authority. For economic libertarians, neoliberalism cast doubt on the collective benefits of publicly funded universities. And for those who support traditional morality, many colleges and universities appeared to be hothouses of anarchy, immorality, and anti-Christian values.

Many secular conservatives also saw universities and their faculties as sources of anarchy and disorder. Even the sober-minded analyst James Buchanan, a future economics Nobel laureate, criticized universities for becoming centers of anarchy, spawned by privileged, draft-exempt students. Their intent, he argued, was to destroy university and societal social order with no plan to replace it other than their own whims. In *Academia in Anarchy* (1970), he and a colleague argued that this development would spiral given the low opportunity costs for anarchists to engage in violence. In turn, there would be a counterdevelopment. The leviathan state would withdraw funds from universities and take other measures to contain the anarchy.[7] This development in their view would mark the move to a more authoritarian society. Universities and individual liberty would be casualties of this trend.

Among evangelicals, science, as opposed to technology, also became suspect as a source of anti-Christian values and thought. In the new political climate these views gained political traction. The alliance between evangelicals and economic conservatives gave them a strong political base at the state and local level to attack universities where they were most vulnerable—the state public funding that most depend on.

CONSERVATIVE POLITICAL TRIUMPH
AND STATE FUNDING POLICIES

What is often unrecognized is that Republicans now dominate most state governments. Seventy percent of state legislatures are in Republican hands. They also control 60 percent of state governorships and 55 percent of state attorney-generals and secretaries of state. In addition, in twenty-five states Republicans have unified control of both the legislatures and governorships, compared to seven in which Democrats have such control (Matthew Yglesias, "Democrats in Denial," *Vox*, October 19, 2015). Republicans are thus in a position in much of the country to put their low-tax, smaller-government proposals into effect. This has led to a general defunding of public institutions, particularly education.

Following the Reagan program at the federal level in the 1980s, many state governments introduced similar programs. Public funding for higher education went into a long, slow decline. The economic crisis of 2008 became politically useful because it created an opportunity for much more severe cuts. Politicians at the state level had a perfect excuse to introduce draconian cuts. State tax bases had shrunk, and voters were calling for income tax cuts as well as cuts in state expenditures. Table 8.2 shows the severity of the cuts that state politicians and governors introduced.

Section A in Table 8.2 shows the average level drop across the fifty states in support per student in inflation adjusted dollars for the period 2007–2013. The drop is severe—almost 30 percent. Section B shows the percentage reductions in state appropriations for full-time students. They are also large, averaging 23 percent across the fifty states. This was occurring at the same time student enrollment was growing by 10 percent (7 percent of which are full time students).

These averages conceal wide variation among states. Spending in Arizona, South Carolina, and Louisiana, for example, was down 40 percent after the 2008 recession. Thirty-seven states have cut funding by more than 20 percent, and nine have cut it by more than 33 percent. Only two states have increased higher education funding. They are the oil-rich states of Alaska and North Dakota.[8]

These budget cuts forced universities to cut back substantially on the numbers of full time faculty. Temporary faculty now do close to 50 percent of the instruction. Cutting faculty is therefore relatively easy to do.

TABLE 8.2 State Funding of Four-Year Public Universities

Average State and Local Revenues per FTE Student*	
2007–2008	$12,748
2012–2013	$9,686
Percentage Change in State Appropriations for Universities 2007–2014	
State Appropriations for Higher Education	–17.5%
State Appropriations for Full-Time Enrolled Students	–23.1%
Student Enrollment Growth	10.0%
Faculty Growth	7.0%

Source: Michael Leacham, Vincent Palacies and Michael Mitchell, States Are Still Funding Higher Education at Below Pre-Recession Levels Report, Center on Budget and Policy Priorities, Washington, D.C. May 1, 2014.
*Source Table 41: Mobile Digest of Educational Statistics, 2013, National Center for Educational Statistics, Washington, D.C.

Over a longer interval, states like North Carolina have made draconian reductions in permanent faculty levels. Thus, the recent cuts are part of a longer-term trend in most states.

University leaders have had to scramble to replace the cuts in state funding. Consequently, tuition has become much more significant in their budgets (see Table 8.3). As a result, average tuition at state universities and colleges has nearly doubled over this period, while tuition at private institutions has grown as well. This change has magnified the gap between wealthy private institutions, where corporate funding and individual philanthropy are significant, and public universities that are losing state funding. The difference between an elite sector and the rest of higher education is growing.

Over the longer haul from 1973 to 2014, tuition has more than tripled in inflation-adjusted dollars, while median family income increased by 5 percent (Center on Budget and Policy Priorities, 2014).[9]

Federal legislative change in the late 1970s made the substitution of tuition for public funds possible (Geiger, 2009). Before this time there were strict legal limits on how much students or their families could *borrow* to pay for college. Private banks made the loans, and the government guaranteed them. The reasoning for limits on borrowing was simple. Keeping loans small helped guarantee that students would repay them. Tuition rates were lower then, so this logic made sense.

However, as the defunding of higher education intensified, colleges and states were eager to find substitutes for the decline in public funding. Congress obliged and took the limits off the amounts that students could borrow in 1978 (see Geiger, 2009). Students, private banks, and

TABLE 8.3 College Costs (Average Undergraduate Tuition, Room, and Board Charges)

Time Periods	Four-Year Public University	Four-Year Private University
1992–1993	$9,772	$24,364
2002–2003	$12,434	$30,220
2012–2013	$17,474	$35,074

Source: Table 40, Mobile Digest of Educational Statistics, 2013, National Center for Educational Statistics, Washington, D.C.
Amounts in constant 2012–2013 dollars.

the federal government are now substantially funding both public and private universities via these loans.

One result is that student debt levels have risen to unimaginable heights. The average student now graduates with over $25,000 in loan debt. This is now a major source of debt in the national economy. The default rate on student loans has also risen substantially.

This change has led to rationing higher education based on family income. Many high-ability students from low-income families do not even consider going to university. If they do, they tend to go to the cheapest one they can find—which are often the lowest-quality institutions. Among low-income, highly capable students who enter college, the rate of college completion is around 30 percent, compared to 80 percent for high-income, highly gifted students (Putnam, 2015; McElwee, 2015). This change has had the effect of lowering U.S. social mobility rates via education compared to Scandinavia and other countries that provide more access. Canada, for example, has a population in which over 50 percent of 25- to 35-year-olds have university BA degrees. The United States, which was once a leader in higher education, is now in sixteenth place in the production of college graduates—behind the Philippines and other third world countries.

RESULTS OF THE CONSERVATIVE COUNTERATTACK

A legitimacy crisis has emerged and opened space for populist movements. Resurgent individualism has aided this development by undermining the legitimacy of *all* elites. As a result, it offered support to a wide variety of movements contesting authority in society. On the right, such movements appealed to less educated groups who resented the control of social institutions by educated elites who they believed neglected their interests. This led to support for authoritarian populist leaders. On the left, movements have grown challenging economic elites. The change in political culture and ecology has opened the door to these developments.

The next chapter examines the rise of a radical form of populism that claims that all elites in society are corrupt and attacks their motives as well as their authority.

CHAPTER 9

The Intensification of Populism and the Declining Legitimacy of Elites

People have had enough of experts
—MICHAEL GOVE, Brexit campaigner, 2016

If the little people, if the real people, if the ordinary decent people are prepared
to stand up and fight for what they believe in, we can overcome the big banks,
we can overcome the multi-nationals. . . . You can go out, you can beat the
pollsters, you can beat the commentators, you can beat Washington.
—NIGEL FARAGE, Brexit campaigner, speaking at a
Donald Trump rally in Jackson, Mississippi[1]

IN RECENT DECADES POPULISM has risen in democracies across the
world (Imig and Tarrow, 2001). Evidence indicates that populist parties'
share of the vote has risen from 5 percent in 1961–1965 to nearly 25 percent in the period 2011–2016 (Dani Rodrik, Global Elections Database,
http://www.globalelectionsdatabase.com/).[2] Globalization has become
tainted with the stigma of unfairness—a theme I will return to. This suggests that many party systems are facing legitimacy crises as globalization, and its discontents, expand (e.g., Stiglitz, 2003). There appear to be
no shortage of lying demagogues, whose followers are perfectly aware of
their mendacity but who believe that they are sending authentic messages
of symbolic protest to elites who are ignoring them (see Hahl, Kim, and
Zuckerman Sivan, 2018).

This chapter examines the rise of radical forms of populism in the
United States. Anti-elitism is a major source of populism historically in
the United States. But resurgent populism is now more radical. No elites
are safe from attack. This is partly because the rise of enhanced individualism has transferred charisma to individuals. The individual is now
the key construct of American society. The authority conferred on the
individual and public opinion has created a culture in which all elites
find their authority contested. This change elevates the power of public

opinion over experts in all institutions. And it diminishes the authority of all institutions.

The distinctive narrative of the new populism is one of distrust of *all* elites and institutions. This includes medicine, universities, the press and media, politics and politicians, science, government, and even banks and corporations. Some are even suspicious of the military as an arm of the deep state. Populists have become more radical in their disdain for elites in all major institutions.

Business may be the one institution immune to this challenge. American civil religion has long defined business as a meritocracy and a major source of progress. In this view business generates practical knowledge that produces modern technologies and wealth, but not elites. This is the basis of the long-term hegemony of business in American society (Thomas, 1989; Lindblom, 1977). An example of the privileged position of business is the fact that the public blamed government, not financial institutions, for the depression of 2008 (Martinelli, 2008).[3]

Other institutions have seen dramatic declines in public confidence. This is a sign of rising public distrust of elites. The press, the presidency, and Congress have been particularly vulnerable. Only local government officials have escaped the stigma of being ineffective, useless, and dangerous to the republic (Jennings, 1998). That is perhaps because such leaders, like businesspeople, are not viewed as elites. They are also often much like their constituents, ethnically and otherwise. Furthermore, they have restricted authority that is limited by the processes of local democracy.

Diffuse suspicion has contaminated most national institutions. For example, it is now common to question the validity of all government statistics, such as the unemployment rate. Many people also tell pollsters that they do *not* believe anything that the government publishes or that the media prints or broadcasts. News from the most prominent newspapers and media in the country has been called "fake." Substantial portions of the public do not believe it. Some believe only news they hear from relatives, close friends, or social media feeds they like.

Higher education, long a venerated institution for its practical consequences in fostering mobility and technical innovation, also faces increasing skepticism—and defunding (see Chapter 8). Bloomberg News

(July 13, 2017; http://fortune.com/2017/07/13/republicans-conservatives
-think-college-is-bad-against-higher-education/) recently reported results
of a survey it had conducted showing that the proportion of people saying
that "colleges and universities have a negative effect on what is happening
in America" increased from 37 percent to 58 percent between 2015 and
2017. This increasing loss of faith in higher education is almost totally
confined to conservative Republicans. Seventy percent of them registered
this complaint in 2017, compared to less than 20 percent of Democrats.[4]

These attacks bear some similarity to those of the 1950s, when academics, particularly in the social sciences and humanities, came under
attack for their alleged communist political affiliations (Lazarsfeld and
Thielens, 1958). The recent attacks, however, are broader. They involve
accusations that scientists have created false knowledge and hoaxes, such
as global warming, in pursuit of money and influence.

Similarly, large segments of the population, particularly conservatives
and evangelicals, feel unconstrained in rejecting scientific theory or facts
that they do not like. Climate change and evolution head the list of taboo
topics in these circles. The population at large increasingly distrusts the
basic objectivity of science. According to Gauchat (2012), the association
of science with public policy in the postwar era has politicized it and led
to growing skepticism about its practitioners and the universities that
house it. Conservatives are especially likely now to be skeptics of science
generally, and willing to defund institutions of science.

Given the general anti-intellectual bent of American culture historically,
the public has always been skeptical of science as opposed to technology
(Hofstadter, 1965). But the general political attacks on science and efforts
to defund it are new and growing. Many federal agencies that rely on scientific research, like the Environmental Protection Agency (EPA), have
defunded it, downgraded it, or dismissed the advice of scientific panels.
This appears to be happening across many federal government agencies.
Industry-linked scientists are now sought for advice instead, further undermining the independence of these agencies as sources of informed policy.

The result of this developing political culture has been to level the
playing field in the political arena. There is now a political ecology favorable to populist movements on both the left and the right. With elites

discredited and on the defensive, there is a great deal of room for populist entrepreneurs and movements to articulate popular grievances.

THE RISE AND DECLINE OF A POWER
ELITE: NEW MODELS OF CITIZENSHIP

Legitimacy crises create room for the emergence of charismatic movements and leaders. From the 1930s to the 1960s, unusual international events and incipient globalization tamped down populism by supporting the rise of a putative power elite in the United States, with some pretensions of guardianship (Dahl, 1971). The Great Depression, followed immediately by World War II and the Cold War, did so by providing temporary legitimacy for a largely liberal-driven elite model of society. A wide variety of social movements developed in the period under review. But these three international events, following upon one another, *restrained* historic U.S. populism. This development also led to a model of citizenship during and after World War II that emphasized political conformity.

With the gradual thawing of the Cold War in the late 1960s and 1970s, the legitimacy of the power elite and the idea of a liberal, activist state collapsed. Attacks from both the right and left opened space for a new model of citizenship that encouraged activism rather than social and political conformity. Many rejected the conformity, political and otherwise, and dutifulness that was associated with the earlier model of citizenship prominent in the 1950s.

During this period the rise of intensified individualism supported this development by increasing the authority and charisma of the individual in society at the expense of institutions and elites. The ongoing educational revolution supported this change by creating large numbers of highly credentialed citizens, whom employers and elites value as agents of modernization and progress (Collins, 1979; Schofer and Meyer, 2005). This change in the status of the citizenry undermined the authority of existing institutions, including the state. Distrust of the latter intensified. Enhanced individualism legitimates the new authority conferred on individuals. Conservatives also cast the state as a potential enemy of progress. An activist state in their view impinged on the freedom of choice of individuals.

The eclipse of citizenship is another development supported by intensified individualism (see Chapter 6). Civic consciousness gave way to individual opinion, and citizen duties became options (Janowitz, 1983). The iconic critiques of American society represented by David Riesman's *The Lonely Crowd* and William Whyte's *The Organization Man* supported this reinterpretation of citizenship by post-1950s generations. On the right, many read Friedrich Hayek's *The Road to Serfdom* and Ayn Rand's *Atlas Shrugged* with approval. They too found support for reinventing their relationship to society and the state. Much of the culture of the post-1960s generations represented a rejection of an earlier model of citizenship in favor of a more liberated and activist model in which the authority of elites and institutions was diminished.

The result was a change in political ecology. With elites under challenge, the playing field of the political arena was now wide open to new groups contesting the status quo. Globalization contributed to this change both by broadening the idea of human rights, thus supporting individualism, and by producing large numbers of people who felt alienated from the new regime of a world economy and culture.

While a variety of groups were pioneering a new, more activist model of citizenship, large minorities on both the right and left were coming to believe that both parties had failed to resolve the key issues of the time: the war in Vietnam, conflicts over civil rights, and the economy at home. Movements on both the right and left emerged challenging traditional elites, starting in the 1960s. On the left the civil rights movement reemerged as a focus of energy, and on the right the Goldwater campaign appeared as a reaction to the 1950s and early 1960s. It challenged both the social liberalism that was emerging and the power of the regulatory state that had emerged in the Great Depression and postwar era.

With the widening split in the population on social and economic libertarianism, polarization began deepening, first among political elites and activists and later among the population at large. Different segments of society held widely differing opinions on what were adequate solutions to these problems. In the political system the result was increasing conflict over the role of government and challenges to traditional morality. In the face of growing complaints about globalization and its effects, politicians did little to resolve these issues. Free trade was part of Republican orthodoxy, and the militarization of foreign policy continued. To many the future looked bleak: stagnant wages at home, more foreign wars, and loss of jobs and industry to China and other low-wage countries and regions. In the meantime, those with a college education were doing well and elites were flourishing (Freeland, 2011; R. Freeman, 2007; Friedland, 1983; Domhoff, 2013). To the population at large the inertia and gridlock in government over these issues indicated that government was either unable or unwilling to deal with issues that were vital to the public.

A decline of the center and fierce attacks on all kinds of elites created a niche for populist movements in the post-1970s. Social movements on the right and left exploded in number and size (see Chapters 5 and 7). And alienated rhetoric about the past failures of American political elites soared, as did political theater. As president, Richard Nixon had unleashed his vice president, Spiro Agnew, to spew vitriol and acidic attacks on his enemies on the left. The publication of the Pentagon Papers, commissioned by defense secretary Robert McNamara in 1967, by the *New York Times* and the *Washington Post* in 1971 undermined the public credibility of government, as did the resignation of President Nixon.

Polarization was growing among elites and was starting to stir among party activists. Assaults on parties from both within and without became common. The Democratic Party was split between progressive and conservative wings and cracks were appearing in the Republican Party, presaging movements in the 1990s like the Tea Party and support for Ross Perot, whose success cost the Republicans the presidential election in 1992 (Lowi, 1996; Rapoport and Stone, 2005). Radical populism's moment had arrived. All elites became targets, and these assaults diminished their authority.

TYPES OF POPULISM

Populism thrives when democracies face legitimacy crises. Third-party movements in the United States have risen when significant segments of the population deemed that the major political parties had failed the people (Rosenstone et al., 1996). For example, in 1992 and 2016, many voters thought that neither party had solutions that were adequate to the scale of the problems. Populist movements and parties emerge in these circumstances, not because they propose adequate policy prescriptions, but because they are able to articulate the rage and anger of voters who are alienated from their own society. What matters is the authenticity of leaders, not their policy solutions or their expertise and track records as leaders. Cries of "drain the swamp" and exhortations about the hoax of global warming are offered instead as proof of the fact that leaders "get it" and are willing to "tell it like it is" (see Hahl et al., 2018).

Populist movements cluster around three types of issues that challenge the existing status quo (Jansen, 2011).The first issue concerns who are proper *members* of the nation-state (Kronberg and Wimmer, 2012). As immigration has increased under globalization, this has become a major issue in many societies. This is a particularly key issue in nation-states that define themselves as ethnic or religious nations. Many groups in the United States believe that while it is a melting pot, it is also a Christian country. They define those who refuse to acculturate, for example, to speak English, or those who are non-Christians as illegitimate members. Many perceive them as enemies and un-American. For example, this was the fate of Japanese Americans in World War II. This is common in eras when there are significant geopolitical or economic threats to the nation.

A second issue concerns the rights associated with membership in the nation-state (Koopmans and Statham, 1999). This includes not only political and legal rights but also social welfare rights like employment, health care, and schooling. For example, many in the United States believe that they are being taxed to pay for benefits that go to people who are not working and will not work (Bartlett, 2012). This fuels their anger over the unfairness of government priorities and against out of touch elites in Washington. The debate here centers on whether people earn economic and other rights in the marketplace or whether government has a responsibility to provide certain basic rights to the population at large.

A third issue concerns the appropriate role of the state in defining and implementing membership rights. One issue this raises in the United States is whether the United States should have a full-employment policy or whether this issue should be left to markets and individuals. Large sectors of the public believe in "workfare, not welfare," that is, that government policies should require welfare recipients to work. They mistakenly assume that jobs are available to any who want to work.

In federal systems like the United States another issue arises: should the national government or local governments have the authority to implement national policies? In the 1930s the United States developed national employment and other policies to deal with the Great Depression, but under pressure from Southern allies in the Democratic coalition, political elites left implementation to the states and local authorities (Katznelson, 2013; Lemann, 2013). Such elites administered policies so that they did not disturb local racial regimes. The result was to disenfranchise blacks and other minorities from the benefits these programs were supposed to confer (Amenta, 1998).

With the spread of globalization there is increasing conflict around all these issues. Some conflicts produce the perception that they are zero-sum games that brook no compromises. Much previous work has focused on economic grievances (e.g., Judis, 2016; Canovan, 1981; Boggs, 1986). The key point is that there are interlocking conflicts that involve both economic and cultural grievances.

The issue of immigration exemplifies this point. While blue-collar workers often view immigrants as threats to their jobs, their foreignness is also an issue, particularly if they belong to non-Western religions. Swedes, for example, complain that walking around a city like Malmo, which has many Middle Eastern migrants, makes them feel like they are in Saudi Arabia. They object to many of the cultural practices of the new Muslim immigrants, particularly the treatment of women. The French complain about burkas on beaches, as a violation of French culture and law about public displays of religiosity.

On the issue of who is a proper member of the nation, globalization is responsible for two different trends, both of which increase tension within societies about legitimate membership. It increases migration from poor countries to the developed world, and it has spawned ideologies that support multiculturalism within societies. This includes the idea of human rights, which pits nations and their definition of citizenship against the claims of immigrant communities to human rights. This is particularly difficult for European societies that have defined themselves as ethnic-religious ones. In Scandinavia, for example, polling shows that attitudes about non-European immigration have become more negative since 2015. This trend is independent of the number of migrants and refugees a country admitted (*The Economist*, July 21, 2018: 38).

Many populist groups in the United States also object to nonwhites or non-Christians claiming the same membership rights as the white majority. The Tea Party argues, further, that such rights are market-based and should only go to those with solid work histories (Bernstein, 2010; McGrath, 2010).

Right-wing populist groups have grown in response to the perceived threats of the advent of a multicultural society. Conservatives and evangelicals who favor public regulation of morality by the state on many issues find the new developments associated with globalization troubling. Such groups no longer feel at home in their own societies. Instead, they imagine that they now reside in a foreign country whose morality they do not accept. Both immigration and the idea of human rights as a civil religion have precipitated this sense of crisis among these groups (Cole, 2012a).

Many of them would like to return to the days when the state regulated morality and created a homogeneous public culture. In their view the changes brought on by immigration, the human rights movement, and intensified individualism have undermined both the religious and moral basis of society and threaten solidarity and patriotism. Evangelical and conservative supporters of right-wing populism detest what they see as anarchy and immorality in society that stems from this trend, such as gay marriage, pornography on the web, social welfare for the "undeserving," affirmative action, and other changes that undermine the family and religion, such as equal rights for women. They have sought to force government to regulate popular morals through strict laws and tough enforcement in such areas as crime, birth control, abortion, illegal drugs, homosexuality, gay marriage, and the death penalty.

One consequence of this set of conflicts is the rise of populist right-wing nativist movements that dispute the fact that "foreigners" are given the same legal and political rights of natives. Many neo-Nazi and white supremacist groups in the United States and Europe have formed and marched under this banner. To them immigrants and minorities are not proper citizens. They do not share the same culture, religion, and language of those who are long-term citizens. In the view of nativists, the government should not give them full citizen rights. They reject the notion of a multicultural society and human rights.

Many on the right are against immigrants, especially those who are carriers of non-Christian cultures (Singer, Hardwick, and Brietell, 2008). And they are decidedly against a multicultural version of America. It is not a global village to them—especially one in which they would be a social and cultural minority. Evangelicals, white nationalists, and many blue-collar workers view immigrants as a social and cultural threat, particularly those with non-Christian religious beliefs. They want a melting pot in which newcomers are coercively assimilated to the "American way of life" (Anderson, 1983). Their imagined community is one where American-ness is valorized and plural identities are subdued or erased. In their view English is the national language, which everyone should speak. Under such pressure many states have enacted symbolic legislation proclaiming English as the state's official language. They also believe that all should believe in the American way, as evidenced by overt patriotism and love of country.

The question they ask is an important one: how does society retain solidarity when diversity is highly valorized? Opinion surveys have shown that historically Americans have had higher levels of patriotism than citizens of other Western countries, that is, love of country (Rose, 1985b). The question these citizens ask is: will this continue under multiculturalism? Their response is that multiculturalism endangers the solidarity and unity of society. And conservatives point to the dangers created by identity politics and single- issue movements that have fragmented U.S. politics and Balkanized it.

Second, globalization has brought with it a redistribution of benefits within societies. In the United States globalization has produced soaring inequality; job losses for blue-collar workers; and a race to the bottom in terms of wages, working conditions, and environmental conditions (Hacker, 2006). For example, the disappearance of jobs in American cities has led to huge rates of unemployment among young black males. In 1980, over 60 percent of low-skilled black men without high school degrees were employed. By 2008, that number had dropped to fewer than 42 percent. When adjusted for incarceration, that figure drops to 26 percent (Sugie, 2018: 1454). One of Martin Luther King, Jr.'s last contributions to the civil rights movement was marching for workers' rights in various cities like Chicago and Memphis. His answer to the question of membership rights was that citizens have a right to a job that pays a wage high enough to support a family. It is the job of government to guarantee that right for all citizens.

In the United States wages have been stagnant despite full employment. The problem is that international agreements have not addressed many of the problems created by globalized trade and manufacturing. The benefits of global trade have largely gone to financiers and corporate executives in the United States. With the decline of unions, workers have been the losers. Without the benefits of a strong safety net like Sweden's for displaced workers, American workers have suffered disproportionately for the gains others have gotten from global trade. Whole industries and regions have suffered from this development.

These changes and soaring inequality have raised an important set of questions that populist movements have seized on. To wit, does citizenship entitle one to a job with decent pay and other social welfare rights? Like King, members of left-wing populist movements like Occupy Wall Street and the Bernie Sanders movement believe that all citizens should be able to expect a right to a decent job (Gitlin, 2012). Furthermore, they believe that government has a responsibility to provide jobs, either through public works programs or by investing in infrastructure and other projects to create the necessary jobs. The black civil rights movement also pushed for a government-backed full-employment policy.

Cultural differences, the perceived economic threat of immigrants to decent jobs, and the right to government benefits all lock in to intensify the sense of loss and anger that many in the United States feel. Tea Party members were livid over such concerns (McGrath, 2010; Bernstein, 2010). In their view benefits are earned in the marketplace. They believe that government benefits should be reserved for those who have paid their dues (Skocpol and Williamson, 2012) Their premise was that anyone who wants to work can find a job. Welfare and old-age benefits should be reserved only for those who had long work histories and had paid into those programs. The indolent in their view should not be coddled and given a living that they did not earn.

While they were not overtly racist, the movement was based on common stereotypes of the poor and minorities as indolent idlers looking for a handout. They were angry about the taxes they were forced to pay to support government programs for the poor and minorities. While they approved of Social Security, Medicare, and Medicaid, they thought that these should be available only to those who had long histories of employment (Skocpol and Williamson, 2012). They, like the conservative wing of the Republican Party, supported programs like workfare rather than welfare—programs that tied welfare benefits to working in paid employment. Many states under Republican dominance enacted such new rules for welfare, and President Clinton enacted them as federal welfare rules.

In Europe, where social welfare rights are generous, there is another concern (Imig and Tarrow, 2001). Given generous social welfare rights, populist movements object to providing similar benefits to new immigrants, who may be unemployable. They argue that society cannot afford to subsidize such populations, who are economically unproductive. Many see these migrant populations as a twofold threat to social solidarity. First, they lack the skills to function in a modern economy and may require permanent subsidies from government. Secondly, their cultural differences and high birth rates threaten the cultural modernity that these nations have managed to achieve. Germans, for example, have been outraged by press reports of public attacks on women by Muslim males. The rise of terrorism has intensified popular feelings that European culture is under attack by immigrants who refuse to assimilate.

Right-wing movements in the United States make similar arguments. On economic issues they are more radical, arguing that markets should determine a person's social welfare benefits. They assume that jobs are plentiful for those willing to work. In their view government should reserve its social welfare programs for citizens who have earned them or are willing to work to receive government subsidies.

Neopopulism now permeates both the right and the left. And the rhetoric these movements use now permeates much of society. Even conservatives, who are structurally aligned with Wall Street and American corporations, have found this rhetoric useful for capturing the support of the white working class, for example, the Reagan Democrats. And they have been successful in this effort. Since the 1990s, blue-collar workers have left the Democratic Party in droves (Teixeira and Rogers, 2000; Teixeira, 1987, 1990). President Obama, for example, lost the white vote in 2008 by 12 percent, but he lost the blue-collar white vote by 30 percent. The South has now become a Republican bastion (J. Glaser, 1996).

SOURCES OF CONTEMPORARY POPULISM

In searching for long-term causes of rising populism in the United States, one underappreciated source of change is the fact that models of *citizenship* have changed. The rise of intensified individualism as the new social reality in all institutional realms in the United States has changed citizens' relationship to the state and nation. In its earlier history, citizenship and the rights it devolved on individuals tied people to the nation-state and diminished the charisma and authority of other bodies (Daalder, 1987), while the nation-state gained charisma and authority. Other bodies like guilds and family lost authority and resources and became subordinate to the state (Ramirez, 2006a).

As individualism has intensified, it has now become the dominant source of agency and charisma. This is classic American individualism that Lipset (1996) saw resurging. The big change, however, is that it is now enhanced and is the major social construct of society (see Chapter 6). This development drains authority and charisma out of the nation-state and all other agencies and elites. They lose authority under this new narrative.

This change has made populism more attractive and legitimates its central claim that the people, not elites, should control society and its institutions. In a fluid society with high education levels, "power to the people" is a winning mantra and increasingly a political trend (Schudson, 1998a). Many recent innovations in politics owe their legitimacy to this cultural change, which empowers voters and citizen movements. Examples are direct primaries and public referenda.[5]

This change has had real consequences that help empower populist movements. One of the most important is that it increases the power of public opinion as a driver of politics. Unfiltered "news" now is a potent source of authority. This has intensified the role that the new social media play and has also increased the power of recently deregulated national media chains in influencing public opinion (see Chapter 10). Both have helped create a polarized polity.

This source of populism has been underappreciated, but many other changes noted in the literature have also radically altered the ecology of the political system. These have drained much of the localism, and democracy, out of the system. Instead of social ties that link citizens to the political system, many perceive that their only links to the political system are through the virtual reality created by the mass media and the rise of social media. They do not feel like active participants in the polity. And they are aware that politicians direct most of their attention toward the big donor class who contribute most of the money that funds the political system.

The growth of government itself has also fueled the rise of populism. It has politicized more areas of society and made them subject to potential government regulation and intrusion. This change has politicized society and propelled activism and mobilization both to protect and to gain rights and resources (Pierson and Skocpol, 2007). This process has also produced a lot of fear and rage that have also fueled populism. The lack of transparency (read corruption) of government intensifies both public anger and estrangement (Norris, 2017). Vote suppression, gerrymandering, and other unfair aspects of the system also alienate voters, particularly minorities and the poor.

The backlash against government welfare programs has generated classic revitalization movements that have diffuse goals and rely on populist rhetoric. Their favorite target is the Washington establishment. Conservatives talk incessantly about the elites in Washington and their supporters in the elite media and liberal universities. In some versions Wall Street is part of this establishment, as opposed to Main Street. All are accused of filtering benefits to themselves and of trying to indoctrinate the country into what are foreign values: socialism, Kenyan anti-colonialism, big government, and recently, New York values (Bartlett, 2012).

Much useful research has also focused on other changes that have led to a disconnect of citizens from the political system (e.g., Crenson and Ginsberg, 2004; Skocpol and Fiorina, 1999; Pierson, 1998, 2007; Putnam, 2000; Pierson and Skocpol, 2007). These include money and politics, the decline of local carriers of political mobilization, and the rise of media politics and social media as the conduits of news and views of social reality. These changes have shifted the scale of resources needed to leverage the system and reduced the openness of the system to those without significant financial resources.

In addition to these developments, the new polarization and hyper-sensitivity to imagined differences may also drive populism. As groups worry that politicians will not tend to their interests, a dynamic of inten-sified populism sets in. As groups project these concerns onto the political system, it is easy for a dialectic to start as each group intensifies its par-tisanship to anchor its agenda in the political system. In a system where compromise signals weakness or failure, each group reacts to provoca-tion by increasing their efforts to rally partisans and convince those on the sidelines to join their cause. The result is nasty, uncivil, and irrational politics (Andris et al., 2015; Shea and Sproveri, 2012).[6]

These splits within parties and among the population at large have made it difficult for the major political parties to govern successfully. Gridlock has created a legitimacy crisis for government. This sense of cri-sis has opened the door for different versions of populism to emerge and dominate the political landscape. When people perceive that the major parties have failed to govern effectively, populism and third parties ap-pear (Rosenstone et al., 1996).

THE TRUMP CAMPAIGN: A CASE STUDY

Right-wing radical populism emerged with vigor in the last presidential election. It is a test case of how radicalized American populism has become. No set of politicians and other elites remained untouched by the critiques and diatribes that Trump and his campaign unleashed. Nor did issues play a key role in his campaign. Sober discussion lost out as attention focused on which group would be the next target for withering criticism and dia-tribe. Nasty rhetoric, not civil conversation, was the rule.

The surprise is that right-wing populism's appeal was high for white men and women without a college degree. Many of the policies the Trump campaign was pushing would not have been in their interests. Deregulating industry and tax cuts for the rich certainly were not. Nor was Trump's misogyny, since many female voters work and have benefited from affirmative action, legal protection from harassment, and other federal rules about the workplace. What appealed to them, however, was not the issues but Trump's witness to their plight and articulation of their sense of loss in a globalized world. Many of his followers were not poor economically, but compared to their parents, many of them felt they were losing ground. This sentiment was common among Tea Party members, for example (Skocpol and Williamson, 2012).

Many of Trump's base among the less educated are people who felt that their status in society was slipping and that others were gaining at their expense under the regime of globalization.[7] For example, polls show that working-class adults who feel that they are worse off than their parents were highly likely to support Trump's populism and his ideas about the damaging effects of immigration on workers' pay. They also felt that the system is rigged against them. Their confidence in major institutions is lower than those who feel that they are at or above their parents' standard of living. And finally, those who feel worse off than their parents are pessimistic about their children's prospects when they become adults (Andrew Cherlin, "The Downwardly Mobile for Trump," *New York Times*, August 25, 2016: A19).

In the 2016 presidential race, candidate Trump's oratory built its appeal to this group of disgruntled Americans by playing up their grievances. His language was crude but crafted to appeal to their vibrant feelings of loss and alienation. While other politicians were tone deaf to their sense of pain and betrayal, the Trump campaign played it to the hilt. And he provided a lengthy list of villains against whom to vent their anger: immigrants, many elites on Wall Street and in D.C., minorities who were using affirmative action to get ahead, the media who overlooked blue collar workers, and corrupt politicians who paid them no attention. His supporters even interpreted his overt lies, which many recognized as untrue, as symbolic protests intended to send a message to Washington elites on their behalf (Hahl et al., 2018).

One popular comment about the candidate was that he speaks our language. His speeches were easily remembered because of the many slogans embedded in them: to wit, "build the wall," "lock her up," "Mexico will pay for it (the wall)," "make America great again." He also used ordinary language and crude stereotypes of others to build his case. The *New York Times* published a content analysis of candidate Trump's speeches and found that a computer analysis showed that their grammatical structure and language was at a fourth-grade level. Ted Cruz's speeches, by contrast, were at a seventh-grade level and sometimes soared to an eleventh- grade level. Trump's speeches were also by and large devoid of any specific policy plans. Unlike Hillary Clinton's speeches, there was little meat for policy wonks or a public interested in practical solutions to major problems. In fact, he turned this flaw into a strength, arguing that uncertainty about his moves was a critical component for winning in future negotiations.

Nate Silver's (2016) analysis of election results shows quite clearly how this appeal to the less educated led to Trump's victory. Trump had claimed during the campaign that he "loved low-educated people." They in turn returned the feeling. According to Silver's analysis of 981 U.S. counties with over fifty thousand people, Trump's victory was assured because he beat Clinton by slim margins in counties with large proportions of people *without* college degrees. He notes that Clinton improved on Obama's margin of victory in forty-eight of the fifty most well-educated counties (those where 45 percent to 51 percent had college degrees). She won these by 25.9 percent versus Obama's win of 17.3 percent (Silver, 2016).

But in the fifty least educated counties where 10 to 13 percent had a college degree, she lost much worse than Obama had: −30.5 percent versus Obama's −.19.3 percent. She lost ground compared to Obama in forty-seven of the fifty counties in this analysis.

This finding holds up even when county level income is controlled. In twenty-two counties where at least 35 percent of the population had a BS or BA but household income was under $50,000, Clinton improved on Obama's performance: +8.8 percent versus +4.4 percent for Obama. On the other hand, in thirty counties where median incomes were $70,000 or higher but 35 percent or less had a college education, Trump edged Clinton by 15.8 percent while Obama lost them by 11 percent in 2012.

Clinton also did better than Obama in educated majority-minority communities where 35 percent of the population had degrees and less than

50 percent of the population were non-Hispanic white. She won by 47.5 percent versus Obama's margin of 41.2 percent. But in nineteen counties where 15 percent or less had college degrees, Clinton struggled. Her victory margin was only 7 percent versus Obama's margin of 10 percent in 2012. Many of Obama's less educated black supporters simply did not turn out for Clinton.

As Silver notes, more research at the individual level and looking at changes over time will be important for understanding the Trump phenomenon. A recent report by the American Association for Public Opinion Research backs up Silver's contentions. The report examined why state polling did such a historically bad job of predicting voting behavior. It concludes that one important reason was that these polls undersampled noncollege voters or failed to weight their data by educational achievement, despite the evidence of a well-documented education gap early in the campaign (Dan Balz, *Washington Post*, May 7, 2017: A-2).

Individual-level research done recently concerning participation in movements against President Trump confirm Silver's picture. The anti-Trump rallygoers are predominantly the college-educated segment of the population. A *Washington Post*–Kaiser Foundation national poll of participants in rallies during the years that Trump has been president found that 20 percent of American adults have attended a rally. These have largely been anti-Trump rallies, as evidenced by the fact that 70 percent of the attendees disapprove of Trump (vs. 54 percent of nonrallygoers). The important finding is that 79 percent of the rally attendees have attended college—50 percent have a BA or higher.[8] The educated have become the vanguard of the anti-Trump movement across the United States.

Education has become an important economic and political dividing line in society (Collins, 1979; Baker, 2014). What is surprising in the American case is the appeal of right-wing populism to voters whose interests would traditionally favor the left. Radical populism bridges this divide by its vehement distrust of *all elites*, redirecting the anger of the less educated to the educated, who control most of society's major institutions. To the less educated, democracy has primarily benefited the educated, who have used it to stack the deck against them (e.g., Schattschneider, 1960; Skocpol and Williamson, 2012). Populist candidates like

Trump are their revenge against political elites who do not listen to them or take their grievances seriously.

As I have pointed out, these grievances are not just economic. Much of the white working class feels that they are losing their place in society, displaced socially, culturally, and politically by foreign groups. Religious, nativist, sexist, and racial rhetoric as well as economic grievances all come into play and point to the real and imagined villains who are usurping their seat at the table.

SOME CONSEQUENCES OF INTENSIFIED POPULISM

With support from a culture of intensified individualism, radical populism has undermined all elite authority. Under this revision of the American creed, society's elites attribute highly enhanced capacities to the public in many areas. This is the era of the rational public and the wisdom of crowds.

One consequence of these changes is to increase the power of public opinion in the political system. It gains weight and gravitas while the role of knowledge diminishes. The public wins and experts/expertise lose out. As a result, public opinion polls become very newsworthy and every major media player is forced to have its own in-house polling service or a contract with a reputable one. Polls, like social media feeds, have become a necessary part of everyday reality. What the public thinks is now important news. This development has greatly lowered the spheres in which the public treats knowledge (vs. public opinion) as authoritative.

This reigning ideology credits the mass public with advanced skills relevant to both democracy and capitalism. For example, many believe that Americans are well aware of their own interests and intelligently attuned to national interests in both domestic and foreign policy (e.g., Page and Shapiro, 1992). The media, for example, highlights and inflates the nation's capacity to voluntarily solve social problems through cooperative action, for example, individual bravery in the Houston and New Orleans floods. By the same token, the media often downplay or disparage government action in favor of citizen action.

Similarly, in the economic sphere, much discourse attributes growth and prosperity to human capital. In this picture, Silicon Valley is the model of future capitalism. Entrepreneurial capitalism is now the image of the economy, despite the reality of the increasing concentration of industry in many sectors via mergers and acquisitions and the importance of public investment in science and research as major sources of innovation. The media and politicians also dramatize American voluntarism, despite evidence that the rate of volunteering and voluntary associations in Scandinavia and Canada is similar. These narratives valorize as well as dramatize this new version of American exceptionalism.

Another change is that elites have lost the exclusive ability to frame public opinion and set the political agenda (Wilensky, 2002). They no longer act as filters over what is fit news for the public. And there are no longer effective vetting processes that determine what is in fact news and what stories are lies put forward to distort popular perceptions of political reality. The intrusion of Russia into the 2016 election via false messages on Facebook exemplifies this danger.

One result is that it is easy for partisans to generate plausible alternative conceptions of reality and market them on social media. The public has no way of discerning the difference between news and "fake news." The universe of facts becomes conflated with "alternative facts" masquerading as social reality. This development massively expands the opportunities for fraud and deception, offered in the guise of actual news and fact. And it massively contributes to political opportunism and contempt for the truth, among both politicians and the public. So far, the giant social media companies have offered no solutions for this new plague of problems that they have created.

The technological displacement of elite control by both the mass media and social media is now complete. This change has led to a historically unprecedented absence of elite media filtering of mass communication. What the media presents is now what conservative media corporations decides is news, along with what directors and network executives think the public wants and will pay for. Media competition and the presence of social media create extremely fast rates of innovation in this effort to please and manipulate the public to maintain viewership and hits on social media sites (see Chapter 10).

This development furthers the shift of politics away from political parties to social movements and the new media. In this environment the distinction between local influentials and cosmopolitan influentials, pioneered in community studies in the 1950s by Lazarsfeld and Merton, is obsolete. The post–mass society has emerged with the masses themselves as opiners and publishers. Both the authority and credibility of the mass media and politicians have been eclipsed by these developments (see Chapter 10).

Intensified populism has helped create a new political ecology. Most important, it has given conservative and antigovernment groups a potent weapon in their battle against government efforts to regulate the economy in the fight against monopoly and inequality. Rebellion against government and the policy sciences give conservative ideologues a platform from which to challenge the active role of government in many areas, such as reducing poverty, stimulating the economy, and reducing unemployment. The rich now have space to oppose any government action that would raise taxes or otherwise affect the operation of economic markets.

Among the very wealthy, neoliberalism has led to a rediscovery of social Darwinism as a legitimate political ideology (see Page et al., 2011; Petracca, 1990). The rich are against almost all entitlements, for lower taxes, and in favor of reducing the national debt. Their belief in meritocracy, and their own merit, permits them to feel totally justified in their exclusiveness and in their rage at government for "coddling" people who do not deserve it. For example, presidential candidate Mitt Romney argued that "undeserving" entitlement seekers composed roughly 47 percent of the American population.

Another sign of this attitude is the renewal of old portrayals of the working class as lacking self-control and discipline. Among intellectuals on the right, there has been an extraordinary outpouring of venom against the working class and the poor. Charles Murray (2011) began this argument by lamenting the decline of family values, the work ethic, and religiosity among poor whites. But he cautioned that the middle class was in part responsible for this decline by fostering and disseminating values and attitudes that were disastrous for poorer communities where kinship and religion were major sources of solidarity. Recently this critique has lost any such nuances and now sees poor whites as perpetrators of their own misery. In the *National Review* in March 2016, for example, Kevin Williamson wrote:

The truth about these dysfunctional, downscale communities is that they deserve to die. Economically, they are negative assets. Morally, they are indefensible. Forget all your cheap, theatrical Bruce Springsteen crap. Forget your sanctimony about struggling Rust Belt factory towns. . . . The white American underclass is in thrall to a vicious, selfish culture whose main products are misery and used heroin needles. Donald Trump's speeches make them feel good. So does OxyContin. (quoted in Jelani Cobb, "Comment: Working Class Heroes," *New Yorker*, April 25, 2016: 33–34).

Similarly, among many ordinary citizens populism encourages dystopian attitudes about society and its prospects. A *Washington Post* poll of seventy-four thousand people across all fifty states conducted by SurveyMonkey (Dan Balz and Emily Guskin, "A Pessimistic Electorate, No Matter the Nov. Result," *Washington Post*, September 8, 2016: A4) showed that 72 percent of likely voters said that the America of today is less reflective of their values than in the past. In no state did more than 33 percent of respondents express a positive view. And five states were outliers in which more than 80 percent said their values are reflected less than in the past. These were largely rural, white states: North Dakota, Kentucky, Oklahoma, West Virginia, and Wyoming.

Among the population at large, radical populism has intensified the distrust of government and other institutions and weakened the idea that society could act collectively to solve social problems. Under this assault of distrust, the idea of society as a collective project vanishes. What replaces it is the notion that politics is the pursuit of privatized self-interests. This change undercuts the notion of taxing everyone to benefit some. Tony Judt and Timothy Snyder (2012: 372) argue that this idea lies at the heart of the modern welfare state (see also Bartlett, 2012). The point is that by doing so in many areas, such as pensions, childcare, employment, and public health, the state makes all people's lives better. Conversely, when politics is privatized, it reduces the state's capacity and responsibility to make good the shortcomings of people's lives. And it removes this responsibility from the conscience of fellow citizens. The idea of *shared* burdens and responsibilities disappears (Judt and Snyder, 2012: 373).

Another consequence is that rational, evidence-based debate gives way to dystopian and utopian outbursts. Other less policy-focused discourse is likely to prevail. Conspiracy theories, for example, are a prominent form of populist dialogue (Hofstadter, 1965). These distract leaders and the public from discussion of pragmatic policy agendas. In politics, wild notions of the threats facing the United States take the place of sober discussion. Under such assaults, elites in the political system are distracted from real problems by being forced to deal with imaginary ones, such as massive voting fraud, deconstructing the administrative state, the hoax of climate change, massive immigration of foreign criminals to the United States, "fake news," and the criminal threat from illegal immigration.

Given the spread of social media and the discrediting of experts and knowledgeable officials, such versions of reality spread readily and find receptive audiences among the public. This makes it easier for quacks and charismatic self-proclaimed leaders to seize control of public debate.

Simultaneously, populism enhances the authority of public opinion so that it has become untamed. The media and public now treat opinions of the public as authoritative pronouncements on many subjects. This change undermines the search for knowledge-based public policies and gives adventurers and demagogues public standing and the ability to appear authoritative. The enhanced standing of public opinion has also led to assaults on rationality and its practitioners in a variety of realms. For example, mistrust of science and scientists is widespread (Gauchat, 2012). In this climate of opinion there are no agreed-upon facts in the public conversation.

Other changes include a paralysis in efforts to improve the operation of government and its effectiveness. In the face of radical populism, attempts to rationalize government fail. Populism encourages the public to believe that running government requires no special competencies or training. In a recent poll, 54 percent of a representative sample of American adults believed that they would do a better job running the country than today's leaders in Washington, D.C. (Balz, 2014). The Pew Research Center also found in 2015 that majorities of Republicans thought that ordinary people could do a better job of running the government than current officials.

Such suspicions also extend to the civil service and state bureaucracies. One result is that policies like term limits for politicians, tightened legislative budgets for staff, and direct popular referenda gain traction. The effect of such policies is to further weaken efforts to develop competent government (e.g., Schrag, 1998).

Lastly, these developments have changed the way American politics works in practice. If rational argument is diminished in the public realm, politics becomes more like a team sport or warfare rather than a national conversation about effective policies to serve the nation. Winning becomes the main and possibly only goal of parties and politicians. Civility declines and the norms/traditions of democratic politics decline. The latter are a weak brake on virulent populism.

In such a system, campaigning becomes much more important, and exciting, than *governing*. Campaigns have even become a public form of entertainment, as the control of elites over candidate selection diminishes. Gone are the dull eminences with extensive résumés. In are newcomers with colorful personalities and histories, ready to rile up politics and boost ratings. Enter the clowns (think Italy, France, Greece) and iconoclasts such as Cruz, Bannon, and Trump.

The next chapter turns to the issue of the emergence of new collective images of society. These are creatures of the changes just described. In the past the dominant view was that consensus on goals and values held society together. Now the dominant view is that society is falling apart from conflict over a wide variety of irreconcilable differences. In the process, the idea of society as a collective social contract disappears. Politics becomes the pursuit of privatized self-interest(s) (see Judt and Snyder, 2012: 373). The next chapter describes the fall from consensus to conflict in the public's imagery of society.

CHAPTER 10

From Consensus to Culture Wars

THE NARRATIVE OF POPULAR CONSENSUS has broken down and public perceptions of a culture war have emerged as the new reality. I discuss this process of breakdown, what is driving it, and some of the consequences of this change in public imagery in this chapter. The critical point is that the widespread perception of discord between groups in society has consequences and can encourage self-reinforcing cycles of conflict. Once disseminated by credible sources they become the new reality.

CHANGING IMAGES OF THE NATION

There is growing evidence that a large sector of the public accepts the image of the United States as a society filled with difficult, and possibly irreconcilable, conflicts. Putnam and Campbell (2010) note that exceptionally large majorities imagine that the country is divided along many lines of conflict: 72 percent of Americans say the country is divided along religious lines; 93 percent believe that it is divided along racial lines; 96 percent see divisions along economic lines; and 97 percent say the country is divided along political lines (Putnam and Campbell, 2010: 516).

While images of the nation have become bleaker, the picture people have of their own local communities has not changed in this direction. Trust of politicians, local institutions like schools and local universities, and other citizens is high at local levels (Jennings, 1998). There are exceptions. Middle-class parents often do not trust big-city public schools and opt to send their children to private or charter schools. But by and large, the evidence indicates that citizens have more confidence in local institutions than national ones. The latter have seen continuous drops in confidence since the 1960s (Tom Smith, 2012).

This pattern suggests that the new collective representations of distrust are largely products of national institutions like the mass media, the new social media, and national political parties. These are the institutions that have been most involved in the divisive ideological conflicts at the national level and in spreading contention.

THE ROLE OF POLITICAL PARTIES IN
ESCALATING CONFLICT IMAGERY

As politics has become polarized around the issues of government regulation of the economy and the regulation of public morality, images of conflict have become the stock-in-trade of political parties. Morris Fiorina, a prominent political scientist, has noted that much of the talk of culture conflict started in the political system in the post-1960s era. In the polarizing debates over civil and economic libertarianism, political parties, along with their media allies, have taken their stances as culture warriors.

Both parties now use this imagery, peppering disputes with the language of war. Arguably, one of the factors that has helped produce such imagery of society is the militarization of society in both foreign and domestic policy. This is a consequence of the rising importance of the national security state beginning in the 1950s (Friedberg, 2000). Both parties facilitated this process. This resulted in the creation of two economies and political systems: the military-industrial complex that is highly funded, regulated, secretive, and nondemocratic, and the civilian economy that is open, relatively unregulated, competitive, and democratic.

This development has had an important influence on politics. Under the mantel of the national security state, domestic as well as foreign policy has become framed in the language of war. For example, the response to the attacks of 9/11 was to declare war on radical Islam, not to start a dragnet for violent, international criminals. Military language is useful in mobilizing the population, but it also produces a politics where differences of degree become differences of kind. One is either an ally or an enemy.[1]

American history since the 1950s is filled with outright declared wars and a corresponding hunt for enemies, domestic and foreign. And each war produces an enemies list of internal and foreign adversaries. Opponents of President Johnson's war on poverty, for example, were presumed to favor poverty under this military linguistic structure. The same is true with the other "wars" that presidents and Congress have launched: the wars for democracy and freedom in Vietnam and Central America, the Cold War, the war on drugs, the war on crime, and the war on terror. Once a war is launched, those who oppose it on policy grounds can be denounced as either naïve, stupid, or un-American. In any case, it becomes legitimate to challenge the motives of those who disagree with the proposed policy. Rational discussion of alternatives becomes diminished.

The imagery of society under siege, both foreign and domestic, that developed in the 1960s fueled another development that enhances the image of society at war. Fears associated with internal racial conflict and urban riots as well as international conflicts enhanced the gun culture. Gallup poll data (https://news.gallup.com poll/guns.aspx) show that support for handgun possession rose steadily after 1959. In 1959, 36 percent of all adults were *not* in favor of a law banning ownership of a gun, other than by the police or military. In 2011, that figure was 73 percent. The National Opinion Research Center (NORC) report on trends in gun ownership from 1973 to 2014, based on the General Social Survey (Gallup, 2011, https://news.gallup.com/poll/150-353/self reported-gun-ownership-highest-in 1993.aspx2015) shows that in 1973, 48 percent of U.S. households had a gun. By 2014 that number had declined to 28 percent. But alongside this trend is another: an increase in Americans who own multiple weapons. *The Guardian* (September 16, 2016; Tom Smith, "Trends," 2015) quotes a Harvard-Northeastern study in 2015 that estimates that about 7.7 million Americans each own between 8 and 140 guns. Women's ownership of guns is also increasing. At the same time, hunting has drastically declined. In 1973, 31 percent said they used guns for hunting. In 2014 this had dropped to 15 percent (Tom Smith, "Trends," 2015). The NORC study also shows that racial minorities are half as likely as whites to own guns

(Hispanics, 11 percent; blacks, 18 percent; whites, 39 percent). Lastly, the clear majority (67 percent) of gun owners say the major reason for owning a gun is for protection (Igielnik and Brown, 2017). These data suggest that it is white fear of minorities, immigrants, and crime that is driving gun ownership.

For men and now women, guns have clearly become a source of security in what they believe is an otherwise fearful world.[2] With this many guns in the hands of citizens, fear of random violence is not irrational.

Furthermore, the widespread distribution of such weaponry enhances the plausibility of armed conflict as a metaphor for society at large. As a result, underlying the talk of culture wars is the everyday possibility of real gun battles in the streets or random shootings at schools, colleges, or other public places. In short, there is good reason for fear of violence.

THE POLITICS OF FEAR

This language of fear and war has also served political purposes. Since the 1960s the Republicans have used the image of society in a state of conflict to attract support. As the party has moved further to the right, these attacks have intensified (Abramovitz and Saunders, 2006; Hacker and Pierson, 2005). To gain the support of evangelicals, Catholics, and working-class Democrats, they launched attacks on cultural libertarianism and have described gays and a variety of others seeking civil rights as outsiders and un-American. The right declared that such groups are claiming rights that fall outside the social contract society has with members. Such groups in their purview are not legitimate members of society, and hence are enemies of morality and a free society based on such morals.

The result of this process is that the language of American politics has become increasingly militarized and filled with fear of outsiders. This language has totally infiltrated the political arena. In the 1968 presidential campaign, for example, candidate Nixon called himself the "law and order" presidential candidate. Trump made similar claims in the 2016 campaign. The underlying imagery, fleshed out by Nixon's vice-presidential running mate, Spiro Agnew, assumed that there were those in society who favored disorder and disruption. Student activists, blacks, antiwar protesters, and liberals were all targeted as members of the party of lawlessness and anarchy. They were the enemy, opposed by candidate Nixon and all right-thinking people like the silent majority who favored lawful behavior. Nixon used this rhetoric to openly court the white South, who had been turned off the Democratic Party by the civil rights legislation sponsored by President Johnson and a Democratic Congress (J. Glaser, 1996). He also used this language to indict any institutions in society like universities and the press that did not agree with his proposals to produce more law and order.

Presidents Reagan and George H. W. Bush also played on this theme of law and order, which had an underlying racist tone. Minorities and the poor figured prominently as enemies. Black "welfare queens" and a convicted black rapist named Willie Horton figured prominently in their campaign advertising. So did "lawless" students and others engaged in civil disobedience. Later presidential candidate Patrick Buchanan popularized the idea of a culture war in his speech to the 1992 Republican National Convention. Since then conservative media have continued this theme. Again in 2004 Buchanan raised the issue of the culture war in his column:

Who is in your face here? Who started this? Who is on the offensive? Who is pushing the envelope? The answer is obvious. A radical Left aided by a cultural elite that detests Christianity and finds Christian moral tenets reactionary and repressive is hell-bent on pushing its amoral values and imposing its ideology on out nation. The unwisdom of what the Hollywood and the Left are about should be transparent to all. (http://www.theamericancause.org/patculture wars.htm)

These perceptions of division and conflict are now prominent as descriptions of American society.

This imagery persists, stoked by Republican losses in the presidential contests of 2008 and 2012 to a black candidate. Populist movements have also used this imagery. Long before presidential candidate Mitt Romney called out a sizable proportion of Americans who he said were addicted to government handouts and would never vote for a Republican, the Tea Party was using the same imagery (Skocpol and Williamson, 2012). After the election of 2002, those who would eventually come to identify with the Tea Party movement distinguished between the reputable body of hardworking Americans and the disreputables, who were not hardworking and were dependent on government handouts, paid for by the taxes of working Americans. One of their popular slogans was "Redistribute my work ethic."

Republican intellectuals like Charles Murray (2011) were also deploring the unraveling of the white working class. They were described as indulging in new lifestyles favoring premarital sex, alcohol, and drugs— all taken from middle-class models. The result, he argued, had been the decline of ethnic, family, and religious ties that bound these communities together. These changes turned the children of a reputable working class into part of the "under-class," whose morality and dysfunction are at war with respectable society.

The Democratic Party has also succumbed to this language of war. Hillary Clinton's infamous comment about supporters of Trump being a "basket of deplorables" is just one instance of the trend to cast anyone who is not a full-throated social libertarian on all issues as the enemy. Issues like abortion and homosexuality have become litmus tests. This has made it difficult to court working-class Catholics, once a bastion of Democratic support. To many liberals in the party these groups are part of the enemy.

On the economy, however, roles have become reversed between the Republican and Democratic parties. The language of class warfare and denouncing corporate monopolies have receded from Democrats' political vocabulary. They now talk about a rising tide lifting all boats and float policies aimed at tweaking out more economic growth to do this. They are now friends of Wall Street and business.

Republicans have strengthened their orthodoxy on government deregulation and denounced efforts to regulate banks and large corporations as unnecessary, harmful to growth, and un-American. Large parts of the party have also adopted militant language against civil libertarianism. To them, government is the enemy. Multiculturalism is also a key enemy, particularly to their Southern base. Other enemies include immigrants, gays, non-Christians, and urban liberals.[3]

Because of the militarization of politics, battles over both social libertarianism and economic neoliberalism have become wars. On the issues of economic libertarianism Republicans have moved to the right, while the Democrats have no coherent perspectives. But the Democratic Party has moved to the left on social liberalism, while Republicans are badly split on the issue of public morality, just as the Democrats are divided on the role of government regulation of the economy.

Battle lines hardened in the 1990s, particularly under speaker of the house Newt Gingrich. Cross-aisle voting has since become a rarity (Andris et al., 2015). Ideology reigns. The ideological center has shrunk. For example, moral stances on taxes and government borrowing have made public finance a charade. Technical fixes to budget deficits have become impossible because of ideological posturing. The mantra of no tax increases and no government borrowing cripples economic policy (Krippner, 2011).

One result is increasing political polarization and divisiveness. In this context of militarized politics, negative campaigning often works (Geer, 2006). Its use is no longer condemned. Political parties now promote images of conflict. Such perceptions have now infected the population at large (see Fischer and Hout, 2006; Baldassarri and Gelman, 2008; Pew Research Center, 2014). Over 50 percent of the public is now in polarized political camps. Those in the middle are shrinking in numbers and have become inactive compared to their polarized counterparts.

THE MEDIA AS PURVEYORS OF CONFLICT

The media has become an important purveyor of conflict as an image of society. With deregulation they have been liberated from older constraints on what news is fit to print. They have turned their attention to fulfilling the public's thirst for scandal, corruption, and celebrity news (Castells, 1997). This change has led the public to believe that society is experiencing exceptional levels of civic discord. Because there had been such little coverage of discord by the media during World War II and in the 1950s, much of the public has come to believe that disorder and crime in society are new and imminent dangers.

Media portrayals, especially TV coverage of events like the 1960s riots, created the image that society has gone from a broad consensus on values to intense and perhaps irreconcilable conflicts. More important is the fact that this picture of a conflicted society was combined with a persistent idealization of earlier periods of consensus, unity, and peace. A glorified vision of the 1930s, 1940s and 1950s has become the touchstone for comparing the post-1970s social order. It is as if the 1930s had never happened. This contrast heightened the power of conservative accounts of society being eroded by crime and immorality.

How did this happen? Much of it involves the revived hegemony of business elites and the role played by a new, more liberated media, focused on profits and politics. It is part of the long story of deregulating capitalism from the restraints pioneered in the 1920s under the Progressives, broadened by the New Deal in the 1930s, and amped up during World War II and the Cold War.

RISING CORPORATE POWER AND THE CHANGING ROLE OF MEDIA

The resurgence of corporate political power in the post-1960s changed the role of the media in society. From 1968 to 1992, during more than twenty years of conservative presidents and administrations, corporations have pushed for less government regulation and have won these battles. The media have been successful in renegotiating their legal charters so that they are now freer to print and broadcast whatever kinds of news stories are most popular and profitable. Some media have also become political propagandists.

At the same time their responsibility to the public has diminished. The public airwaves are now theirs to use practically as they please. For example, industry groups like Clear Channel Radio and the Murdock Group can now dictate to local stations partisan news scripts or commentary that they must broadcast for a prescribed number of minutes a day. On social media, blogs like Gateway Pundit can stream conspiracy theories and false news stories, such as the idea that mass shootings are hoaxes, complete with actors portraying themselves as victims.

Once freed from tighter government regulation, the media became purveyors of news stories that featured conflict, crime, and disorder in society (McChesney, 2004). There were strong commercial incentives for broadcasting and publishing such news. It boosted ratings and profits. "Bad news travels, good news dies" was a common maxim in the news business (Fallows, 1996). But there were also political motives at play. As capitalist enterprises, they had a stake in fostering images of society that would enhance support for parties that shared their ideological view of society and the responsibilities of corporations and the media (see Auletta, 2011). They and their advertisers had a strong interest in fostering deregulation of the economy and dramatically loosening government control (Schudson, 1978, 1996).

The decline of local media abetted this process. The new media outlets are part of larger conglomerates that are primarily interested in corporate profits and political influence. The news industry has been politicized by this process to the point that the public identifies all the news media as biased, in either a liberal or conservative direction (Pew, online, 2004; 2014; 2017).

These changes occurred largely because of the success of the attack on liberalism and the modern welfare state in the late 1960s and 1970s. It ushered in a new political climate and new suppositions about the role of corporations and the media in society. The idea that corporations and the media had any fiduciary responsibility to the public quickly faded. Instead, neoclassical economists argued that their responsibility was to act as agents for shareholders, to whom they had a fiduciary responsibility. This view won out.[4]

For media companies, this meant that increasing current ratings, subscriptions, use, and advertising revenue became major goals of corporate elites. It also created a dilemma. If they were public trusts and had to broadcast vetted news stories a standard number of hours a day, how could they increase their advertising space and develop programs with wide audience appeal? The answer was to renegotiate their legal status in society.

A major change took place concerning the social and legal responsibilities of the media in the 1980s under President Reagan. The underlying definition of the mass media changed. Instead of public trusts they became opinion spaces. Before this, the unified media system was held together by elite political and legal agreements. Near monopolies of the public radio waves, and later TV channels, were accepted and deemed permissible, under the claim that safeguards were in place to ensure that the American public got objective news and information, not propaganda, from the networks. The FCC monitored the media and used their authority to penalize media that egregiously violated their legal charters (Lemann, 2005).

This system of constraints turned the news media into both filtering agencies and opinion leaders. A set of standards was honored that recognized sharp distinctions between public and private spheres and that gave the news media a guardian role over what the public had a right to know. For example, the health issues of Presidents Wilson, Roosevelt, and Kennedy were not discussed, though reporters were well aware of them. The private lives of political and other leaders were respected and regarded as irrelevant to their public roles. It was thus off-limits to the media. This continued in the post–World War II era. Radical criticism of administration policy and the private lives of politicians were off-limits to the press.

This role began to change in the post–1960s era, particularly during the Vietnam War era. As public opinion became conflicted, the major media now began to veer toward presenting news that increased readership, viewing, ratings, and profits, instead of filtering the news. Release of the Pentagon Papers by the *Washington Post* and the *New York Times* in 1971 is perhaps a watermark for this change. It initiated one of the first legal tests of the right of the press to publish news of government documents on the Vietnam war that the Nixon administration kept secret under the cover of national security.

The challenge to what was called the "fairness doctrine" that regulated the media came to a head in 1985 under the Reagan administration. It cumulated in 1987 in a new decision by the FCC. Then chairman Mark Fowler persuaded his fellow commissioners to abolish the fairness doctrine. Starting in 1948 it had required radio stations, news media, and later TV to "devote a reasonable amount of time" to public issues and to present different viewpoints on these issues. Instead, Fowler insisted that TV was just *"another appliance"* (italics added) and was not a finite and supremely influential broadcast medium. He was backed by a pair of Reagan appointees and in the courts by Robert Bork and Antonin Scalia. Later he was supported politically by President George H. W. Bush himself (Kevin Baker, *New York Times*, March 25, 2012: SR 5). Legally, the successful challenge to the fairness doctrine in 1985 also had a dramatic impact in altering the regulation of *partisan* coverage of political issues (FCC, 1985).

The successful challenge to the fairness doctrine had several corporate benefits. It increased profitability, since the media could now focus on ratings and adjust content to fit popular tastes. It also affected content. The media were now free to present partisan viewpoints that were politically in tune with key constituencies. And it gave media corporations unprecedented power over public opinion in pursuit of their own corporate interests.

One immediate result was that broadcasting companies and news media in general became less constrained as public trusts under law and were freer to compete for viewers by emphasizing conflict, scandal, and corruption.

Another result was that the media's self-defined and legal public role as news filters and opinion leadership changed. News became a commercial product with few restrictions on its content or reliability. This dictate also applied to political news. Networks became unfettered in this respect and were able to become the loudspeakers for political viewpoints and parties.

THE PURSUIT OF PROFITS AND POLITICS: CHANGED UNDERSTANDINGS OF NEWS

These changes challenged many of the underlying assumptions governing media. Under older standards of journalism, networks and news media acted as if there were a standard, objective version of the news that was independent from opinion. Objectivity was enshrined as a mainstream standard of good journalism. This meant that facts, which are expensive, were important. There were many beats and reporters to cover them, so much more information was available. Opinion, which is cheaper, was less important (Fallows, 1996; McChesney, 2004; Schudson, 1991, 1978, 1996a).

Broadcasters and others also assumed that news was a serious business, separate from entertainment. Presenting news was a civic duty and part of networks' legal responsibility as license holders of the public airwaves. News programs were thus longer and more serious in style. Newscasts were not designed to entertain.

The networks worked under the legal presumption that broadcast news was a *public service* and therefore not a profit-making part of the business. News programming was subsidized by profits from other parts of the business. Active FCC oversight reinforced this conception of network responsibility. It had the legal authority to do this under the fairness doctrine (Lemann, 2005).

In addition, broadcasting news was a prestigious business, as it was presumed to be the most important work for the public that networks did. Therefore, having a highly reputable and authoritative news department was a source of institutional pride and occasioned heavy investment that was not expected to pay for itself (McChesney, 2004).

And lastly, there was an understanding that federal regulators would be vigilant, though often politically motivated, overseers of media accountability (e.g., Lemann, 2005). News media were defined as public interest groups with special responsibilities, not special interest groups.

This survey of institutional assumptions is not meant to imply that the media were unbiased in earlier periods or that they reflected a wide variety of opinion. News coverage usually was markedly conservative (see Gitlin, 1980; Gans, 1979, 2004). Newspapers, for example, had a long history of being conservatively biased on economic issues (Schudson, 1978). In the 1930s, for example, the *New York Times* and many other papers railed against the Social Security program proposed by Roosevelt and demonized it as a source of economic recession and job loss.[5] Similar attitudes prevailed about the minimum wage as a job destroyer.

Furthermore, media bias was apparent in the narrow range of authoritative opinion given coverage. Dissent from mainstream views went uncovered and unrepresented. As Tocqueville observed, democracy in America gave many a voice, but the views expressed were markedly similar. News media were one of the institutions that gave American business its ideological hegemony in American society (Lindblom, 1977).

Similarly, disorders were not given prominence as group conflicts. Lawlessness, riots, and labor unrest were presented as the work of criminals, outsiders, and agitators (Schudson, 1996a: 113–169). This became particularly prominent in the 1950s under the threat of communism and with the growth of a national security state. Similarly, civil rights and

Southern racism went largely uncovered in the mainstream media. Coverage intensified in 1956 when President Eisenhower sent troops into Little Rock, Arkansas to enforce school desegregation. But it died down afterward until the freedom rides started in 1961.

One result of the guardian role of the media was that the "news" presented by the networks, radio, and the press largely *avoided* conflict. Racial, religious, and other conflicts were played down. The media did not present an image of society as rife with enduring conflicts between groups. This began to change in the 1960s (Iyengar, 1992; Iyengar and Kinder, 1988).

THE CHANGING MEDIA AND NEW IMAGES OF SOCIETY

Deregulation of the media and change in their legal status led to new understandings about the role of the media in society. Several radical shifts occurred in the late 1960s and 1970s that challenged the older working arrangements surrounding the media and produced new assumptions. Though not exhaustive, I note a few of the most notable changes.

Conceptions of the news itself changed. News was no longer viewed as objective and untainted by political ideology. There were multiple voices and sources. Even more significantly, the news itself became contested territory. Vietnam was the first war in which there were two public sides in the conflict that had legitimate representation: the pro-war faction and the antiwar faction. Walter Cronkite's newscasts on the Vietnam War after 1968 became a lightning rod of this process. To supporters and opponents of the war, the news was now perceived as partisan (see Gitlin, 1980). This was a dramatic change that opened the way for an overtly politicized media system.

It was also the beginning of open political partisanship by national media. After the 1985 fairness decision, right-wing radio came into its own. Right-wing-networks like Clear Channel became major media conglomerates with no obligations to broadcast any conflicting views. Clear Channel, for example, owned 850 radio stations across the country in the early twenty-first century. Its conservative competitor Cumulus had 570 radio stations across the country at the time. Rush Limbaugh's extremely popular radically conservative talk show appeared on 600 stations, 125 of which are owned by Clear Channel.[6] In 1996 the Murdoch-owned Fox Network entered the fray. Conservative politicians and advocates saw their ideas amplified as the weight of Rupert Murdoch's media empire was thrown into the balance on their side.

The legal definition of the media also changed. The media became defined by political elites and their owners as ordinary corporations, not as public trusts. Thus, ratings and profitability became the primary goal of news/media corporations. For example, once elites in news media discovered that the program 60 *Minutes*, launched in 1968, was a commercial success, executives demanded that news departments be profitable.

As a result, media corporations, like others, came to be viewed as special interests with their own special—often political—purposes and motives. With deregulation and lowered federal oversight, the networks and other news media, as licensees of the public airwaves, were under less pressure to act as public trusts (see McChesney, 2004: 48ff). Hence, they are free to pursue private, proprietary goals. News and public accountability have taken a backseat to profitability.

With news shows expected to turn a profit, there were sustained efforts to find the least expensive ways to do news and public service programming. The cheapest way to do this is to employ "talking heads" rather than reporters, as the Fox News Channel demonstrated (McChesney, 2004: 78). Investigative reporting and other forms of journalism are expensive and time-consuming. The effort to increase profits led to a trend toward more opinion and less reportage.

Journalists now measure success by their celebrity status rather than by professional journalistic norms. And without regular beats, reporters' political coverage tends to be based on individual motives and political tactics/strategy rather than substantive policy analysis. Analysis focuses more on the horse race aspect of politics rather than the distinctive goals of candidates and parties. For the same reason, news programs have also become shorter (for detailed discussions of these changes, see Fallows, 1996; Schudson, 1978, 1991, 1996a; Lemann, 2005; Cunningham, 2004).

After 1985, the effort to build audiences and profits led to a diminishing distinction between news and entertainment. News was expected to be entertaining to increase ratings and advertising revenues. One result is that a star system developed in broadcasting and print (see Fallows, 1996: chap. 3; McChesney, 2004). A few stars at the top, who can produce high ratings, are paid huge salaries—what Fallows calls the "gravy train." The rest make relatively low salaries. News shows are now expected to be entertaining. Other parts of television, once viewed as entertainment, are seen by audiences as sources of serious news. For example, TV comedy shows, particularly late shows, are seen by younger audiences as serious purveyors of political news, as are individual blogs on the Internet (Pew Research Center for People and the Press, 2004a, 2004b; Baumgartner and Morris, 2006). There are thus numerous sources of *unvetted* news that are used by viewers and readers for multiple purposes. These changes helped pave the way for the new social media.

As media markets have been consolidated into a few big corporations, the content of news has also changed. It is now both more national and focused on the major urban centers and Washington. It is also disproportionately attuned to issues that the affluent find important (Gans, 2004; McChesney, 2004; Cunningham, 2004). The wealthy are, after all, the target of much advertising. Ad revenue is the economic mainstay of TV and print media as well as the corporations that control the new social media.

Another change is that there are fewer reporters and fewer beats covered. There is thus less overall news, particularly for working-class readers.

And as reporters have become fewer in number but better paid and college educated, they themselves are attracted to stories and issues that appeal to elite audiences with whom they increasingly identify (Cunningham, 2004; Fallows, 1996). Hence, a new kind of bias creeps into news reporting. The result is that alternative views, such as working-class issues and perspectives, are often neglected or given limited visibility and credibility. The upbeat side of this development is that there is more reportage on women and minority communities, as more women, young people, and people of color become journalists and bloggers. Thus the Black Lives Matter and #MeToo movements have gotten mainstream news coverage.

This set of changes unfettered the news media in many ways. First, it made possible the advent of media that had political advocacy as part of their overt agenda: Fox News, MSNBC, Clear Channel, and so on. The media no longer saw themselves as filters of news or as opinion leaders.

The media are also now freer to report conflict and disorder in society. And being freed from their function as a filter of news for the public, they were quick to seize on the narrowing distinction between public and private space for their own purposes of profit and political advantage. The private lives of politicians, for example, are now open for investigation and reportage. The wall of secrecy that had shielded Roosevelt's health issues and Kennedy's sexual life shattered. They are also free to give voice to the ideology of their clients and audiences. In short, the search for crime, scandal, charismatic leaders, and celebrity is unleashed to satisfy the public's thirst for villains, heroes, and public figures that they can identify with (see Castells, 1997).

SOCIAL MEDIA AS PURVEYORS OF CONFLICT

Social media have also become a key source of communication and influence in society in the last twenty years. For example, the last presidential election may have been won primarily by effective use of social media. Like the Obama campaign, the Trump campaign made heavy use of social media a key strategy. Through a British company, Cambridge Analytics, they were also able to get their hands on the personal profiles of fifty million Facebook subscribers who took a psychographic test about their preferences.[7] What they did with this information is not known, but it is suspected that they targeted groups of undecided voters with false stories about candidate Hillary Clinton. If true, this amounts to a massive disinformation campaign designed both to sway undecided voters and to suppress the vote among weak Clinton supporters.

While this conclusion is speculative, we do know some facts that corroborate how effective social media can be in spreading false news and enhancing social conflict. In an article published in *Science*, Sinan Aral and his colleagues analyzed all Twitter messages during the years 2006–2017. They found that false stories spread faster and further than true ones. They also found that humans were much more responsible for this trend than bots. Lastly, they discovered that these effects were more pronounced for false *political* stories than for any other type of false news.[8]

It is unclear why this is so. The authors speculate that the novelty and drama of lies in the form of conspiracy theories and plots captivates users. While we do not know the answer to this question, the fact that false political news travels further and faster than true stories is disturbing in a democracy that depends on people sharing the same documented facts.

Another study reported by Zeynep Tufekci,[9] an investigation of YouTube for the *Wall Street Journal*, found that YouTube often fed far-right or far-left videos to users who watched relatively mainstream news sources. When they clicked a link for more information, they got extremist content. Such extremist tendencies were evident for a wide variety of material. The author guesses that YouTube's recommender algorithm has a bias toward inflammatory content. It seems possible that the reason for this bias is that YouTube's algorithms are biased in favor of content that produces the highest volume of traffic—and profits.

Third, Facebook's own research shows how effective its mass communications can be in altering people's psychology. In 2012 it tweaked the feeds of nearly seven hundred thousand users without their permission. It sent one group more posts containing "positive emotional content" and the other posts with more "negative emotional content." In 2014 Facebook declassified the experiment and published the results. Subsequent analysis of users' feeds showed that people with the happier feeds acted happier in subsequent messaging and vice versa.[10] The authors called the results "massive-scale emotional contagion." This suggests the potential power such media have and the enormous damage that the spread of false stories may do.

While much is unknown about the effects of social media, it seems clear that it has dramatically changed how the political system works. The mass public and interested actors have now become opiners and editors. Together they help create public opinion and powerful images of society.

The problem currently is that much of this opinion is false and often politically motivated and inflammatory. For example, the following is a list of some of the sites set up on Reddit that were later taken down by the company: r/Jailbait (sexually suggestive photos of good-looking women), r/Jewmerica, r/ChokeABitch, r/Coontown (a racist site), r/Physical_Removal (a white nationalist site), r/KillAllJews (a Nazi site), and r/SexWithDogs.

Reddit managers, for example, have to deal with this problem every day and try to decide if they should ban a site such as r/GentlemenBoners, a soft-porn site. The difficult problem is that private corporations are now in the business of policing the First Amendment. This role puts them in an untenable position. Their business model and profits depend on the volume of messages they can generate, while effective policing requires them to ban sites and reduce profits.

Social media have arguably contributed to creating images of dysfunction, conflict, and corruption in society. Deregulation has allowed high-tech companies like Facebook to develop such platforms with no responsibility for how they are used. Facebook, YouTube, Twitter, and Reddit provide users with uncensored platforms on which almost anyone can spread false stories, rumors, conspiracy theories, and vitriol to millions of users. The algorithms used appear to be totally focused on producing the highest volume of use since this is the route to the highest profits.

THE CULTURE WARS NARRATIVE AND ITS EFFECTS

Such collective representations arguably have far more impact on people's perceptions of others than has been attributed to them (Iyengar, 1992; Iyengar and Kinder, 1988). Dominant perceptions of the "nation at war," for example, permit people to publicly demonize groups who are targeted as suspects, such as immigrants. It also abets polarization of the population into separate camps that become increasingly politicized.

The media have helped spread polarization, often deliberately, as part of their corporate mission. The result is distortion of the news by reason of corporate interest. This has helped spread conflict from elites to the mass public. It also has helped sharpen political conflict by presenting inflated perceptions of conflict in society at large. In recent decades, the result has been the growth of political language that is nasty and uncivil. The result is irrational politics (Andris et al., 2015). Populism has fed on such perceptions of irreconcilable conflict.

The changed image of American society has had many other wide-ranging effects on the American polity. First, it has been responsible for Americans' increased distrust of national institutions and of the news media itself (Norris, 1999). If society is believed to be composed of warring factions, then the neutrality or impartiality of *all* institutions becomes suspect. Paranoid ideas of the "deep state" now find an audience (see Hofstadter, 1965). Radical anti-elitism is also given support by media skepticism and false advertising on such topics as global warming and pollution. The media also erode the authority of many institutions by demeaning the motives, talents, and commitments of many groups such as civil servants, politicians, scientists, teachers, and so on. Similarly, the old definition of patriotism ("we are all in the same boat") fractures. The constant depictions of conflict and disorder help create the distinct impression that we are not all in the same boat. Instead we are in vessels that are at war with each other. Politics becomes defined as a zero-sum game rather than an effort to increase overall prosperity and well-being.[11]

Trust of the media itself also declines. For many, all media are believed to be biased and no source of news is trusted. For the population at large, this suspicion breeds contempt for truth. Ideology becomes the stand-in for objective discussion. In such a world there are no common facts, only opinions.[12]

As these data suggest, the media have become vehicles of partisanship.[13] According to David Carr, a *New York Times* media observer, "all over the internet, and on cable TV, posses are forming, positions are hardening, and misinformation is flourishing. Instead of debating how we as a culture are going to proceed, an increasingly partisan system of news and social media has factionalized and curdled."[14]

DECLINING TRADITIONS OF CITIZENSHIP AND COMMUNAL RITUALS

Media depictions of polarization and loss of community may well be one reason for the decline of many communal rituals that were part of citizenship. Collective representations affect whether people imagine that they are part of a civic community. Feelings of belonging influence their willingness to participate in its established rituals. Where there is little sense of community or a sense of a divided community, people may withdraw from society into homogeneous ghettoes and isolate themselves from others. They may also invent their own rituals of community that signal their distinctiveness.

Voting is one significant community ritual in democratic societies. In the United States, it has undergone a long-term decline since the 1960s (Burnham, 1984, 1995; Teixeira, 1987, 1990; Teixeira and Rogers, 2000; Stanley and Niemi, 2006: 14–15, tables 1-1 and 1-2). Since voting is largely a symbolic exercise for individuals, a declining sense of community can have a significant impact on such feelings of civic duty (Shienbaum, 1984). Once the sense of civic duty declines, such activity is likely to become both socially and psychologically optional, much like military service. Many will then choose to withdraw from these activities. The role of citizen itself undergoes a drastic alteration under these circumstances.

Participation in many other communal rituals also declines when a sense of community vanishes. This includes activities such as volunteering and participating in local community life, including social and political organizations (Wuthnow, 2002; Putnam and Campbell, 2010). There is some evidence that these activities are in decline. So are many *local* voluntary associations (Skocpol and Fiorina, 1999). Many of these are dying.

Americans' sense of obligation and duty to the collectivity has changed. The most patriotic generations were those born between 1890 and 1946 (Janowitz, 1983; Putnam, 2000). If the United States is no longer an imagined community, then one does not owe it loyalty and a willingness to sacrifice for it. Putnam and Campbell (2010: 87) offer a striking instance of this change, which parallels the generational changes in patriotism earlier reported. They observe that religious attendance in the 1950s was "less an act of piety than an *act of civic duty*." Many respondents reported that they were asked by others to join their church.[15] Now even religion cannot overcome the larger feeling of Americans that society is divided and contains people with irreconcilable attitudes and cultures. Currently, religion may unite believers, but it does not act as a bridge to other communities.

Other changes have emerged that may also be problematic for democracy. Images of a society in conflict legitimate identity politics and a zero-sum game political mentality (Judt and Snyder, 2012). This may make governing more difficult because it undermines willingness to compromise. It may also legitimate extremism, if groups come to see others as outsiders who have no legitimate standing. This may be the current case with such political identities. Whether it is the wave of the future is uncertain.

The future is also being molded by new forms of solidarity that are emerging, just as older forms are dying. Some forms of political identity, for example, may be more fluid and open to coalition building (see Castells, 1997). "Identity politics" for some may therefore be an opening gambit to gain entry to the political system as a legitimate contender. This seems to be characteristic of ethnic politics historically. Once in the system, ethnic politicians found it necessary to participate in normal coalition building. This was, of course, not true of the South on the issue of racism. It was an inextricable feature of Southern life and politics. But it seems to have been characteristic of the competitive politics of the urban north. Perhaps the moral here is that the effect of identity politics will depend on features of the larger political system, particularly its openness.

NEW IMAGES OF SOCIETY

While media images of conflict arguably have deleterious influences on national solidarity, part of the current conflict is over what kind of society we will become. The traditional answer was that America is a "melting pot" of races and ethnicities. The new answer is that we are a pluralistic "mosaic" of such groups. Under the influence of the latter model, new sources of social identity and solidarity have emerged. They are based on more pluralistic models of nationhood and more fluid personal identities. In politics, for example, while voting has suffered a decline, participation in social movement forms of politics has risen (Kamens, 2009; Judis, 2016). People are choosing movements rather than established parties to express their political identities because they offer a wider choice for unsanctioned viewpoints.

A wide array of rituals has arisen under a more pluralistic model of society. These affirm this form of national solidarity (Mirel, 2010). Plural identities, such as African American, have become common and are widely accepted as legitimate. Such display is no longer seen as undermining one's claim to be a good "American." The same is true for public dress codes. They have become less uniform, even in corporate settings, particularly the high-tech sector, where informality is encouraged. Patterns of speech have also become less hierarchical, even in large corporations that have elaborate status hierarchies. Corporate bonding and leadership have become the watchwords. And to keep expensive talent, managers have learned to be more respectful to their younger subordinates. There are now textbooks for managers on how to treat millennials and other newer generations in the workplace. *Respect* is the new corporate watchword. Formal deference has been downgraded, though not discarded.

Many other social rituals have also changed and become less constrained. Religious and ethnic intermarriage is becoming common. Even interracial dating and intermarriage is increasing. Living together is common and generally approved. Social life has also become more spontaneous and less formal. "Hooking up" as a form of dating has become common. Sexting has become a new form of communication via social media. Personalized identities blossom. Body art, for example, is more common among younger generations as an expression of personal and social identity. Language even in public places has become less formal. The use of slang in the classroom is common, and lectures are less formal and stilted. Currently, even the president can swear in public.

Some of these changes reflect a greater openness of language and popular culture to the diversity of American society. It is a sign that we are moving slowly toward a more pluralistic society.

CHAPTER 11

Conclusion

WHAT IS THE FUTURE of democracy in the United States? I can, of course, only speculate, but I do so relying on the fact that there is considerable continuity in the major constitutive elements of any political system. This is particularly true of fundamental conceptions of the political community: definitions of membership, their rights/responsibilities, and notions of the proper relationship between state and nation.

THE FUTURE OF CITIZENSHIP
UNDER INDIVIDUALISM

One of the important questions is: can individualism effectively function as the basis for a viable political community? There is much skepticism on this issue (see Bell, 1973; Levin, 2016).

It is hard to imagine another source of national solidarity in the United States. Secularization has advanced to the point that it challenges traditional definitions of proper citizenship. putting such definitions on the defensive. Many aspects of citizenship are dead. The idea that the United States is a white, Christian nation is under successful challenge. Racism, of course, is still prevalent and white nationalism is celebrating a public revival, but it is hard to imagine that politicians could successfully brand the country as a white nation again, though some are trying. Similarly, it is unlikely that any party could successfully float the idea that the United States is a Christian country. We are too far down the path to multiculturalism for that to be successful, though it is still a minority position that is alive and well. Nor will a combination of these work as a national source of solidarity, that is, as a white, Christian country.

There have been critical moments in this transition. The election of John F. Kennedy in 1960 signaled the end of the white Anglo-Saxon Protestant (WASP) domination of both the presidency and national politics. It did not, however, challenge the domination of white men in politics and elsewhere, or that of the white Christian population, but that too is changing. These ideas are, of course, still in play, but given the changing composition of the country and the rising power of blacks, Hispanics, Catholics, women, other ethnic groups, and the young it is unlikely that white Christian males can again be successful as symbols of the national community (Anderson, 1983). Barack Obama's presidency successfully challenged some of these stereotypes of the community, and Hillary Clinton's candidacy and the #MeToo movement are challenging male supremacy as a national source of pride and solidarity.

However, there is a major impediment to solidarity, even given the success of multiculturalism. That is economic inequality. Unemployment and underemployment undermine the ability of many citizens to act and credibly portray themselves as legitimate members of society. Stable employment in the United States has been and is a major source of human dignity. Unemployment or erratic foraging for temporary jobs undercuts the ability of many to act and see themselves as responsible citizens, that is, being successful family providers. In the eyes of mainstream society such people are not proper citizens.

Those invoking the mantle of individualism lay much blame on such people for shirking their responsibility to be employed (Ehrenreich, 2012). This rhetoric has sharpened in conservative circles since the Reagan era, when commentators denigrated "welfare queens" and many others for relying on publicly funded support. At the same time, politicians have eroded the weak social safety nets that had existed, and many are calling for further assaults, such as higher retirement ages for Social Security.

Culture-of-poverty ideas have also resurfaced that lay the blame squarely on the culture of the poor for their misery (Murray, 2011).

This situation undermines the ability of enhanced individualism to bolster national solidarity. For example, working-class white men often see themselves pitted against women and minorities for scarce jobs and resent affirmative action. This trend began in the 1970s and particularly the 1980s under President Reagan (Kinder and Sanders, 1996). In an economy in which decent jobs are scarce for the less educated, these reactions are understandable. While these are economic conflicts, politicians and many men frequently frame them in language that invokes race, gender, or ethnicity as sources of the problem (Lamont, 1997). Such groups then become objectified as villains who deserve hostility. This occurs in part because popular prejudices frame these conflicts with concrete images of undeserving predators taking jobs from others who are more worthy. The stigmatized groups then become objects of popular anger and rage. This happens in part because it is much easier to blame concrete individuals or groups than abstract processes like automation or artificial intelligence for reducing blue-collar jobs for white men. At any rate, these changes have fueled blue-collar anger at both political parties. This is partly the basis for the Trump movement. He won heavily in communities dominated by white men and women without college degrees.

Without family supporting jobs for all those who can and want to work, we will continue to be separated into two distinctive and unequal societies. One sector consists of legitimate citizens who are full participants in society, and the other is composed of second-class citizens who are unemployed or working erratically at minimum-wage jobs that do not support family life. The former inhabit niches in society that allow for the exhibition of solidarity with neighbors and the community. The affluent sector stigmatizes the latter as disreputable, who often end up living in areas where such solidarity is weak. What the conservative political scientist Edward Banfield called "amoral familism," an adaptation he witnessed in poverty-stricken southern Italy, emerges as a survival tactic in these environments. In such a culture, family members trust only one another. The job of male members is to protect the honor of the family.

Under the canopy of individualism, even family cohesion fades for such people. This predicament leaves the poor with guns and the police as sources of security.

The success of the United States in the global politico-economic order will play a significant role in determining the fate of national solidarity. If inequality lessens in response to successful world economic integration and political stability, more members of society will find their prospects improving and become defined by fellow citizens as legitimate members of society, independently of their race, ethnicity, gender, or religion. They will in short become defined as proper citizens and people capable of trust. The communities that form will be those that individuals choose to join based on their own personal identities. The fluidity of these identities may even increase the likelihood of many cross-cutting ties between groups and lead to new forms of cohesion and solidarity. This form of modernity appears akin to what Mirel (2010) forecast in his book *Patriotic Pluralism*. This is the optimistic version of what is in store for a society whose social organization is based on the individual.

However, under circumstances where globalization continues to produce soaring inequality in the United States, a much darker scenario is likely (Wuthnow, 1980). In this case there is every likelihood that the affluent classes will opt for multicultural models of society based on fluid modernity and liberalism on civil and legal rights. The less affluent will opt for less tolerant models in self-defense and find themselves in anomic communities dominated by economic woes and unemployment. The better-off poor will retreat into homogeneous ghettos and try to rely on family and community solidarity to deal with a harsh economic environment. This has already happened for many (Cahn and Carbone, 2010; Murray, 2011). They may also opt for reactionary social/religious movements and populist authoritarianism politically as another seeming bulwark to their distress. No common political community would emerge under these circumstances.

In this scenario it is also likely that civil society will become further militarized in defense against the poor and "disreputable" segments of society. This pattern already exists in low income areas of cities and poor communities. Movements of resistance have arisen to contest these conditions, for example, the Black Lives Matter movement. But, as happened during the urban riots of the 1960s, many politicians and their constituencies will support a military presence in these areas to prevent the spread of crime, violent conflict, and rioting. Police departments are already using military riot gear and other military surplus equipment. In many areas police have extensive experience in using tough and violent tactics against suspects, particularly minorities. And the language of "war" is already part of the national political vocabulary for describing appropriate responses to national problems. The gun culture is alive and well, and much of the white population is already well armed, trained, and ready to shoot. Gun violence has already become common. It may escalate under persistent and high inequality.

THE FUTURE OF IDEOLOGICAL POLARIZATION

Daniel Bell framed the problem of growing conflict in society as follows: "in the 19th and early-20th centuries we had, in America, individualism in the economy and regulation in morals; today we have regulation in the economy and individualism in morals. Politically, there may be a communal society coming into being; but is there a communal ethic? And is one possible?" (Bell, 1973: 482–483). Bell was writing in the 1970s when there was still government regulation of the economy left over from the Cold War. The country is now in a phase where much deregulation has occurred and inequality is soaring. The question now is: can the country develop a communal ethic when politicians have freed both morality and the economy from many prior restraints?

One way to answer this question is to consider whether the current political fault lines will continue to intensify. The two cultural fault lines in society are as follows: (1) should the nation deregulate morality by state and society to advance civil liberties for all? and (2) should government regulate the economy to reduce inequality and promote growth and innovation? The divide on each of these axes has become strong, but the main trends are clear. Majorities are in favor of extending civil legal and political rights, such as gay rights and civil rights to minorities. They are also in favor of deregulating the economy. Deregulation of morality and deregulation of the economy are the main trend lines. Vocal minorities, however, contest both trends.

In the case of public morality, many changes toward more social and legal equality have already happened in the United States and elsewhere. This is part of the international movement for human rights (Cole, 2012a, 2012b). In a globalized world such evolution happens quickly, for example, decriminalizing adultery and homosexuality (Frank, Camp, and Boutcher, 2010). For example, before 1985 the majority in the United States were against homosexual legal rights and gay marriage. By 2012 a majority of the population supported both.

In the United States the expansion of personal liberty and choice is at the heart of enhanced individualism. The spread of human rights is thus likely to continue. Civil liberalism finds support among corporate elites, minorities, the middle classes, and the young. Therefore, over time polarization on this front is likely to decline, as increasingly large majorities come to favor civil liberties.

The following trends favor this development. Current polling data support the idea that the young favor the expansion of civil liberties. Younger millennials who came of age during the Great Recession of 2008 report more concern for others and less interest in material goods than older millennials (Emily Smith and Jennifer Aaker, *New York Times*, December 1, 2013, Sunday Review: 1, 4). This compassion may be the basis of strong beliefs in the equality of all people and equal rights.

Among younger generations, such as Gen X and the millennials, surveys also show that traditional religious orientations are fading. Jonathan Merritt calls this phenomenon the rise of the Christian left (*The Atlantic*, July 29, 2013: 1–4). These cohorts are becoming more moderate or progressive in religious orientation. And many more are becoming nonreligious in their social orientation.

While church attendance and social-political conservatism have fused on the right, for a large minority of youth secular views on social issues are common. In addition, this trend gains further support from the increase in diffuse spirituality. A minority of Americans (14 percent in 2008) say they are spiritual but not religious. This trend is particularly true among younger age cohorts (Chaves and Anderson, 2012: 228ff). This is important because declining church attendance of younger age cohorts releases them from the hold of older traditions on social issues. Many people are now free to be religious or spiritual and at the same time in favor of gay rights, abortion, and premarital sex—all of which are anathema to religious conservatives. Millennials are particularly likely to take these social stances (Pew Research Center Report, Feb., 2010.

This change will come more slowly to areas that lack competitive political systems and remain backwaters of authoritarianism. Thus poorer, less economically developed areas and whole regions may be more resistant than others. Barrington Moore's famous quip will apply to these areas: "no bourgeoisie, no democracy." With the current fusion between church attendance and conservatism on civil liberties, the South and other more religious sectors of the country will continue to oppose this otherwise mainstream trend. But if economic development and more democracy expands to these areas, its corporate elites and middle classes are likely to push for social libertarian regimes. As a result, on this axis of conflict, there may be less controversy over time as the population that supports deregulating morality and extending legal and political rights becomes a robust majority.

On the issue of government regulation of the economy to reduce inequality and promote growth, it is hard to see a political path to a breakthrough. Any kind of corporatist decision making that involves the state and industry has been antithetical to the American tradition (see G. Wilson, 1982; Katznelson, 2013; Lembruch and Schmitter, 1982). To achieve more equality requires continually active state regulation of the economy and corporate practices, government support for unions, and higher tax rates generally, but particularly on corporations and the wealthy. The current policy at the federal and state levels is currently for more deregulation and lower tax rates.

Ironically, the development of intensified individualism has provided ideological support for a deregulated economy with its attendant inequality.[1] This narrative frames the state as an enemy of expanded personal liberty. One significant model of the future in the eyes of many is Silicon Valley and the high-tech industry in general. Labor unions are weak in this sector, as is government regulation. High-tech elites, however, are prominent supporters of the ideology of civil rights and equality, though in practice such high-tech corporations are often hothouses of misogyny and "whiteness." Current research suggests that these biases are prominent parts of the culture of science, engineering, and computer science at major institutions.[2] However, despite their support for civil rights ideology, high-tech corporate elites are hostile to both unions and government regulation.

Such attitudes, however, may be changing among the recent birth cohorts. Polling data shows that among the young, confidence in government institutions is rebounding. These findings suggest that the long-run ideological hegemony of neoliberalism may be ending among some of the youngest birth cohorts. Both the oldest and the youngest birth cohorts now show more confidence in government and institutions dependent on government than the middle cohorts (T. Smith, "Trends," 2012: 192ff, table 7.7). From 1973 to 2006 confidence in government, education, medicine, the military, the executive branch, science, Congress, and the Supreme Court has risen among the *youngest* birth cohorts.

The Pew Research Center report (February 2010) also shows that millennials are more pro-government than older generations. They are more likely to support the idea that the government should do more to solve problems (by 8–14 percentage points) than older generations. The Pew Research Center Report (July 3, 2013) also reports that millennials are less traditionally patriotic than older generations. They are less likely to view America as the greatest country in the world. They reject older notions of patriotism. This stance may make them open to practices of other countries that the United States could adapt to solve problems.

Working-class voters may also be more open to an activist government on economic issues than many politicians currently imagine. There is evidence that Trump voters would support more collectivist, though nonsocialist, policies on social welfare. Economic inequality is also a major concern of these voters. Research among Trump voters conducted by Hart Research Associates indicates that there is widespread support for social welfare policies that would create more equality (Garin, 2017). This research used focus groups of Trump voters in fourteen battleground states and a large-scale survey that oversampled *less-educated populations*. The results indicate that majorities of these voters are against many of the policy priorities of Republicans and Trump himself. Their most prominent concerns are with health care, but Republican plans in other areas also worry them. These Trump voters are against privatizing Medicare and cuts in Medicaid spending. They also do not support repealing the Affordable Care Act before presenting a replacement plan, and they are against the effort to cut off funding for health care services by Planned Parenthood. In addition, they are for raises in the federal minimum wage, against tax cuts that would primarily benefit the rich, and against large tax cuts for corporations).

These data suggest that there may be support for an active government program on economic issues among the young and working-class voters. Second, other data reaffirm that the search for meaning and authenticity has become a major motive among the young. This may open them to more tolerance on issues of public morality. Third, growing support for government suggests that younger generations may be rethinking the logic of neoliberalism. For instance, they may be more willing to accept the idea that education, government, and other institutions provide *collective* goods and services that are valuable. This ideology is at the heart of modern welfare states (Judt and Snyder, 2012). Support among Trump voters for New Deal–like policies in health care and the economy also indicates that there is working-class support for policies that deal with social inequality.

The major question is: how will the Democratic Party respond to pressure for more equality versus corporate donors' concerns with government regulation? It may be that a major political realignment could lead to an effective fight against inequality. How this might happen is difficult to imagine. The current electoral system with its nontransparency and voter suppression does not augur well for such change (see Norris, 2017). Whether social movement politics can overcome such inertia is an open question.

While these changes offer hope, polarization on economic equality will continue if the Democratic Party cannot develop nonsocialist collective solutions to these problems. Currently, there is strong corporate and political support favoring deregulation of the economy. Changing the status quo will require a new political alignment. It seems unrealistic to imagine that current demographic trends will produce a movement that would be able to overcome current antipathy to government efforts to reduce inequality.[3] First, the demographic changes are not large. They do not presage a tidal wave of support necessary for dramatic change. Second, these changes are primarily among the young, whose involvement in politics is inconsistent and lower than older age groups. And lastly, to be politically effective a political movement will have to emerge to translate such personal changes into highly organized and well-funded organizations to mobilize large sectors of the population for change.

In addition, the Democratic Party may not be able to respond with radical, nonsocialist programs that would appeal to working-class voters. American labor unions have become weak in numbers and political strength. The Supreme Court has recently made it harder for unions to fund themselves. And such constraints may become more severe as the Court considers other cases involving unions' rights.

Furthermore, the liberal-labor alliance has vanished. Corporations have become the dominant political actors, both as funders and as controllers of the mass media, for example, the ubiquity of Fox News nationally. They even control the platforms of social media and can regulate the dominant content produced there.

One result of these efforts has been a steadily declining political support for measures that strengthen government regulation of corporations. Even the modest efforts of the Dodd-Frank Act to control banks and financial institutions to prevent another occurrence of massive bank failure like 2008 are under ferocious attacks that have been legislatively successful.

If these trends are not just transitory, one plausible result is that a social divide will continue. A more civil libertarian society will exist simultaneously with one that harbors enormous economic disparities. It is unlikely that this could be a successful political community with a common political ethic. It excludes too much of the population from participating.

If this happens, politicians will continue to invoke the classic American strategy of popular mobilization via education to reduce inequality. Liberals and conservatives will rely on schools to create a more competitive economy and egalitarian society. As Christopher Jencks (1972: 265) put it almost fifty years ago at the end of his book *Inequality*:

As long as egalitarians assume that public policy cannot contribute to economic equality directly but must proceed by ingenious manipulations of marginal institutions like the schools, progress will remain glacial. If we want to move beyond this tradition, we will have to establish political control over the economic institutions that shape our society. This is what other countries call socialism. Anything less will end in the same disappointment as the reforms of the 1960s.

This is a strategy that will not work. Absent government policies to decrease monopolistic concentration in many economic sectors, and to reward firms for investing in the economy to increase innovation, productivity, and employment, education will not function as a ladder of social mobility. Elevated levels of mobility occur when the economy expands and absorbs large numbers of people into better-paying, more productive jobs, for example, the large-scale movement of rural workers to the urban factory economy. Tax policy is one way to achieve such changes by rewarding firms that reinvest profits in plants and innovation with tax breaks. There are many other tools government could use for such purposes. It does, however, require an activist government that has enough popular support to buck the resistance of the corporate community. This is a tall order to fill.

Historian Sean Wilentz (2016) has argued that one of the keys to American politics is the continuous struggle against inequality. The other key is the importance of political parties and partisanship in producing changes that mitigate the effects of American-style capitalism on inequality. With the rise of neoliberalism and the demise of a Democratic alternative, deregulated capitalism and inequality have been on the rise since the 1970s.

There is, however, one scenario in which a challenge to neoliberalism might arise and become effective. If increasing support for civil libertarianism produces enormous popular momentum for the extension and implementation of voting rights and legal equality, the electorate might expand and become more active. If this happens, a real fight against inequality might materialize. There is no telling how fast this might happen. The current funding crises of many states might propel such issues to the forefront, led by organized groups such as teachers—often against the advice of their own unions. Currently vote suppression rules stifle many possibilities for change (Norris, 2017).

At present the faltering struggle against inequality works against such change by diminishing hope. Working-class wages have been stagnant and labor force participation has dropped (see Hacker, 2006; Soss et al., 2007; Stiglitz, 2003; Sugie, 2018) "Deaths of despair" have increased. Anne Case and Angus Deaton, Princeton economists, have shown that since 1998, deaths from preventable causes (alcoholism, opioid addiction, and obesity) have risen for every birth cohort. In short, for much of the population the life span is contracting rather than growing longer.

Under current conditions the status quo is likely to continue. One of the Trump campaign promises and current policy directions is to further deregulate the economy to allow more space for private sector growth and innovation. The "blue wave" that helped the Democrats take over the House may stem this tide. But any effective drive will depend on Democratic unity around a program that has wide popular support. This is a tall order, given the competition within the party that will emerge among prospective presidential candidates ahead of the 2020 elections.

In the meantime, Wall Street is gearing up for a new, unprecedented level of mergers, acquisitions, share buybacks, and bank profits. Absent a clear antitrust set of policies and the will to enforce them, such consolidation in the economy is likely to expand and intensify. The almost certain result will be increasing inequality between regions and between sectors of the population. The Silicon Valleys will prosper, while the cities and regions like Flint and western New York will fall further behind, increasing the divide between the haves and have-nots. It is unlikely that this will produce a productive economy with decent jobs for everyone willing to work, and more equality.

If this scenario plays out, gridlock may continue. It is hard to see how an inclusive political community could emerge and function in the face of widespread political polarization on the role of government in the economy. Bell's pessimism in 1973 may turn into an accurate prediction of the future in twenty-first-century America. The new tax law, for example, produced income gains of $5 billion for workers and $175 billion for corporations. Corporations currently have plans—and are busy enacting them—to use most of this windfall to buy back shares—at record levels. This means increasing the stock price of their own corporations, enriching shareholders, investors, and executives of the company in the process. According to Matt Philips of the *New York Times* (February 27, 2018: B1–B2), American corporations have announced $175 billion in planned buybacks—the largest amount ever unveiled in a single quarter. Such investments lift the stock price but typically do not expand their workforces or result in new plants or technologies.[4]

Currently, the United States is a divided society.[5] The affluent sector of society enacts Mirel's (2010) patriotic pluralism, but it does so by excluding the lower social classes from political life altogether (think vote suppression and gerrymandering) or by selective inclusion. The solution to this problem is to incorporate the legitimate fears of working-class whites into a program that is socially inclusive. If the Democratic Party takes a left-of-center tack and focuses on economic rights and policies that provide decent employment for those without college degrees (see Geoghegan, 2014), this may be possible. Whether the Democratic Party could coalesce around such a program is the question.

THE RISE OF POPULISM AND ITS FUTURE: PERSISTENT CRISIS?

The uncomfortable truth about the Trump campaign is that, like the Brexit campaign, it is perfectly timed to ride a mood of popular revolt—against neo-liberal economics, against the bankers who emerged with impunity from the 2008 financial meltdown, against what Farage called "global capitalism," against seemingly uncontrolled immigration and against the politicians behind growing workplace precariousness and a pervasive sense of personal control lost to impersonal forces.[6]

—ROGER COHEN

Historically, when political crises arise in the United States, populist politics emerge (Huntington, 1981; Rosenstone et al., 1996). This logic suggests a series of questions about the future of politics in the United States. The first is, are populist politics the wave of the future? A plausible hypothesis is that major party failure is likely to occur much more frequently in the future, unless political polarization declines. Such failure is, of course, as much a matter of perception as factual reality.[7] The sources of such definitions of the situation are readily visible. And the availability of social media makes it much easier for movements outside or within parties to reconstruct reality such that it casts doubt on the integrity and/or competence of sitting governments. Trump is an expert in this art. Others are waiting in the wings.

A second question is: what will be the effects of such movements? It may not be far-fetched to imagine that populist authoritarianism might emerge from the new politics. Tocqueville noted that this is part of American tradition, and it fits in with both anti-elitism and individualism as narratives of society. He foresaw this danger in an egalitarian, individualist society and saw signs of it coming under the presidency of Andrew Jackson (see also Meacham, 2008). We have already had a taste of this kind of authoritarianism under President Trump. He has already been successful beyond anyone's (including his) wildest dreams. And the Republican Party is now substantially under his control. His legions of loyal supporters will "primary" any opponent who criticizes the president. The recent Republican primaries have demonstrated the danger of challenging this president.

Under conditions of real or perceived economic failure, many may find populist authoritarianism a promising solution. Current evidence indicates that in a legitimacy crisis, a substantial sector of the public perceives lying demagogues as presenting a deeper truth about the system and achieving authenticity despite their known mendacity (Hahl et al., 2018). This research shows that Trump supporters knew he was lying but did not care. For them even the lies were part of his symbolic protest about uncaring elites—a message that they applauded.

This outcome may also work in practice. It has many advantages. It would keep the American creed alive, at least in appearance. Second, it would appear legitimate because it was the result of elections. And third, formal legal rights would remain on the books but suffer disimplementation in fact. The devil would lie in the details. Such changes are happening elsewhere, even more quickly—for example, in Hungary and Poland.

Here again the world economy and political order will play a leading role. A failing global economy and political order could make conditions much worse. And some of Trump's policies may hasten this reality. Under this scenario, the future would be much bleaker. For example, it may well be the basis for draconian reductions in individual legal rights. Political majorities may support repression as a popular antidote to political or economic collapse. And a garrison state would be available to enforce such order.

Democratization would fail, but the appearance of democracy would survive. One result would be complete failure to implement political, legal, and social rights that are formally on the books. The United States would become a Potemkin village. This was a classic way for Russian officials to fool the czar concerning prosperity in the provinces: build a well-painted village that was only a shell for him to inspect from his coach. A sitting populist presidential regime in the United States could play a similar trick by leaving current laws and programs in place but not enforcing or funding them.

Already there are ominous signs. Old-fashioned nationalism is reemerging complete with racist and nativist undertones. This scenario is not new in the United States or elsewhere. For example, during the early twentieth century, President Theodore Roosevelt was hostile to immigrants, who were coming to the United States in large numbers. He questioned their fitness as citizens, saying:

We wish no further additions to the persons whose affection for this country is merely a species of *pawnbroker patriotism* [my italics]—who's coming here represents nothing but the purpose to change one feeding trough for another feeding trough.[8]

A version of this attitude has surfaced in many places when globalization failed, for example, during World War I in the United States; after World War II; and during decolonization. In tough times the "man on the white horse" is a promising symbol of societal redemption in a populist, egalitarian democracy. Many saw President Eisenhower in those terms—a military man who could save the country from the "red scare."

This speculation raises another question: what happens when populism fades after the demise of its founder? We may have another five years of the Trump regime, but what happens then? The historical evidence suggests some possibilities. First, it often leads to a retreat from globalization. Brexit is one contemporary example. Driven by populist anger in the declining industrial areas of the North and lassitude and overconfidence of both elites and voters in the prosperous South, Britain now faces a painful exit from the European Union that prefaces substantial economic losses (Judis, 2016). It may also lead to a retreat from liberalism on civil rights, once anti-immigrant fervor becomes law. Second, the transition often results in substantial losses of democracy as heirs of charismatic leaders try to institutionalize their political control over state and society. Isolationism promotes this because it removes the elites from external economic and political sanctions for their behavior. The result is often the emergence of one-party states, which are dictatorships in fact, such as Venezuela after Chavez, Cuba under Castro, Zimbabwe under Mugabe and his wife, South Africa after Mandela, post-Weimar Germany, and Chile after Allende. In some cases, like Chile and 1930s Germany, few people foresaw this turn of events. It happened so quickly under both Hitler and Pinochet.

Another aftermath of such movements is factionalism and anarchy (see R. Kaplan, 1997, 2000). In Libya and Iraq, the breakdown of the state has led to both factionalism and the inability of government to govern. The result for many is anarchy.[9] In any case the chances for democracy are slim.

Neither of these outcomes are likely to happen in the twenty-first century to a high-tech, industrial power like the United States. But there are other ways that a nation can become less democratic. If the retreat from global ties, trade, and alliances continues, the United States will lose sight of its role in supporting democracy, security, and liberal values abroad. Like Trump it will see these relationships as one-off transactions that are zero-sum games. And politicians will measure the success of these changes only in dollars—not in enhanced security or international economic stability. This will encourage other nations to do the same, including using military or geopolitical threats whenever possible, for example, China in the South China Sea, Russia in Eastern Europe and Europe, and North Korea in the peninsula and Sea of Japan.

Such tensions in the absence of solid alliances might provoke even more militarization of foreign and domestic policy in the United States.

This has already happened, but it could go much further. Politicians could use national security claims to bolster policies such as greater militarization of police forces, particularly in urban, anti-regime areas and neighborhoods where minorities and immigrants congregate. Conservative critiques of universities and science could lead to more draconian policies vis-à-vis these institutions, such as reduced funding for science, not related to military or industrial needs; diversion of university funding to technical schools and for-profit colleges; and fierce attacks on the liberal arts and outspoken faculty. Reducing funds for Medicare and raising the retirement age for workers to pay for tax cuts and increased military spending are other possibilities along with further deterioration of social safety nets.

Some of this is already happening, but it could get much worse. Leaders might seal off borders and increase patrols to keep out immigrants and curtail freedom of movement in these areas as part of this policy of border policing. Lastly, vote suppression might continue or even intensify under the guise of preventing voter fraud. Local party groups already implement such policies. This is an effective shield from widespread public visibility.

These are just some of the tactics that a sitting U.S. presidential regime could use to reduce democracy to maintain control. Democracy would survive, but with grave limitations. Many would not find a legitimate space. Some of this has already happened, for example, arbitrarily closing voter registration in Ohio, decertifying voters who miss arbitrary cutoff dates, and militarization of local police. It is, however, an open question as to how far this could go. Once instituted, such changes might be hard to reverse by a new administration, for example, if it involved congressional legislation. There are also signs of declining democracy vis-à-vis civil rights under the Trump administration.[10]

Whether such a fate is in store depends on whether a majority will arise to support democratization. This will depend heavily on the success of the United States in the global order. The continuation of high levels of inequality might intensify a deterioration of democracy.

A final question is: how can the United States restrain populism and its irrational politics yet retain space for legitimate public debate? One current obstacle to solutions is the contemporary disdain and hatred for the political class. Widening the opportunity for political participation may be part of the solution to this problem.

In the transformation of American politics, two changes have collided. The political changes described previously have drained *localism* out of the system, along with much *democracy*. Mass politics becomes an activity that engages only a minority of society. Working-class participation has been dropping. Trump, for example, won the election with 46 percent of the popular vote. While polarization has raised voter turnout rates a little, they are still low compared to Europe and to earlier historical periods.[11] For example, in the 2016 presidential election the total turnout was 54 percent of eligible voters. In local and state primary races, turnout is lower, often involving only 20 to 40 percent of eligible voters (see Cancela and Guys, 2016; Teixeira and Rogers, 2000). For example, in the last mayoral election (2014) in Washington, D.C., 27 percent of eligible voters turned out. In the most recent election (2018) the turnout was 17 percent. The voting population is disproportionately composed of the middle and upper classes, whose interests the system now serves. Many others know that the tilt of the system is toward the upper classes and drop out (see Schattschneider, 1960).

The organization and functioning of the electoral system itself is responsible for some portion of this problem. Currently, it breeds anger, dropout, and a sense that the system is both unfair and rigged (Norris, 2017).[12] According to comparative research, the United States ranks below Western Europe, the Baltic states, and even Costa Rica in the nontransparency (read corruption) of its elections. State laws to suppress the vote include rules on voter identification that are difficult and expensive for poor people to comply with; limiting the number of polling places available, thereby extending waiting time to vote; limiting voting to the workweek; outdated and malfunctioning equipment at the polls, resulting in breakdowns; uninformed officials at the polls; and confusing information for voters about polling locations. Some represent tactics that politicians use to reduce voting. Thirty-two states, for example, currently have voter ID requirements that increase the expense and inconvenience for poorer voters, such as obtaining a driver's license for people who do not own a car. In short, a twenty-first-century society has a nineteenth-century voting system—underfunded, backward, and discriminatory.

One major antidote to this problem is to fix the political system to make it more transparent and less corrupt. The effort to fix the electoral system is straightforward. Then one could tackle other problems of corruption, such as money in politics. But it will require large-scale funding and stamina to challenge the inertia and self-interests of political parties and the minority whose interests they serve.

These are some of the questions the United States faces in extending democracy. The most challenging task will be persuading the electorate that there are solutions to these problems. This has traditionally been the role of political parties, but it is unclear if either is up to this daunting task. The Republicans are willing captives of the president, and his hardcore base has nowhere else to go. Psychological research suggests that they will continue to pursue this wildly irrational gamble. People who are betting to recoup massive losses tend to make such irrational choices. And much of Trump's and the Republican Party's base believes that they are trying to snatch victory from defeat by any effort that promises success.

The big question is whether the Democratic Party can develop an agenda for achieving mass economic mobility that will lift all boats. This will require direct efforts to tilt the economy in favor of workers and the middle class. One of their biggest hurdles will be convincing voters that such plans to relieve soaring inequality are viable and that these policies can achieve good effects without destroying the economy. They will also have to make the case that ordinary people can make a difference if they mobilize and get their friends and relatives to participate and vote. This will be difficult. Given the present state of politics there are many reasons to doubt that it will work.

Notes

1. This is also partly due to the self-censorship the mass media engaged in up to the late 1960s (see Chapter 10). News of conflict, race riots, and mob activities like lynching was purposely kept out of the news as was political conflict, industrial strikes, black protest movements, and crime. When these events were covered, papers and local radio presented them as activities of individual misfits, loners, communists, or foreigners. Similarly, the private lives of politicians and other public figures were defined as non-newsworthy. In this way the media helped maintain the myth of the virtuous American past of peace, consensus, and tranquility in social and political life.

2. This is an argument variously suggested by Lipset (1990, 1996), Martinelli (2008), and others.

3. In challenging times, politicians can fan the flames of nationalism and increase its salience, particularly for the less educated and less privileged.

4. This is true internationally as well (Shavit et al., 2007).

5. Another vivid illustration of the effects of such embeddedness come from anthropological studies of people with schizophrenia in the United States and India. Both groups hear "voices." But the voices give these people radically different messages consonant with the different political cultures of these countries. In India, where caste taboos and obligations are key features of citizens' identities, people with schizophrenia report that they are told to do domestic chores like "going to the kitchen to prepare food" or in some cases to do counternormative actions often focused on sex. Others are told to do things like eating raw sewage or committing taboo sexual acts that violate caste and societal norms. In the United States, where individualism and self-reliance are important characteristics of the citizen role, people with schizophrenia hear more violent messages and commands. Americans' "voices" more often command them to go to war; to commit suicide; or to commit violence against someone, for example, "taking their eyes out with a fork," or "cutting off someone's head and drinking their blood" (Luhrmann, 2012, 2013). Thus, even people with mental illness are told different things by the voices they hear depending on the dominant narratives embedded in their cultures.

CHAPTER 2

1. Dab Bilefsky, "Tougher Test on Citizenship Stumps Even Native Danes," *New York Times*, July 8, 2016, A-4.

2. This vision of society triumphed because it found an important carrier: the post–Civil War Republican Party. The party became the institutional carrier of a rationalized ontology that featured the following narrative: autonomous individuals using rational calculation to subdue a mechanical (vs. ecological) nature under the guidance of an abstract God (Thomas, 1989: 136). The Republican Party became a carrier of a religious

view of nationalism that enshrined individualism, anti-statism, and millennial nationalism as prominent aspects of its ideology. With the defeat of the Democrats and their counter-ideology of a stronger national center in the election of 1896, the Republican ideology of "national individualism" persisted.

3. The timing of institutional development also affected this outcome. The fact that a thriving economy appeared on the scene *before* the emergence of a bureaucratic state gave capitalists space to develop legitimacy as prominent sources of innovation, wealth, and morality in society (Shefter, 1977; Heidenheimer, 1982). As a result, business became a privileged group in society and has sustained its prominence and ideological hegemony (Lindblom, 1977).

4. A decentralized, weak government also favored the growth of capitalism and the hegemony of business culturally as an institution (Lindblom, 1977). Towns and counties had every incentive to support economic innovation, local industry, and agriculture. Prosperity created jobs, wealth, and the willingness to pay local taxes for improvements (Mann, 2012). And the adoption of British common law was favorable to capitalists in dealing with labor and unions (Orren and Skowronek, 2004). It took the view that such practices obstructed free markets and were thus illegal.

5. See George Saunders, "Trump Days," *New Yorker* (July 11–18, 2016): 50–62.

6. While Philip Converse argued that the American public was "untainted by ideology," it is likely that just the opposite is true. Their views are tainted by the prevalence of American civil religion. For example, modern economists and political scientists are often surprised at how irrational the American public is in its attitudes toward social and economic policy. In his book *The Myth of the Rational Voter*, Caplan (2007) argues that three major public biases have led to bad public policies. The biases of Americans are (1) general opposition to free trade and international competition, sometimes referred to in popular and political parlance as "job killers"; (2) a general disposition to favor capitalist institutions and individual enterprise and to oppose unions and other efforts to regulate "free enterprise"; and (3) opposition to government and collective solutions to social and economic problems. Thus, both elites and mass publics are suspicious of Keynesian solutions to economic problems; they are also against free trade and immigration; and they are convinced that government should not and cannot develop effective regulatory systems that cushion the effects of the business cycle and mitigate the likelihood of catastrophic depressions. In addition, many economists like Jeffrey Sachs (see Chapter 5) are shocked at how hollowed out and incompetent the American state is for formulating and enacting effective public policies.

Thus, while Caplan (2007) sees massive public ignorance and consequent irrationality as the result of badly educated individuals, it seems more plausible to see these as evidence of a deeper systemic problem: American citizens have fewer politico-economic ideologies to choose from than Europeans. And those available ideologies are more xenophobic and suspicious of collective solutions to societal problems (e.g., Lipset, 1963; Lipset and Raab, 1970).

7. Recent analyses of American conservatism have made this point clear. In their survey of American conservatism, for example, Micklethwait and Wooldridge (2004) note how different the attitudes of U.S. conservatives are from their British and European counter-parts. The former are virulent anti-statists while the latter have often supported the development of social welfare states on pragmatic and moral grounds. There is also a strong element of Social Darwinism in the ideology of American conservatives that is absent in Europe. Skocpol and

Williamson (2012), for example, found that Tea Party members support federal programs that benefit them, such as Medicare, Social Security, and veterans' benefits, but oppose extending them to "undeserving" groups like minorities and the poor, who in their view have not "earned" these benefits by hard work. A popular slogan on signs at Tea Party gatherings is "Redistribute my Work Ethic." The very rich are even more conservative and oppose almost all government programs that involve redistribution of wealth to provide more universal social welfare programs like Medicaid, Medicare, and Social Security (Page, Bartels, and Seawright, 2011). Their belief in Social Darwinism as a governing ideology is complete.

Antigovernment ideologies are even more widespread in the United States than these examples suggest. Surveys indicate that distrust of government is high and has been growing since the 1950s (Putnam, 2000; Lane, 1999; Steurle et al., 1998).

8. On the other hand, public opinion in Eastern Europe and Islamic nations soundly *rejects* the idea that politicians should be open about their religious beliefs. Their *means* are significantly lower on this item. For example, only 28 percent of the former and 12 percent of the latter agree with this statement. While they support religious elites, both populations are wary of ordinary politicians using religion or secular religious ideologies to support their legitimacy.

9. However, Eastern Europeans and citizens of Islamic countries soundly *reject* these two propositions about the role of religious elites in politics. In these mono-religious cultures, both populations favor and expect the participation of religious elites in politics. Only 12.1 percent of Eastern Europeans agree with the first statement and 14.1 percent agree with the second. Those in Islamic societies are similar: 13.8 percent agree with the first statement and 19.2 percent with the second. It appears that in countries where a dominant religion is linked to nationalism, the fact that religious elites participate in politics is viewed as normal and to be expected.

10. The standard deviations, however, are similar (2.6 for the United States, 2.5 for Western Europe, 2.7 for Eastern Europe, and 2.8 for Islamic societies).

11. There is also much less variance in the American case than in Europe—and especially Eastern Europe and Islamic societies (standard deviations are 2.2, 2.5, 2.8, and 2.9). For example, 13 percent of Americans believe in extreme inequality (9 or 10 on the scale) versus 9 percent of Western Europeans.

12. For example, 2 percent of Americans strongly endorse expanding the public sector (scores of 9 or 10 on this scale) versus 6 percent of Western Europeans, while 20 percent of Eastern Europeans and 24 percent of those in Islamic societies favor public sector growth. However, there is less variance around the American and Western European means than in Eastern Europe and Islamic societies (standard deviations are 1.9, 2.2, 2.8, and 2.7).

13. Only 3 percent of Americans give credence to "luck and connections" as a narrative of success (scores of 9 or 10) versus 8 percent of those in Islamic societies, 7 percent in Western Europe, and 12% in Eastern Europe. However, 48 percent of citizens of Islamic societies endorse scale values 1 and 2—the strongest support for the narrative of individualism. This compares with 31 percent of Americans, 22 percent of Western Europeans, and 28 percent of Eastern Europeans. There is less variance in American opinion than in Western Europe, Eastern Europe, and Islamic societies (standard deviations are 2.2, 2.5, 2.8, and 2.9).

CHAPTER 3

1. These societies also have transparent tax and social welfare policies that are broad-based and universalistic. Furthermore, they use both carrots (e.g., job training programs)

and sticks (e.g., loss of welfare benefits for school truants) to keep national budgets in check and social welfare spending sleek and relatively effective. Just as important, they have a corps of long-term, well-trained civil servants who help shape and monitor policies (see *The Economist*, February 2–8, 2013, Special Report: 1–16). None of these characterize the American state.

2. In a *New York Times* poll in 2010, 31 percent of the public admitted to not knowing what most Americans paid in federal taxes. Among the rest, most grossly *overestimated* the average tax rate. Twelve percent of the public at large and 17 percent of Tea Party members believed that the average *federal* income tax rate is between 30 and 40 percent. In fact, 86.5 percent pay less than 10 percent; 12.9 percent pay between 10 and 20 percent; and 0.6 percent pay above 20 percent (Bartlett, 2012: 33, table 4.3). Even the wealthiest taxpayers face rates below these popular estimates. In 2008 the average federal tax rate of the four hundred wealthiest taxpayers was 18.11 percent (Bartlett, 2012: 34, table 4.4). And these rates have been coming down. In 1992, before the Bush tax cuts, the four hundred wealthiest paid an average 26.38 percent federal income tax.

3. *Washington Post*, "Tax Breaks and the Invisible Welfare State," March 3, 2012: A2; Mettler, 2011.

4. Only tax-phobic Switzerland has fewer. One immediate result is a high rate of noncompliance in reporting income. This trend is growing. Between 1990 and 2005 the rate of nonreporting of taxable income went from 10.3 percent to 14.8 percent—a 33 percent increase. One reason for this increase is that few people are ever audited (Bartlett, 2012: 156–157).

5. This example comes from Dhruv Khullar, "Unhealthy Politics in Congress," *New York Times*, October 26, 2017.

6. In addition, such policies create lower administrative costs and eliminate bias against those of younger age cohorts (Wilensky, 2002). Historically, researchers have found that they promote economic growth and competitiveness (Lindert, 2004; Wilensky, 2002).

7. This includes tax expenditures that consume economic resources without showing up in the budget or in standard measures of government as a share of GDP.

8. Steinmo (2010) has argued that this calculation shows that the United States is an advanced welfare state. But it is also apparent that these expenditures disproportionately benefit the wealthy. They do not fund universal benefits and extend social citizenship throughout society.

9. In Scandinavia, for example, the narrative of nationhood produces a communitarian culture in which the state emerged as the corporate representative of the national community. Their states had, as a result, considerable legitimacy as such. State authority derives legitimacy from its official role in representing a religious-ethnic community (see Boli, 1989, on Sweden; Jepperson, 2002). The public views state action as promoting what is referred to as "statist individualism," that is, individual autonomy and social mobility promoted through state action, such as inexpensive higher education and high subsidies for all students. In France and Germany, state development and nation building took different forms, but in those countries as well the state is representative of society and an agent for its collective interests (see Jepperson, 2002; E. Weber, 1979; Brubaker, 1992). In France, the state has legitimacy to act and has support if it is perceived as doing so effectively. Mark Lilla, a French journalist, argues that if public officials there look responsible, the public leaves them alone to do their jobs. Public trust will continue if they make evident progress. An example of this view of the state is the title of politician Alain Juppé's book.

To inaugurate his presidential campaign in 2016 he published a book called *For a Strong State*. It's hard to imagine an American politician arguing that the federal government should be given more autonomous bureaucratic power as the main representative of society.

10. Furthermore, because U.S. parties have not been policy-oriented, ideological entities, they have had no difficulty in absorbing and co-opting dissident groups under their own diffuse banners (Shefter, 1977). Dissenting groups do not suffer stigma from this arrangement because they can argue that the dominant party they are associated with articulates and supports their interests.

CHAPTER 4

1. The avowed purpose was to make government more efficient and effective by ridding it of patronage appointments. But it was also an attack on urban political machines by Progressives and corporate elites (Weinstein, 1968). The effects of this change were mixed. In some cities this movement dispersed power by curtailing patronage and instituting other reforms such as citywide elections. Where a professional city management form of government was instituted, it produced centralized authority without much popular accountability (Weinstein, 1968).

2. A brief survey of the historical landscape illustrates this point. If a state-centered system is considered as the fusion of executive, bureaucracy, and legislature into one governmental collectivity (Nettl, 1968), then the American "state" historically has been a weak one. The American system was for some time peculiarly "governmentless" (e.g., Rose, 1985b) a system of "courts and parties" with patronage linkages to civil society and without a well-developed administrative core (see, e.g., Skowronek, 1982; Skocpol and Ikenberry, 1982). Organizationally, the system represented a "Tudor polity" with "fusion of functions and division of powers" (Huntington, 1968). Much public collective action was organized by local government instrumentalities, or through governmental delegation to private actors. The political system often relied on the construction and manipulation of property rights as a means for establishing authority and resolving disputes (see Horowitz, 1977; Bright and Harding, 1984).

3. I am indebted to John Boli for this insight.

CHAPTER 5

1. See Neal Lane and Michael Riordan, "The President's Disdain for Science," *New York Times*, January 5, 2018: A27.

CHAPTER 6

1. In response to these changes, political scientists often argue that people have distinct "action repertoires." Instead of explaining these changes, they reify the idea of individual choice in politics, as modern economics has done. In this context, the idea of the rational public surfaces and is accepted and lauded by politicians, academics, pollsters, and the public (e.g., Page and Shapiro, 1992).

2. The Baylor surveys on religion found a good deal of anti-science sentiment among the public and especially conservatives. For example, political and religious conservatives all agree with the statement that "We rely too much on science and not enough on faith." Similarly, these groups reject the idea that "Science will eventually provide solutions to most of our problems" (see Froese and Bader, 2010: 185, table A.6). And they reject basic

theories of modern science. They agree, for example, that "Creationism should be taught in the public schools" and reject the idea that "Humans evolved from primates over millions of years" (Froese and Bader, 2010: 187, table A.7, and 188, table A.8). They also agree that "Embryonic stem cell research is always wrong." They are both anti-statist and anti-science. They disagree, for example, that "The government is spending too little on science." These findings indicate that even educated evangelicals and religious conservatives reject key elements of science: its optimism about the role of reason in guiding human societies and the key theory of evolutionary biology.

3. The decline in voting in the United States, however, has been steeper than in other advanced democracies (roughly from 65 percent in the 1950s to 50 percent of the eligible electorate in the post-1960 period). This is largely because the United States has no working-class parties that integrate blue-collar groups into the polity (e.g., for the 1970s and 1980s, see Dennis, 1970, 1978; Dalton et al., 1984; Abramson and Aldrich, 1979; Abramson et al., 1986; Dalton, 2002a, 2007). Less educated and lower-income Americans are not well represented either by political parties or by the state(s). Both the poor and the working class are therefore rightfully suspicious of both political parties, politicians, Congress, and the national government as well (see Hacker and Pierson, 2010; Wuthnow, 2002). Therefore, their participation is lower than that of low-income groups in other democracies (G. Powell, 1980, 1986).

4. However, the evidence does not entirely support this belief. Putnam (2000), for example, found that the highest levels of interpersonal trust are found in the least developed and least democratic states of the United States—Louisiana and Mississippi. In highly developed and educated sections of the country, the plausibility that "we are all in the same boat" has been eclipsed by a highly individualized culture.

5. One result is that there is important universal agreement across nations and regions on one component of human rights: the right of individuals to physical integrity, which means freedom from torture, arbitrary arrest, and personal abuse by the state or agents of the state (Ramirez, Suarez, and Meyer, 2006; Cole, 2012b; Cole and Ramirez, 2013). Other aspects of human rights are still contested, for example, Western-style freedoms such as freedom of speech and the right to freely associate.

CHAPTER 7

1. *Washington Post*, October 4, 2017: C1, C5. The article focused on the comedian Jimmy Kimmel hitting the right notes on health care legislation and the Las Vegas massacre versus tone deaf politicians.

2. And citizens are generally more aware of central government than local governments (see, e.g., Jennings, 1998; Nachmias and Rosenbloom, 1980: 240ff).

3. For example, in 1995 over a thousand lobbyists and farm representatives testified before Congress regarding pending farm legislation. In the 1970s, about thirty farm organization representatives and lobbyists showed up to testify when farm bills were discussed (NPR, September 20, 1995; Browne, 1983).

4. Theodore Lowi usefully calls attention to the importance of the increasing discretionary character of federal activity, such as discretionary investment guarantee programs, reaching magnitudes equivalent to 16 percent of GNP in 1978 (from 12 percent in 1956; Lowi, 1978a: 288), and federal revenue sharing and block grants to localities (Lowi, 1978a; Lowi and Ginsberg, 1996). Devolution and block grant strategies of the 1990s have a similar character.

5. Similarly, the incomes of corporate and hedge fund executives depend on federal tax policies that treat income derived from stock speculation differently than that for ordinary productive labor. The disclosure, for example, that 2012 presidential candidate Mitt Romney paid only 15 percent federal tax on millions of dollars of income from investing was a shocking revelation to much of the public. This outrage led to the Buffett rule: to wit, that billionaires should be taxed at rates higher than their secretaries.

6. Furthermore, most major segments of the U.S. populace also receive some pork barrel stake in defense-related production and expenditure (Shefter, 1977). Direct dependence on government for take-home pay reached about 29 percent of total employment in 1976 (estimate of Rose and Peters, 1978: 258). This figure includes central and local government employees, employees of government-owned industries, and employees of private suppliers to government. This value is near those of several large European countries—due to the United States' particularly large "covert public sector," for example, the defense establishment (see Friedberg, 2000).

7. The OECD median that year was 22.52 percent (Lindert, 2004, vol. 1: 12–13, table 1.2). Only Japan had a lower rate of social transfers, though Australia was only slightly ahead of the United States (Lindert, 2004, vol. 2: 14, fig. 1.1).

8. In 1940, for example, the Washington press corps numbered about 700 members. In the year 2000, membership was over 1,800. TV and radio in 1960 had about 200 reporters covering Washington politics. By the year 2000 it was over 2500 (Stanley and Niemi, 2006: 176, table 4-1). And an increasing number of blogs and special news sources focus on specific government institutions and substantive areas of interest, such as defense and agriculture. Furthermore, a growing segment of the public follows presidential campaigns on TV (Stanley and Niemi, 2006: 180, table 4-5).

CHAPTER 8

1. James Surowiecki, "Trump's Other Tax Ploy," *New Yorker*, October 17, 2016: 29.

2. See for example, journalist Eric Levitz's op-ed in the *New York Times*, November 1, 2017, arguing that "America Is Not a 'Center-Right Nation.'"

3. The study is by two political scientists, Gregory Ferenstein and Neil Malhotra of Stanford University. It is under peer review. Karl Russell has summarized the results: *New York Times*, September 7, 2017: B1, B6. It includes a survey of six hundred tech elites and surveys of Republican and Democratic donors and voters.

4. Both quotes are from Michelle Goldberg, "Why Young People Hate Capitalism," *New York Times*, December 5, 2017: A25.

5. Even the provenance of this development is cause for suspicion for Hamburger. He notes that action taken by the Interstate Commerce Commission in 1887 was the first instance of such activity. Its success in centralizing administrative law at the federal level inspired imitation by other government bodies. Hamburger claims that the inspiration for this action came from Prussia, following Otto von Bismarck's successes in expanding the administrative authority of the center. In this view, the push to expand federal administrative authority was an innovation that was a direct import from Europe with its tradition of strong, central states. Therefore, both the provenance of the idea and the actual practice are *foreign* to the American model of government and unconstitutional.

6. These studies recognize that there was, and is, conflict. But Fischer and Hout (2006) argued that it is not uniform, nor is it stationary. Some periods have more conflict than others. As the authors admit, there may have been episodes of intense cultural conflict

like the 1920s and the 1960s, which served as historical markers of change. But these period effects are not well captured by contemporary polling data (Fischer and Hout, 2006: 223–224). On attitudes toward premarital sex, wives working, and homosexuality there are uniform shifts over time toward greater liberalism. Conflict morphs into the uniformity that Tocqueville noted was so characteristic of the U.S. polity. Individualism and equality, he observed, produced a slide toward social conformity.

7. In a later essay (Buchanan, 2005) reflecting on the 1970 book, he admitted that this analysis was a stretch but cautioned that it was a product of the time. The book was prescient in one regard: that conservative discontent with universities would lead to drastic funding reductions.

8. On the positive side, in 2013 forty two states raised student funding by 7.2 percent. But student enrollment grew by 10 percent during this period, thus spreading these resources over a larger population.

9. Again, there is much variation between states. Since 2013 tuition has risen by more than 40 percent in ten states and more than 20 percent in twenty-nine states (Center for Budget Priorities and Policy, 2014).

CHAPTER 9

1. Roger Cohen, "Trump and Britain Big Disrupter," *New York Times*, August 30, 2016: A21.

2. These data were presented in an article in the *New York Times*, January 31, 2018: B1–B2, by Eduardo Porter. Parties were coded as populist if that term was in the name of the party, if the term *populist* occurred in party literature, or if knowledgeable sources like newspapers described the party and its ideology as populist.

3. I owe this insight to my colleague John Boli.

4. This is even true of Republican respondents who themselves have a college education. This does not mean that these respondents will not encourage their children to go to college. They told pollsters that they would. The implicit point is that they doubt the efficacy of higher education for other people's children.

5. Unwanted intrusion of government into people's private affairs has been a staple of the American creed. It thrives on the far right of the Republican Party. And it finds a ready audience among corporate elites and increasingly among working-class voters, who have come to see the state as an enemy. Even the very liberal technocrats in areas like Silicon Valley are hostile to government regulation and the power of unions in the workplace (see Chapter 6). And many Democratic voters are wary of the taxing and regulatory power of the state. Many of the latter voted for Trump, who won overwhelmingly among blue-collar voters.

6. John Boli suggested this idea to me in personal communication.

7. Declining American hegemony has intensified feelings of loss and stoked conflict over the future direction the American nation-state should take (Zolberg, 2002). Myths of cultural superiority die hard among ex-hegemonic powers. They are a source of hubris that undermines change. Such a history appears to haunt Britain, for example. While England has diluted its national identity and clings to the special partnership with the United States as a source of superpower status, its conservative elites are hostile to the European Union. And within the EU, the British and Irish populations are the least likely to identify with Europe and the EU (for evidence see Fligstein, 2008: 143ff, 156). England seems to want the trade advantages associated with a large common market, but without any dilution of

national sovereignty. A history of hegemony, it appears, may reinforce path dependence, rather than opening the way for potential new models of national political development.

8. The results of this poll were published in the *Washington Post*, April 7, 2018: A1, A7.

CHAPTER 10

1. I am indebted to John Boli for this insight.

2. See Adam Hochschild, "Gun Culture," *New York Review of Books* 55, no. 6 (April 5, 2018): 4–10.

3. Eric Hauser, an advisor for the AFL-CIO, argues that "people have been angry for more than a generation about their difficulty in moving ahead despite their best efforts. There has been too much acceptance on the part of elites, including Democrats, that a little bit of trying is good enough." Their stance as warriors on social libertarian issues combined with their appeasement on economic ones has cost them the support of blue-collar voters.

4. One result was to change how corporate elites were compensated. The latter were increasingly turned into shareholders by the strategy of using stock options as rewards for performance. Success was increasingly defined as increasing share prices. This tactic was supposed to align their interests with those of the corporation. Profitability in the short run became a major goal for corporate executives because of this new metric of success.

5. David Leonhardt, "When Jobs Are Bountiful and Pay Isn't," *New York Times*, October 25, 2006: C1.

6. Brian Stelter, "Talk Radio Face-Off Approaches," *New York Times*, April 2, 2012: B1.

7. See the *New York Times*, March 18–20, 2018. This information was gained without the permission of the users and was given to Cambridge Analytica and the Trump organization for free.

8. Sinan Aral, "How Lies Spread Online," *New York Times*, March 11, 2018: 6. The research was published in *Science*, March 8, 2018.

9. Zeynep Tufekci, "YouTube, the Great Radicalizer," *New York Times*, March 6, 2018: 6.

10. See Andrew Marantz, "Anti-Social Media," *New Yorker*, March 19, 2018: 64. Users were livid when Facebook published the news. It has since ceased doing such research or admitting that it does it.

11. Survey evidence confirms that confidence and trust in most social institutions has declined since the 1950s. Trust in fellow citizens has also declined (Putnam, 2000; Lane, 1999; Steurle et al., 1998; Paxton, 1999; Lipset and Schneider, 1983; T. Smith, "Trends," 2012). The dissemination of such conflict imagery by parties and the media may also be one of the reasons that Americans have lost confidence in many of their basic institutions and in each other.

Trust and confidence in the media itself has also plummeted (Pew Research Center for People and the Press, 2004a; 2010). There have been steep drops in the believability of the press and TV between 1985 and 2002 (Pew Center for the Study of the Press, 2004: 4–6). The same survey found that newspaper believability fell from 80 percent to 59 percent. The major TV networks' credibility ratings also dropped during this period from 80 percent to 65 percent. And local news saw declines in viewers' credibility ratings. Earlier studies report similar findings, starting in the 1970s (Fanet al., 2001).

12. The following empirical data indicate how far this process has come for the population at large. Distrust of the media has grown, and people read or view primarily media

whose viewpoint they agree with (*Washington Post*, January 12, 2004: A6). Distrust of the media is now pronounced among *highly politicized* groups. In 2004, 47 percent of conservative Republicans and 36 percent of liberal Democrats reported that the media are biased in favor of the other party (*Washington Post*, January 12, 2004: A6). Overall, 39 percent of the adult population reported seeing media bias, whereas 38 percent did not. Over time this perception of bias has *increased* considerably. In 2010, 82 percent of the population reported finding bias in news coverage! This doubt does not spare even the most reputable media, such as the *New York Times*, MSNBC, Fox News, and the *Wall Street Journal* (Pew, 2010).

Diverse groups, however, see distinct kinds of bias in the news. The perception of bias is highly colored by political identification. 43 percent of the public says the bias of news media is a liberal one, while 23 percent think it is a conservative one. And Republicans are far more skeptical of most major news sources than Democrats (Pew Center, 2010: 5). The exception is Fox News. 41 percent of conservatives believe all or most of its news reporting while only 21 percent of Democrats respond this way. These findings suggest that the neoliberal critique of the news has been effective.

As one would expect, the choice of news outlets is also strongly affected by ideology. Pew put together a portrait of four groups in terms of their choices of news sources. For a Tea Party supporter the two most popular choices were Rush Limbaugh and Glenn Beck. For a gay rights supporter, the *New York Times* and the *Colbert Report* came in first and second. For National Rifle Association (NRA) supporter, Rush Limbaugh and Sean Hannity were the most popular choices. And for libertarians, the *Wall Street Journal* and the *Colbert Report* were the most popular, but these choices were nowhere as popular as the number one and two for the other groups (Pew, 2010: 5.

13. Hand in hand with this trend is the fact that viewing and reading habits have become more politicized over time (Pew, 2004). Twenty-nine percent of Republicans (vs. 14 percent of Democrats) choose the conservative Fox News channel as their primary source of campaign news. This has undoubtedly increased.

14. For example, the shooting of black teenager Trayvon Martin in Florida produced polarized accounts of what happened, justifying either the shooter or the victim (David Carr, "A Shooting and Instant Polarization," *New York Times*, April 2, 2012: B1).

15. Whether religion provides an integrating link between communities is a subject of empirical debate. The evidence is unclear on whether religious participation forges unity across the community by providing links between different social networks. Putnam and Campbell (2010: 1–37, 443ff) claim that it does and thus unites Americans. But their evidence is weak on this point and contradicts the conclusions of more sophisticated analyses (see Sherkat, 2012). DiPrete and colleagues (2011) analyze the General Social Survey data from 2006 using network analysis and find that the hopes that broader social networks provide "bridging" social capital are not supported. They find that while Americans are not as isolated as extreme estimates would suggest, the larger acquaintanceship networks are perceived to be as segregated as the smaller ones. Furthermore, they find that while people do not always know the religiosity, political ideology, family behaviors, or socioeconomic status of their acquaintances, perceived social divisions are high in these larger acquaintanceship networks. They conclude that the major challenge to social integration today comes from the tendency of many Americans to isolate themselves from others who differ on race, political ideology, level of religiosity, and other salient aspects of social identity.

CHAPTER 11

1. I am indebted to John Boli for this insight.

2. A recent study by the National Academies of Science (June 7, 2018) found that 50 percent of women in university science programs experienced sexual harassment from fellow students *and* professors. This ranged from disparaging public comments about them to unwanted sexual fondling and rape.

3. For a more optimistic view see Kensworthy (2014).

4. This example also indicates how far the American economy has come in terms of deregulation. The *Times* article referenced earlier also notes that until the early 1980s, stock buybacks were considered borderline illegal because it opened the company up to charges of manipulating their share price. But in 1982 the Securities and Exchange Commission adopted a rule that gave the green light to most such share repurchases, if certain guidelines were followed. Corporations then started using more of their profits to buy back their own shares, giving investors bigger pieces of the company. This pattern has continued. The result is that twenty years ago companies spent four times as much on new plants, research, and development as they did on buybacks. This is one way that inequality stultifies economic growth and a full-employment economy.

5. There is much other adverse news on the economy. Wealth inequality has dramatically worsened. This is particularly true in families with children under age eighteen. A policy paper by two researchers at Duke and Northwestern shows that between 1989 and 2013, the bottom 50 percent of income earners lost 260 percent during this period. The next 40 percent lost 6 percent. Those at the bottom ended up with a median net worth of –$233, that is, in debt. The next 40 percent had a median net worth of $68,974. At the top, the 1 percent gained an average of 156 percent while the next 9 percent gained an average of 54 percent. At the top, median net worth was $5.2 million, while the next 9 percent had a net worth of $584,850 (*New York Times*, May 20, 2018: A-7). The elderly (families with no children and one person over sixty-five) have, however, done well during the same period. This is largely due to the lower costs of education and housing prices they experienced. The bottom 50 percent gained 70 percent during this period, while the top 1 percent gained 69 percent. The median net worth of the bottom 50 percent is $46,020, while that of the top 1 percent is $11.3 million (*Washington Post*, March 31, 2018: A12). If other benefits of the law are factored in, the richest Americans will get a tax break of $51,140 while the poorest will get a $60 break.

Middle-class jobs have also disappeared as firms have merged and introduced labor-saving technology. The result is that most of the gains in productivity have benefited the incomes of the top 10 percent, and particularly the 1 percent who exercise financial control over the economy. For example, the Tax Policy Center estimates that the new tax bill will give families in the top 1 percent a $33,000 tax cut while those in the poorest income bracket will get a rebate of $40. (Christina Gibson-David and Christine Percheski, "The Wealth Gap Hits Families Hardest," *New York Times*, May 20, 2018, Opinion Section: 7).

6. Roger Cohen, "Trump and Britain's Big Disrupter," *New York Times*, August 30, 2016: A21.

7. Obamacare is a case in point. Critics can point to the fact that premiums have gone up and many can no longer choose the doctors and health networks that they have had in the past. Proponents argue that the Affordable Care Act increased access to insurance for more than twenty million people and lowered the overall rate of increase in health care costs. It did so by allowing young people to stay on their parents' insurance until age

twenty-six, forced insurance companies to accept enrollees regardless of previous health conditions, and leveled the price that insurance companies could charge enrollees. What both sides failed to acknowledge is that adding large numbers of sicker (e.g., rural populations) people who had never had insurance before to the health care insurance rolls would increase medical costs and cut profit margins for insurance companies. And under these conditions many insurers would pull out of such health care markets, decreasing competition, increasing prices, and leaving a vacuum and a legal nightmare about whether the federal government could step in and set up federal exchanges when states wouldn't set up their own.

8. Quoted in Julie Zauner, "Behind the (Trump) Music," *Washington Post*, June 9, 2018: B2. The article deals with the history of the song "God Bless America."

9. Under these circumstances villagers often support radical movements like ISIS. The trade-off for them is personal and family security and government that works in exchange for absolute obedience. The radicals provide law and order, clean streets, regular garbage pickup—in short, a working government versus violent anarchy. See "The ISIS Files," *New York Times*, April 8, 2018: Special Report.

10. The Justice Department under its chief Jeff Sessions, for example, is trying to roll back both LGBT rights and voting rights by backing cases that challenge established legal principles and twenty years of Justice Department policy. Under Sessions, the Justice Department is backing cases involving extreme racial gerrymandering of voting districts in Ohio, which previous Justice Departments refused to support. There is also an attack on immigrants, Muslims, and undocumented workers and children from Mexico and Latin America. Nativism has gone through a renaissance—with support from the White House. Neo-Nazi groups, while small, have reemerged in public and so have other hate groups like the Ku Klux Klan. They feel empowered enough to present their racial hatred in public without fear of sanction. Social media is buzzing with hate speech.

11. These are just some of the major studies of this problem: Burnham, 1984; Franklin, 2004; Teixeira and Rogers, 2000; H. Allen and Allen, 1981; Axelrod, 1972; Kleppner, 1982; Ladd, 1978; G. Powell, 1986; Zukin et al., 2006.

12. See also Eduardo Porter, "How Dysfunction Threatens U.S. Democracy," *New York Times*, January 4, 2017: B1.

References

Aberbach, Joel, Robert Putnam, and Bert Rockman. 1981. *Bureaucrats and Politicians in Western Democracies*. Cambridge, MA: Harvard University Press.

Abramovitz, Alan, 1984, "National Issues, Strategic Politicians, and Voting Behavior in the 1980 and 1982 Congressional Elections." *American Journal of Political Science* 28, no. 4 (November): 710–721.

Abramovitz, Alan, and Kyle Saunders. 2006. "Exploring the Bases of Partisanship in the American Electorate," *Political Research Quarterly* 59 (June): 175–187.

Abrams, Richard. 2006. *America Transformed: Sixty Years of Revolutionary Change, 1941–2001*. Cambridge, UK: Cambridge University Press.

Abramson, Paul. 1977. *The Political Socialization of Black Americans: A Critical Evaluation of Research on Efficacy and Trust*. New York: Free Press.

Abramson, Paul, and John Aldrich. 1979. "The Decline of Electoral Participation in America." *American Political Science Review* 76 (September): 502–521.

Abramson, Paul, John Aldrich, and David Rohde. 1986. *Change and Continuity in the 1984 Elections*. Washington, DC: Congressional Quarterly Press.

Agranoff, Robert. 1978. "The New Style of Campaigning: The Decline of Party and the Rise of Candidate Centered Technology." In *Parties and Elections in an Anti-Party Age*, edited by Jeff Fishel, 230–240. Bloomington: Indiana University Press.

Agre, Phil. 2003. "The Practical Republic: Social Skills and the Progress of Citizenship." In *Community in the Digital Age: Philosophy and Practice*, 201–224. Lanham, MD: Rowman and Littlefield.

Alexander, H., 1979. *Political Finance*, Vol. 5. Beverly Hills, CA: Sage.

———. 1980. *Financing Politics: Money, Elections, and Political Reform*, 2nd ed. Washington, DC: Congressional Quarterly Press.

Alford, Robert, and Roger Friedland. 1975. "Political Participation and Public Policy." *Annual Review of Sociology* 1: 429–479.

Allen, Frederick Lewis. 1931. *Only Yesterday: An Informal History of the 1920s*. New York: Perennial.

Allen, H., and K. W. Allen. 1981. "Vote Fraud and Data Validity." In *Analyzing Electoral History: A Guide to the Study of American Voter Behavior*, edited by Jerome M. Clubb, William H. Flanigan, and Nancy H. Zingale, 153–195. Beverly Hills, CA: Sage.

Almond, G. and S. Verba. 1963. *The Civic Culture*. Princeton, NJ: Princeton University Press.

Amenta, Edward. 1998. *Bold Relief: Institutional Politics and the Origins of Modern American Social Policy*. Princeton, NJ: Princeton University Press.

Anderson, Benedict. 1983. *Imagined Communities: Reflections on the Origin and Spread of Nationalism*. London: Verso Books.

Andrain, Charles, and David Apter. 1995. *Political Protest and Social Change*. New York: New York University Press.

Andres, Gary. 1985. "Business Involvement in Campaign Finance: Factors Influencing the Decision to Form a Corporate PAC." *PS: Political Science and Politics* 18, no. 2: 210–220.

Andris, Clio, David Lee, Marcus Hamilton, Mauro Martino, Christian Gunning, and John Selden. 2015. "The Rise of Partisanship and Super-Cooperators in the U.S. House of Representatives." *PLOS One* (April 21): 1–9.

Angwin, Julia, and Sarah McBride. 2005. "Radio's Bush-Bashing Air America Is Back in Fighting Form." *Wall Street Journal*, January 20.

Associated Press and NORC Center for Public Affairs Research. 2014. "The People's Agenda: America's Priorities and Outlook for 2014." http://www.apnorc.org/projects/Pages/the-peoples-agenda-americas-priorities-and-outlook.aspx.

Attewell, Steven. 2012. "Competing Visions of the Past." New America Foundation Series on the Social Contract Initiative, Washington, DC, December.

Auerbach, Joel D. 1981. *Western Democracies*. Cambridge, MA: Harvard University Press.

Auletta, Ken. 2011. "Media Births and Deaths." *New Yorker*, December 6.

Axelrod, R. 1972. "Where the Voter Came From: An Analysis of Electoral Coalitions 1952." *American Political Science Review* 66 (March): 11–20.

Azmanova, Albena. 2011. "After the Left-Right (Dis)continuum: Globalization and the Remaking of Europe's Geography." *International Political Sociology* 5: 384–407.

Badie, Bertrand, and Pierre Birnbaum. 1983. *The Sociology of the State*. Chicago: University of Chicago Press.

Bailyn, Bernard. 1967. *The Ideological Origins of the American Revolution*. Cambridge, MA: Harvard University Press.

Baker, David P. 2014. *The Schooled Society*. Stanford, CA: Stanford University Press.

Baker, David P., and G. LeTendre. 2005. *Global Similarities and National Differences*. Stanford, CA: Stanford University Press.

Baldassarri, Delia, and Andrew Gelman. 2008. "Partisans Without Constraint: Political Polarization and Trends in American Public Opinion." *American Journal of Sociology* 114, no. 2 (September): 408–447.

Balz, Dan. 2014. "Why So Many Americans Hate Politics." *Washington Post*, August 23. https://www.washingtonpost.com/politics/why-so-many-americans-hate-politics/2014/08/23/e56dbaf0-18d5-11e4-9e3b-7f2f110c6265_story.html?utm_term=.68cf4bcb8173.

Banfield, Edward, and James Q. Wilson. 1963. *City Politics*. Cambridge, MA: Harvard University Press.

Barry, Jeffrey. 1999. "The Rise of Citizens' Groups." In *Civic Engagement in American Democracy*, edited by Theda Skocpol and Morris Fiorina, 367–395. Washington, DC: Brookings Institution Press.

Bartlett, Bruce. 2011. "What Your Taxes Do (and Don't) Buy for You." *New York Times*, June 7. https://economix.blogs.nytimes.com/2011/06/07/health-care-costs-and-the-tax-burden/.

———. 2012. *The Benefit and the Burden*. New York: Simon and Schuster.

Bauman, Zygmunt. 2013. *Liquid Modernity*. New York: Polity Press.

Baumgartner, Jody, and Jonathan Morris. 2006. "The Daily Show Effect: Candidate Evaluations, Efficacy, and American Youth." *American Politics Research* 34: 341–367.

Beck, Colin J., G. S. Drori, and John W. Meyer. 2012. "World Influences on Human Rights Language in Constitutions: A Cross National Study." *International Sociology* 27, no. 4 (May): 483–501.

Beck, Paul Allen. 1974. "A Socialization Theory of Partisan Re-Alignment." In *The Politics of Future Citizens*, edited by Paul Niemi, 199–219. San Francisco: Jossey-Bass.

Becker, Gary. 1994. *Human Capital Revisited*. Chicago: University of Chicago Press.

Beckett, Katherine. 1994. "Setting the Public Agenda: "Street Crime and Drug Use in American Politics." *Social Problems* 41, no. 3: 425–444.

Beer, S. H. 1971. "Group Representation in Britain and the U.S." In *Political Sociology*, edited by A. Pizzorno, 191–207. Baltimore: Penguin.

Bell, Daniel. 1960. *The End of Ideology*. New York: Doubleday.

———. 1973. *The Coming of Post Industrial Society*. New York: Basic Books.

Bellah, Robert. 1975. *The Broken Covenant*. New York: Seabury Press.

Bellah, Robert, Richard Madsen, William Sullivan, Ann Swidler, and Steven Tipton. 1996. *Habits of the Heart*, updated ed. Berkeley: University of California Press.

Bellah, Robert, and Steven Tipton, eds. 2006. *The Robert Bellah Reader*. Durham, NC: Duke University Press.

Bendix, Reinhardt. 1964. *Nation Building and Citizenship*. New York: Wiley.

———. 1978. *Kings or People*. New York: Basic Books.

Beniger, James Jr., and Susan Herbst. 1990. "Mass Media and Public Opinion: Emergence of an Institution." In *Change in Societal Institutions*, edited by Maureen T. Hallinan, David M. Klein, and Jennifer Glass, 211–231. New York: Plenum Press.

Bernstein, J. M. 2010. "The Very Angry Tea Party." *New York Times*, June 13. https://opinionator.blogs.nytimes.com/2010/06/13/the-very-angry-tea-party/.

Berger, Peter. 1967. *The Sacred Canopy*. New York: Doubleday Anchor Books.

Berger, Peter L., and Thomas Luckmann. 1967. *The Social Construction of Reality*. New York: Doubleday Anchor Books.

Berkovitch, Nitza. 1999. "The Emergence and Transformation of the International Women's Movement." In *Constructing World Culture*, edited by John Boli and George Thomas, 100–127. Stanford, CA: Stanford University Press.

Bibby, J., J. Gibson, C. Cotter, and R. Huckshorn. 1983. "Trends in Party Organizational Strength, 1960–1980." *International Political Science Review* 4, no. 1: 21–28.

Bibby, J., and Robert Huckshorn. 1978. "The Republican Party in American Politics." In *Parties and Elections in an Anti-Party Age*, edited by Jeff Fishel, 55–66. Bloomington: Indiana University Press.

Block, Fred. 1987. *Revising State Theory: Essays in Politics and Post Industrialism*. Philadelphia: Temple University Press.

Block, Fred, Richard Cloward, Barbara Ehrenreich, and Frances Piven. 1987. *The Mean Season: The Attack on the Welfare State*. New York: Pantheon Books.

Bobo, Lawrence, James Kluegel, and Ryan Smith. 1996. "Laissez Faire Racism: The Crystallization of a 'Kinder, Gentler' Anti-Black Ideology." In *Racial Attitudes in the 1990s: Continuity and Change*, edited by Steven Tuch and Jack Martin, 17–162. Westport, CT: Praeger.

Boggs, Carl. 1986. *Social Movements and Political Power: Emerging Forms of Radicalism in the West*. Philadelphia: Temple University Press.

Boies, John. 1989. "Money, Business and the State: Material Interests, Fortune 500 Corporations, and the Size of Political Action Committees." *American Sociological Review* 54, no. 5 (October): 821–833.

Boli, John. 1989. *New Citizens for a New Society*. New York: Pergamon Press.

Boli, John, and George Thomas, eds. 1999. *Constructing World Culture*. Stanford, CA: Stanford University Press.

Boli, John, and M. A. Elliot. 2008. "Facade Diversity: The Individualization of Cultural Difference." *International Sociology* 23, no. 4: 540–560.

Boli-Bennett, John. 1979. "The Ideology of Expanding State Authority in National Constitutions, 1870–1970." In *National Development and the World System*, edited by John Meyer and Michael Hannan, 222–238. Chicago: University of Chicago Press.

Bonikowski, Bart, and Paul DiMaggio. 2016. "Varieties of American Popular Nationalism." *American Sociological Review* 81, no. 5 (October): 949–981.

Boswell, Terry, and Albert Bergesen, eds. 1987. *America's Changing Role in the World System*. New York: Praeger.

Boyer, Paul. 2012. *American History: A Very Short Introduction*. New York: Oxford University Press.

Braungart, Richard. 1971. "Family Status, Socialization and Student Politics: A Multivariate Analysis." *American Journal of Sociology* 77 (July): 108–130.

Brehm, John. 1989. "How Survey Non-Response Damages Political Analysis." Paper presented at the annual meeting of the American Political Science Association, Atlanta, GA.

———. 1993. *The Phantom Respondents*. Ann Arbor: University of Michigan Press.

Bright, Charles, and Susan Harding, eds. 1984. *Statemaking and Social Movements*. Ann Arbor: University of Michigan Press.

Broder, D. 1972. *The Party's Over: The Failure of Politics in America*. New York: Harper and Row.

Brody, Richard. 1978. "The Puzzle of Political Participation in America." In *The New Political System*, edited by A. King. Washington, DC: American Enterprise Institute.

Bromley, Patricia, John W. Meyer, and R. O. Ramirez. 2011. "Student-Centeredness in Social Science Textbooks, 1970–2008: A Cross National Study." *Social Forces* 90, no. 2: 547–570.

Brook, Daniel. 2007. *The Trap*. New York: Times Books.

Brooks, Clem, and Jeff Manza. 2013. "The Politics of Publics: The Public Mind in the Short and Long Term." *American Sociological Review* 78, no. 5 (October): 727–749.

Brown, L. 1983. *New Policies, New Politics: Government's Response to Government Growth*. Washington, DC: Brookings Institution Press.

Browne, William. P. 1983. "Mobilizing and Activating Group Demands: The American Agriculture Movement." *Social Science Quarterly* 64 (March): 19–34.

Brubaker, Rogers. 1992. *Citizenship and Nationhood in France and Germany*. Cambridge, MA: Harvard University Press.

Bruni, Frank. 2012. "Rethinking His Religion." *New York Times*, March 24. https://www.nytimes.com/2012/03/25/opinion/sunday/bruni-a-catholic-classmate-rethinks-his-religion.html.

Buchanan, James M. 2005. "Reflections After Three Decades." In *Anarchy, State and Public Choice*, edited by Edward Stringham. Cheltenham, UK: Edward Elgar.

Buchanan, James M., and Nicos Devletoglou. 1970. *Academia in Anarchy: An Economic Analysis*, New York: Basic Books.

Burawoy, Michael. 2012. "Review Essay: The Great American University by Jonathan Cole." *Contemporary Sociology* 41, no. 2 (March): 139–150.

Burnham, Walter Dean. 1970. *Critical Elections and the Mainsprings of American Politics*. New York: Norton.

———. 1965. "The Changing Shape of the American Political Universe." *American Political Science Review* 59, no. 1: 7–28.

———. 1984. "Political Parties, Political Mobilization, and Political Demobilization." In *The Political Economy: Readings in the Politics and Economics of American Public Policy*, edited by Thomas Ferguson and Joel Rogers, 140–148. Armonk, NY: Sharpe.

———. 1995. *The American Prospect Reader in American Politics*. Chatham, NJ: Chatham House.

Burstein, Paul. 1985. *Discrimination, Jobs and Politics*. Chicago: University of Chicago Press.

Bybee, Carl R., Jack M. McLeod, William D. Luetscher, and Gina Garramone. 1981. "Mass Communication and Voter Volatility." *Public Opinion Quarterly* 45, no. 1: 69–90.

Cahn, Naomi, and June Carbone. 2010. *Red Families vs. Blue Families: Legal Polarization and the Creation of Culture*. New York: Oxford University Press.

Cancela, Joao, and Benny Guys. 2016. "Explaining Voter Turnout." *Electoral Studies* 42 (June): 264–275.

Canovan, M. 1981. *Populism*. New York: Harcourt, Brace.

Caplan, Bryan. 2007. *The Myth of the Rational Voter: Why Democracies Choose Bad Policies*. Princeton, NJ: Princeton University Press.

Caplow, Theodore. 1991. *American Social Trends*. New York: Harcourt Brace Jovanovich.

Cappell, Charles, and David H. Kamens. 2006a. "The Politicization of the Media and the Rise of Media Distrust, 1973–2004: Explanations for the Long-Term Decline of Confidence in the American Media." Unpublished manuscript.

Cappell, Charles, and David Kamens. 2006b. "Politicized Media Systems and Public Distrust of the Media, 1974–2004." Unpublished manuscript.

Cappella, Joseph, and Kathleen Hall Jamieson. 1997. *Spiral of Cynicism: The Press and the Public Good*. New York: Oxford University Press.

Castells, Manuel. 1997. *The Power of Identity*. London: Blackwell.

Cavanagh, T., and James Sundquist. 1985. "Contours of a New Re-Alignment." In *The New Direction in American Politics*, edited by John E. Chubb and Paul E. Peterson, 33–69. Washington, DC: Brookings Institution Press.

Cavanagh, T. E. 1982–83. "Dispersion of Authority in the U.S. House." *Political Science Quarterly* 97, no. 4: 623–639.

Charles, Maria, and Karen Bradley. 2009. "Indulging Our Gendered Selves: Sex Segregation by Field of Study in 44 Countries." *American Journal of Sociology* 114, no. 4: 924–976.

Chaves, Mark, and Shawna Anderson. 2012. "Continuity and Change in American Religion, 1972–2008." In *Social Trends in American Life: Findings from the General Social Survey Since 1972*, edited by Peter Marsden, 212–238. Princeton, NJ: Princeton University Press.

Chirot, Daniel. 1977. "The American World System (1945–1975)." In *Social Change in the Twentieth Century*, by Daniel Chirot, 149–184. New York: Harcourt Brace Jovanovich.

Choi, Joon Nak. 2011. "External Influences on U.S. Think Tanks: Epistemic Communities and Vast Conspiracies." Unpublished manuscript, Shorenstein Asia-Pacific Research Center, Stanford University.

Christian Science Monitor. 2011. "Could You Pass a US Citizenship Test?" January 4. https://www.csmonitor.com/USA/2011/0104/Could-you-pass-a-US-citizenship-test/Who-signs-bills newspaper/

Clark, Burton. 1972. "The Organizational Saga in Higher Education." *Administrative Science Quarterly* 17: 178–183.

Club, Jerome. 1985. "Federalism and the Bias for Centralization." In *The New Direction in American Politics*, edited by John E. Chubb and Paul E. Peterson, 273–307. Washington, DC: Brookings Institution Press.

Club, Jerome, William Flanigan, and Nancy Zingale. 1980. *Partisan Realignment: Voters, Parties and Government in American History*. Beverly Hills, CA: Sage.

Chubb, John, and Paul Peterson. 1985. "Re-Alignment and Institutionalization." In *The New Direction in American Politics*, edited by John E. Chubb and Paul E. Peterson, 1–33. Washington, DC: Brookings Institution Press.

Cobb, Roger, and Charles Elder. 1983. *Participation in American Politics: The Dynamics of Agenda Building*. Baltimore: Johns Hopkins University Press.

Cohen, Michael, James March, and Johan Olsen. 1972. "A Garbage Can Model of Organizational Choice." *Administrative Science Quarterly* 17, no. 1 (March): 1–25.

Cohen, P. C. 1982. *A Calculating People: The Spread of Numeracy in Early America*. Chicago: University of Chicago Press.

Cole, Wade. 2012a. "A Civil Religion for World Society." *Sociological Forum* 27, no. 4 (December): 937–960.

———. 2012b. "Human Rights as Myth and Ceremony: Re-Evaluating the Effects of Human Rights Treaties, 1981–2007." *American Journal of Sociology* 117, no. 4 (January): 1131–1171.

Cole, Wade, and F. O. Ramirez. 2013. "Conditional De-Coupling: Assessing the Impact of National Human Rights Institutions, 1981–2004." *American Sociological Review* 78, no. 4: 702–725.

Coleman, James. 1974. *Power and the Structure of Society*. New York: Norton.

———. 1982. *The Asymmetric Society*. Syracuse, NY: Syracuse University Press.

———. 1986. *Individual Interests and Collective Action*. Cambridge, UK: Cambridge University Press.

Collins, Randall. 1994. *Four Sociological Traditions*. New York: Oxford University Press.

———. 1979. *The Credential Society: A Historical Sociology of Education and Stratification*. New York: Academic Press.

———. 1992. *Sociological Insight*. New York: Oxford University Press.

———. 1999. "The European Sociological Tradition and 21st Century World Sociology." In *Sociology for the 21st Century*, edited by J. Abu-Lugod, 26–42. Chicago: University of Chicago Press.

Collins, Randall, and Neal Hickman. 1991. "Altruism and Culture as Social Products." *Voluntas* 2, no. 2: 1–16.

Commager, Henry Steele. 1960. *The Era of Reform, 1830–1860*. New York: Van Nostrand Reinhold.

Congressional Budget Office. 2007. *Federal Support for Research and Development*. June. Washington, DC: Congressional Budget Office.

Converse, Philip. 1972. "Change in the American Electorate." In *The Human Meaning of Social Change*, edited by Angus Campbell and Philip Converse. New York: Macmillan.

———. 1976. *The Dynamics of Party Support*. Beverly Hills, CA: Sage.

Costa, Donna, and Mathew E. Kahn. 2001. "Understanding the Decline in Social Capital, 1952–1998." Working Paper 8295. Cambridge, MA: National Bureau of Economic Research.

Cotter, C., and J. Bibby. 1980. "Institutional Development of Parties and the Thesis of Party Decline." *Political Science Quarterly* 95, no. 1: 1–29.

Crenson, Matthew, and Benjamin Ginsberg. 2004. *Downsizing Democracy*. Baltimore: Johns Hopkins University Press.

Crotty, W. J., and G. Jacobsen. 1980. *American Parties in Decline*. Boston: Little, Brown.

Crouch, Colin. 2004. *Post-Democracy*. Cambridge, UK: Polity Press.

Crozier, M. 1964. *The Bureaucratic Phenomenon*. Chicago: University of Chicago Press.

Cunningham, Brent. 2004. "Across the Great Divide: Class." *Columbia Journalism Review* 3 (May–June): 1–16.

Curtis, James E., Douglas Baer, and Edward Grebb. 2001. "Nations of Joiners: Explaining Voluntary Association Membership in Democratic Societies." *American Sociological Review* 66, no. 6: 783–805.

Curtis, James E., Edward Grebb, and Douglas Baer. 1992."Voluntary Association Membership in Fifteen Countries." *American Sociological Review* 57, no. 2 (April): 139–152.

Daalder, Hans. 1987. "European Political Traditions and Processes of Modernization: Groups, the Individual and the State." In *Patterns of Modernity, Vol. 1: The West*, edited by S. N. Eisenstadt, 22–43. New York: New York University Press.

Dahl, Robert. 1957. "Decision-Making in a Democracy: The Role of the Supreme Court in National Policy-Making," *Journal of Public Law* 6 (Fall): 279–295.

———. 1971. *Polyarchy: Participation and Opposition*. New Haven, CT: Yale University Press.

———. 1984. *A Preface to Democracy*. New Haven, CT: Yale University Press.

———. 1994. "The New American Political (Dis)Order." In *The New American Political Order*, by Austin Ranney. Berkeley: University of California Press.

Dalton, Russell. 2002a. *Citizen Politics: Public Opinion and Political Parties in Advanced Industrial Democracies*. New York: Chatham House.

———. 2002b. "Political Cleavages, Issues and Electoral Change." In *Comparing Democracies* 2, edited by L. LeDuc, R. Niemi, and P. Norris, 189–209. London: Sage.

———. 2007. *Democratic Challenges*. Oxford, UK: Oxford University Press.

Dalton, Russell, Scott Flanagan, and Paul Allen Beck. 1984. *Electoral Change in Advanced Industrial Democracy: Realignment or De-Alignment*. Princeton, NJ: Princeton University Press.

Dalton, Russell J., and Martin P. Wattenberg. 1993. "The Not So Simple Act of Voting." In *Political Science: The State of the Discipline*, edited by A. Finifter. Washington, DC: American Political Science Association.

Danner, Mark. 2006. "Iraq: Bush's Fantasy War." *New York Review of Books* (December 21): 81–97.

Demos. 2013. "Stacked Deck: How the Dominance of Politics by the Affluent and Business Undermines Economic Mobility in America." February 28. https://www.demos.org/stacked-deck-how-dominance-politics-affluent-business-undermines-economic-mobility-america.

Dennis, Jack. 1970. "Support for the Institution of Elections by the Mass Public." *American Political Science Review* 74 (September): 833.

———. 1978. "Trends in Public Support for the Party System." In *Parties and Elections in an Anti-Party Age*, edited by Jeff Fishel, 3–22. Bloomington: Indiana University Press.

Diamant, Alfred. 1981. "Bureaucracy and Public Policy in Neo-Corporative Settings: Some European Lessons." *Comparative Politics* 14: 101–124.

Diamond, Sigmund. 1958. "From Organization to Society: Virginia in the Seventeenth Century." *American Journal of Sociology* 63, no. 5 (March): 457–475.

DiMaggio, Paul, John Evans, and Bethany Bryson. 1996. "Have Americans' Social Attitudes Become More Polarized?" *American Journal of Sociology* 102, no. 3 (November): 690–755.

DiPrete, Thomas A., Andrew Gelman, Tyler McCormick, Julien Teitler. and Tian Zheng. 2011. "Segregation in Social Networks Based on Acquaintanceship and Trust." *American Journal of Sociology* 116, no. 4 (January): 1234–1283.

Djelic, Marie-Laure. 2001. *Exporting the American Model.* Oxford, UK: Oxford University Press.

———. 2002. "Does Europe Mean Americanization? The Case of Competition." *Competition and Change* 6, no. 3 (December): 1–18.

Dobbin, Frank. 1994. *Forging Industrial Policy: The U.S., Britain and France in the Railway Age.* Cambridge, UK: Cambridge University Press.

Dobbin, Frank, and Erin Kelly. 2007. "How to Stop Harassment: Professional Construction of Legal Compliance in Organizations." *American Journal of Sociology* 112, no. 4: 1203–1243.

Domhoff, G. William. 2013. *The Myth of Liberal Ascendancy: Corporate Domination from the Great Depression to the Great Depression.* Boulder, CO: Paradigm Press.

Douglas, Mary, and Stephen Tipton. 1982. *Religion and American Spiritual Life in a Secular Age.* Boston: Beacon Press.

Downs, A. 1967. *Inside Bureaucracy.* Boston: Little, Brown.

Drake, Bruce, and Jacob Poushter. 2016. "In Views of Diversity, Many Europeans Are Less Positive Than Americans." Pew Research Center, July 12. http://www.pewresearch.org/fact-tank/2016/07/12/in-views-of-diversity-many-europeans-are-less-positive-than-americans/.

Drori, Gili, John Meyer, Francisco Ramirez, and Evan Schofer. 2003. *Science in the Modern World Polity.* Stanford, CA: Stanford University Press.

Drori, Gili S., John W. Meyer, and Hokyu Hwang. 2006. *Globalization and Organization: World Society and Organizational Change.* Oxford, UK: Oxford University Press.

Durkheim, Emile. (1912) 1961. *Elementary Forms of Religious Life.* New York: Macmillan.

Easterbrook, Gregg. 1986. "Washington: The Business of Politics." *Atlantic Monthly* 258, no. 4 (October): 28–38.

Eckstein, Harry. 1966. *Division and Cohesion in Democracy: A Study of Norway.* Princeton, NJ: Princeton University Press.

The Economist. 2012. "Special Report: For Richer, for Poorer." October 13. https://www.economist.com/special-report/2012/10/13/for-richer-for-poorer.

Edsall, Thomas. 1984. *The New Politics of Inequality.* New York: Norton.

Edsall, Thomas, with Mary Edsall. 1991. *Chain Reaction: The Impact of Race, Rights and Taxes on American Politics.* New York: Norton.

Edwards, Bob, and Michael W. Foley. 1998. "Civil Society and Social Capital Beyond Putnam." *American Behavioral Scientist* 42, no. 1: 124–139.

———. 2001. "Much Ado About Social Capital." *Contemporary Sociology* 30, no. 3: 227–230.

Egan, Rachel. 1996. *Buying a Movement: Right Wing Foundations and American Politics.* Washington, DC: People for the American Way.

Ehrenreich, Barbara. 2012. "Twisting the Phrase 'Culture of Poverty.'" March 16. https://billmoyers.com/2012/03/16/twisting-the-phrase-culture-of-poverty/.

Eisenstadt, S. N., ed. 1987. *Patterns of Modernity, Vol. 1: The West*. New York: New York University Press.

Eisinger, Peter. 1973. "The Conditions of Protest Behavior in American Cities." *American Political Science Review* 67, no. 1 (March): 11–28.

———. 1974. "Racial Differences in Protest Participation." *American Political Science Review* 68, no. 2 (June): 592–606.

Elkin, Stephen, and Karol Soltan, eds. 1999. *Citizen Competence and Democratic Institutions*. University Park: Pennsylvania State University Press.

Enoke, C. H. 1981. "The Growth of the State and Ethnic Mobilization: The American Experience." *Journal of Ethnic and Racial Studies* 4: 123–136.

Epstein, E. 1979. "The Emergence of Political Action Committees." In *Political Finance*, edited by H. Alexander: 125–159. Beverly Hills, CA: Sage.

Etzioni, Amitai. 2001. "Is Bowling Together Sociologically Lite?" *Contemporary Sociology* 30, no. 3: 223–224.

Fainstein, S. S., and N. Fainstein. 1976. "The Future of Community Control." *American Political Science Review* 70, no. 3 (September): 905–923.

Fallows, James. 1996. *Breaking the News: How the Media Undermine American Democracy*. New York: Vintage Books.

Fan, David, Robert Wyatt, and Kathy Keltner. 2001. "The Suicidal Messenger: How Press Reporting Affects Public Confidence in the Press, the Military and Organized Religion." *Communication Research* 28: 826–852.

FCC (Federal Communications Commission). 1985. *Report Concerning the General Fairness Doctrine Obligations of Broadcast Licensees*. 102 F.C.C. 2d 143.

Ferguson, Thomas, and Joel Rogers, eds. 1984. *The Political Economy: Readings in the Politics and Economics of American Public Policy*. Armonk, NY: Sharpe.

Fiala, Robert. 2006. "Educational Ideology and the School Curriculum." In *School Knowledge in Comparative and Historical Perspective*, edited by Aaron Benavot and Cecilia Braslavsky, 15–35. Hong Kong: Springer.

Finer, S. E. 1970. *Comparative Government: An Introduction to the Study of Politics*. London: Pelican Books.

Fiorina, Morris. 1996. *Divided Government*. Boston: Allyn and Bacon.

Fiorina, Morris, et al. 2004. *Culture War? The Myth of a Polarized America*. New York: Longman.

Fischer, Claude. 2010. *Made in America*. Chicago: University of Chicago Press.

Fischer, Claude, and Michael Hout. 2006. "When Americans Disagreed: Cultural Fragmentation and Conflict." In *Century of Difference: How America Changed in the Last One Hundred Years*, 212–240. New York: Russell Sage.

Fischer, Claude, and Greggor Mattson. 2009. "Is America Fragmenting?" *Annual Review of Sociology* 35 (August): 435–455.

Fishel, Jeff. 1978. "American Political Parties and Elections: An Overview." In *Parties and Elections in an Anti-Party Age*, edited by Jeff Fishel, xi–xxxiii. Bloomington: Indiana University Press.

Fitzgerald, Frances. 2007. "The Evangelical Surprise." *New York Review of Books* (April 26): 31–35.

Flacks, Richard. 1967. "The Liberated Generation: An Exploration of the Roots of Student Protest." *Journal of Social Issues* 23, no. 3: 52–75.

———. 1972. *Youth and Social Change*. Chicago: Markham.

Flanagan, Scott, and R. J. Dalton. 1984. "Parties Under Stress: Realignment and De-Alignment in Advanced Industrial Societies." *Western European Politics* 7, no. 1: 7–23.

Fligstein, Neil. 2008. *Euroclash: The EU, European Identity, and the Future of Europe*. New York: Oxford University Press.

Fligstein, Neil, Jonah Brundage, and Michael Schultz. 2017. "Seeing like the Fed: Culture, Cognition and Framing in the Failure to Anticipate the Financial Crisis of 2008." *American Sociological Review* 82, no. 5 (October): 879–909.

Flora, Peter, and Arnold Heidenheimer, eds. 1982. *The Development of Welfare States in Europe and America*. New Brunswick, NJ: Transaction Books.

Foucault, M. 1991. *The Foucault Effect: Studies in Governmentality*. Chicago: University of Chicago Press.

Fourcade, M. 2006. "The Construction of a Global Profession: The Trans-Nationalization of Economics." *American Journal of Sociology* 112, no. 1 (July): 145–195.

Fourcade-Gourinchas, M., and Sarah Babb. 2002. "The Rebirth of the Liberal Creed: Paths to Neo-Liberalism in Four Countries." *American Journal of Sociology* 108, no. 3 (November): 533–580.

Fox, Cybil. 2012. *Three Worlds of Relief: Race, Immigration and the American Welfare State from the Progressive Era to the New Deal*. Princeton, NJ: Princeton University Press.

Frank, David, Bayliss Camp, and Steven Boutcher. 2010. "Worldwide Trends in the Criminal Regulation of Sex, 1945–2005." *American Sociological Review* 75, no. 6 (December): 867–893.

Frank, David, John W. Meyer, and David Miyahara. 1995. "The Individualist Polity and the Centrality of Psychology." *American Sociological Review* 60, no. 3 (June): 360–377.

Frank, David J., and Jay Gabler. 2006. *Restructuring the University*. Stanford, CA: Stanford University Press.

Frank, David J., and John W. Meyer. 2002. "The Profusion of Individual Roles and Identities in the Postwar Period." *Sociological Theory* 20, no. 1 (March): 86–105.

Frankel, Jeffrey. 2012. "Sex, Money, Red States and Blue States." *Vox* (October 2). http://voxeu.org/article/which-50-states-practise-personal-responsibility.

Franklin, Mark N. 2002. "The Dynamics of Electoral Participation." In *Comparing Democracies 2: New Challenges in the Study of Elections and Voting*, edited by L. LeDuc, R. Niemi, and P. Norris, 148–168. London: Sage.

———. 2004. *Voter Turnout and the Dynamics of Electoral Competition in Established Democracies Since 1945*. Cambridge, UK: Cambridge University Press.

Freedland, Jonathan. 2007. "Bush's Amazing Achievement." *New York Review of Books* (June 14): 16–22.

Freeland, Christine. 2011. "The Rise of the New Global Elite." *The Atlantic* 307, no. 1: 44–55.

Freeman, Joshua. 2012. *American Empire, 1945–2000: The Rise of a Global Power and the Democratic Revolution at Home*. New York: Viking Press.

Freeman, Richard. 2007. *America Works: Critical Thoughts on the Exceptional U.S. Labor Market*. New York: Russell Sage.

Friedberg, Aaron. 2000. *In the Shadow of the Garrison State*. Princeton, NJ: Princeton University Press.

Friedland, Roger. 1983. *Power and Crisis in the City: Corporations, Unions and Public Policy*. New York: Schocken Books.

Friedman, Lawrence. 1973. *A History of American Law*. New York: Simon and Schuster.

———. 2004. *Law in America*. New York: Modern Library.

Froese, Paul, and Christopher Bader. 2010. *America's Four Gods*. New York: Oxford University Press.

Gaddis, John Lewis. 2005. *The Cold War: A New History*. London: Penguin.

Galbraith, John Kenneth. 1971. *The New Industrial State*, 2nd rev. ed. New York: New American Books.

Gans, Herbert. 1979. *Deciding What's News*. New York: Random House.

Gans, Herbert J. 1988. *Middle American Individualism: Political Participation and Liberal Democracy*. New York: Oxford University Press.

Gans, Herbert, 2004, *Democracy and the News*, Oxford: Oxford University Press.

Garin, Geoff. 2017. "Survey of Voters in 18 Battleground States," 1–11. January 3. Washington, DC: Hart Associates.

Gauchat, Gordon. 2012. "The Politicization of Science in the Public Sphere: A Study of Public Trust in the U.S., 1974–2010." *American Sociological Review* 77, no. 2 (April): 167–188.

Geer, John G. 2006. *In Defense of Negativity: Attack Ads in Presidential Campaigns*. Chicago: University of Chicago Press.

Geiger, Roger. 2009. "Culture, Careers, Knowledge and Money: Change in American Higher Education Since 1980." Keynote address to German Gesellschaft für Amerikastudien, Jena, Germany, June 4.

Geoghegan, Thomas. 2014. *Only One Thing Can Save Us: Why America Needs a New Kind of Labor Movement*. New York: New Press.

Gerbner, George, Larry Gross, Michael Morgan, and Nancy Signorielli. 1984. "Political Correlates of Television Viewing." *Public Opinion Quarterly* 48, no. 1: 283–300.

Gibson, J., C. P. Cotter, J. Bibby, and R. Huckshorn. 1983. "Assessing Party Organizational Strength." *American Journal of Political Science* 27, no. 2 (May): 193–223.

———. 1985. "Whither the Local Parties? A Cross Sectional and Longitudinal Analysis of the Strength of Party Organizations." *American Journal of Political Science* 29, no. 1: 139–161.

Giddens, Anthony. 1983. *The Constitution of Society*. Berkeley: University of California Press.

———. 1986. *The Nation-State and Violence*. Berkeley: University of California Press.

Ginsberg, Benjamin. 1984. "Money and Power: The New Political Economy of American Elections." In *The Political Economy: Readings in the Politics and Economics of American Public Policy*, edited by Thomas Ferguson and Joel Rogers, 163–179. Armonk, NY: Sharpe.

———. 1986. *The Captive Public: How Mass Opinion Promotes State Power*. New York: Basic Books.

Ginsberg, Benjamin, Theodore Lowi, and Margaret Weir. 2005. *We the People*. New York: Norton.

Ginsberg, Benjamin, and Martin Shefter. 1985. "Institutionalizing the Reagan Regime." Paper presented at the annual meeting of the American Political Science Association, August 25–September 2.

———. 1999. *Politics by Other Means: The Declining Importance of Elections in America*, rev. ed. New York: Norton.

Gitlin, Todd. 1980. *The Whole World Is Watching: The Mass Media in the Making and Unmaking of the New Left.* Berkeley: University of California Press.

———. 2012. *Occupy Nation: The Roots, Spirit and Promise of Occupy Wall Street.* New York: It Books.

Glaser, James. 1996. *Race, Campaign Politics and Realignment in the South.* New Haven, CT: Yale University Press.

Glaser, William A. 1965. "Television and Voting Turnout." *Public Opinion Quarterly* 29, no. 1: 71–86.

Glazer, Nathan. 1975. "Toward an Imperial Judiciary?" *Public Interest* 41 (Fall): 104–110.

Goffman, Irving. 1961. *Encounters.* Indianapolis: Bobbs-Merrill.

Goldfarb, Jeffrey C. 1991. *The Cynical Society: The Culture of Politics and the Politics of Culture in American Life.* Chicago: University of Chicago Press.

Goodin, Robert, and H. D. Klingemann. 1996. *A New Handbook of Political Science.* Oxford, UK: Oxford University Press.

Gourevitch, Peter. 1986. *Politics in Hard Times.* Ithaca, NY: Cornell University Press.

———. 2002. "Reinventing the American State: Political Dynamics in the Post–Cold War Era." In *Shaped by War and Trade,* edited by Ira Katznelson and Martin Shefter, 301–330. Princeton, NJ: Princeton University Press.

Greeley, Andrew. 1997. "The Other Civic America." *American Prospect* (May–June): 68–73.

Greenberg, Edward, and Benjamin Page. 1997. *The Struggle for Democracy.* New York: Longman.

Grey, T. 1975. "Do We Have an Unwritten Constitution?" In *Stanford Legal Essays,* edited by J. Merryman, 179–194. Stanford, CA: Stanford University Press.

Grodzins, Morton. 1960. "American Political Parties and the American System." *Western Political Quarterly* 13, no. 4 (December): 978–980.

Habermas, Jürgen. 1973. *Legitimation Crisis.* Boston: Beacon Press.

———. 1991. *Toward a Rational Society.* Boston: Beacon Press.

Hacker, Jacob S. 2006. *The Great Risk Shift: The Assault on American Jobs, Families, Health Care and Retirement.* New York: Oxford University Press.

Hacker, Jacob S., and Paul Pierson. 2005. *Off Center: The Republican Revolution and the Erosion of American Democracy.* New Haven, CT: Yale University Press.

———. 2010. *Winner Take All Politics.* New York: Simon and Schuster.

Hadensius, Axel. 1985. "Citizens Strike a Balance: Discontent with Taxes, Discontent with Spending." *Journal of Politics,* 5, no. 3: 349–363.

Hahl, Oliver, Minhae Kim, and Ezra Zuckerman Sivan. 2018. "The Authentic Appeal of the Lying Demagogue: Proclaiming the Deeper Truth About Political Illegitimacy." *American Sociological Review* 83, no. 1 (February): 1–34.

Hall, John. 2002. "Review of Contentious Europeans." *American Journal of Sociology* 108, no. 3: 719–720.

Hallen, Daniel, and Paolo Mancini. 1985. "Political Structure and Representational Form in U.S. and Italian News." In *New Directions in Journalism Research,* edited by Lara Furhoff and Pertti Hemanus, 48–66. Stockholm: University of Stockholm.

Hamburger, Philip. 2014. *Is Administrative Law Unlawful?* Chicago: University of Chicago Press.

Hamilton, Richard F., and James D. Wright. 1986. *The State of the Masses.* New York: Aldine de Gruyter.

Handler, E., and J. Mulkern. 1982. *Business in Politics: Campaign Strategies of Corporate Political Action Committees*. Lexington, MA: Lexington Books.

Hannan, Michael T., and Glenn R. Carroll. 1992. *The Dynamics of Organizational Populations*. Oxford, UK: Oxford University Press.

Hazen, Don. 2005. "The Right-Wing Express." AlterNet, February 6. https://www.alternet .org/story/21192/the_right-wing_express.

Hartz, Louis, 1955. *The Liberal Tradition in America*. New York: Harcourt, Brace and World.

———. 1964. *The Founding of New Societies*. New York: Harcourt, Brace and World.

Heclo, Hugh. 1977. *A Government of Strangers: Executive Politics in Washington*. Washington, DC: Brookings Institution Press.

———. 1978. "Issue Networks and the Executive Establishment." In *The New American Political System*, edited by Anthony King, 87–107. Washington, DC: American Enterprise Institute.

Heerwig, Jennifer. 2018. "Money in the Middle: Contribution Strategies Among Affluent Donors to Federal Elections, 1980–2008." *American Journal of Sociology* 123, no. 4 (January): 1004–1063.

Heidenheimer, Arnold. 1982. "Education and Social Security Entitlements in Europe and America." In *The Development of Welfare States in Europe and America*, edited by Peter Flora and Arnold Heidenheimer, 269–307. New Brunswick, NJ: Transaction Books.

Heidenheimer, Arnold J., Hugh Heclo, and Carolyn Adams. 1983. *Comparative Public Policy*, 2nd ed. New York: St. Martin's Press.

Herbst, Susan. 1993. *Numbered Voices: How Opinion Polling Has Shaped American Politics*. Chicago: University of Chicago Press.

Hetherington, Marc J. 2005. *Why Trust Matters: Declining Political Trust and the Demise of American Liberalism*. Princeton, NJ: Princeton University Press.

Hicks, Alexander. 2006. "Comment on Somers and Block." *American Sociological Review* 71, no. 3: 503–511.

Hicks, Alexander, and Joya Misra. 1993. "Political Resources and the Growth of Welfare in Affluent Capitalist Democracies, 1960–1982." *American Journal of Sociology* 99, no. 3: 668–711.

Hirschman, Albert. 1977. *The Passing and the Interests*. Princeton, NJ: Princeton University Press.

Hobsbawm, Eric. 1999. *On the Edge of the 20th Century*. New York: New Press.

Hobsbawm, Eric, and T. Ranger. 1983. *The Invention of Tradition*. Cambridge, UK: Cambridge University Press.

Hofstadter, Richard. 1962. *Anti-Intellectualism in American Life*. New York: Knopf.

———. 1965. *The Paranoid Political Style in American Politics*. New York: Knopf.

Holmberg, Soren. 1999. "Down and Down We Go: Political Trust in Sweden." In *Critical Citizens*, edited by Pippa Norris, 103–123. Oxford, UK: Oxford University Press.

Horowitz, Donald. 1977. *The Courts and Social Policy*. Washington, DC: Brookings Institution Press.

Hout, Michael. 1988. "More Universalism, Less Structured Mobility: The American Occupational Structure in the 1980s." *American Journal of Sociology* 93, no. 6 (May): 1358–1400.

Howe, Mark DeWolfe. 1965. *The Garden and the Wilderness: Religion and Government in American Constitutional History.* Chicago: University of Chicago Press.

Huber, Evelyne, and John D. Stephens. 2001. *Development and Crisis of the Welfare State.* Chicago: University of Chicago Press.

Huchshorn, Robert, James Gibson, Cornelius Cotter, and John Bibby. 1986. "Party Integration and Party Organizational Strength." *Journal of Politics* 48, no. 4 (November): 976–992.

Huntington, Samuel. 1968. *Social Order in Changing Societies.* New Haven CT: Yale University Press.

———. 1981. *American Politics: The Promise of Disharmony.* Cambridge, MA: Belknap Press.

———. 1984. "Congressional Responses to the 20th Century." In *The Political Economy: Readings in the Politics and Economics of American Public Policy*, edited by Thomas Ferguson and Joel Rogers, 180–202. Armonk, NY: Sharpe.

Igielnik, Ruth, and Anna Brown. 2017. "Key Takeaways on Americans' Views of Guns and Gun Ownership." Pew Research Center, June 22. http://www.pewresearch.org/fact-tank/2017/06/22/key-takeaways-on-americans-views-of-guns-and-gun-ownership/.

Imig, Doug, and Sidney Tarrow. 2001. *Contentious Europeans: Protest and Politics in an Emerging Polity.* New York: Rowman and Littlefield.

Inglehart, Ronald. 1977. "Political Dissatisfaction and Mass Support for Social Change in Advanced Industrial Society." *Comparative Political Studies* 10, no. 3: 455–472.

———. 1981. "Post Materialism in an Environment of Insecurity." *American Political Science Review* 75, no. 4: 880–901.

———. 1990. *Culture Shift in Advanced Industrial Society.* Princeton, NJ: Princeton University Press.

Inkeles, Alex, and David H. Smith. 1974. *Becoming Modern.* Cambridge, MA: Harvard University Press.

Isaac, Larry, Steve McDonald, and Greg Lukasik. 2006. "Takin' It from the Streets: How the Sixties Mass Movement Revitalized Unionization." *American Journal of Sociology* 112, no. 1 (July): 46–97.

Isaacs, Julia, Isabel Sawhill, and Ron Haskins. 2008. *Getting Ahead or Losing Ground: Economic Mobility in America.* Washington, DC: Brookings Institution Press.

Iyengar, Shanto. 1992. *Is Anyone Responsible? How TV Frames Political Issues.* Chicago: University of Chicago Press.

Iyengar, Shanto, and Donald Kinder. 1988. *News That Matters: TV and American Opinion.* Chicago: University of Chicago Press.

Jackson, J. S. III, and R. Hitlin. 1981. "The Nationalization of the Democratic Party." *Western Political Quarterly* 34, no. 2 (June): 270–287.

Jacobson, G., and S. Kernell. 1983. *Strategy and Choice in Congressional Elections*, 2nd ed. New Haven, CT: Yale University Press.

James, David R. 1988. "The Transformation of the Southern Racial State: Class and Race Determinants of Local-State Structures." *American Sociological Review* 53, no. 2: 191–209.

Janda, K. 1983. "Cross National Measures of Party Organizations and Organizational Theory." *European Journal of Political Research* 11: 319–332.

Janowitz, Morris. 1970. "Patterns of Collective Racial Violence." In *Political Conflict*, 171–207. New York: Quadrangle Books. ·

————. 1978. *The Last Half Century: Social Change and Politics in America*. Chicago: University of Chicago Press.

————. 1983. *The Reconstruction of Patriotism: Education for Civic Consciousness*. Chicago: University of Chicago Press.

Jansen, Robert S. 2011. "Populist Mobilization: A New Theoretical Approach to Populism." *Sociological Theory* 29, no. 2: 75–96.

Jencks, Christopher. 1972. *Inequality: A Reassessment of the Effect of Family and Schooling in America*. New York: Basic Books.

Jenkins, Craig, and Craig Eckert. 1986. "Channeling Black Insurgency." *American Sociological Review* 51, no. 6: 812–830.

Jennings, M. Kent. 1998. "Political Trust and the Roots of Devolution." In *Trust and Governance*, Vol. 1, edited by Valerie Braithwaite and Margaret Levi, 218–245. New York: Russell Sage.

Jennings, M. Kent, and Richard Niemi. 1981. *Generations and Politics: A Panel Study of Young Adults and Their Parents*. Princeton, NJ: Princeton University Press.

Jennings, M. Kent, Jan W. Van Deth, Samuel Baves, Dicter Fuchs, Felix Heughs, Ronald Inglehart, Max Kaese, Hans Dieter Klingemann, and Jacques Thomassen. 1989. *Continuities in Political Action: A Longitudinal Study of Political Orientations in Three Western Democracies*. Hawthorne, NY: Aldine de Gruyter.

Jepperson, Ronald L. 2002. "Political Modernities: Disentangling Two Underlying Dimensions of Institutional Differentiation." *Sociological Theory* 20, no. 1: 61–85.

Jepperson, Ronald L., and David Kamens. 1985. "The Expanding State and the Changing Character of Participation and Legitimation: On the Transformation of U.S. 'Civic Culture.'" Paper presented at the annual meeting of the American Political Science Association for a panel on Political Transformation in Liberal Democracies, New Orleans, August 16.

Jepperson, Ronald, and John W. Meyer. 1991. "The Public Order and the Construction of Formal Organizations." In *The New Institutionalism in Organizational Analysis*, edited by Walter W. Powell and Paul J. DiMaggio, 204–232. Chicago: University of Chicago Press.

————. 2011. "Multiple Levels of Analysis and Limitations of Methodological Individualisms." *Sociological Theory* 21, no. 1 (March): 54–73.

Jessop, Bob. 1987. *Studies in State Theory*. New York: Polity Press.

Johnson, Chalmers. 2004. *The Sorrows of Empire: Militarism, Secrecy and the End of the Republic*. Henry Holt & Co.: N.Y.

Jones, Bryan D. and Walter Williams, 2008, *The Politics of Bad Ideas: The Great Tax Cut Delusion and the Decline of Good Government in America*. New York: Pearson Longman.

Judis, John B. 2016. *The Populist Explosion*. New York: Columbia Global Reports.

Judt, Tony. 2004. "Dreams of Empire." *New York Review of Books* (November 4): 38–41.

————. 2005. "The New World Order." *New York Review of Books* (July 14): 14–18.

Judt, Tony, with Timothy Snyder. 2012. *Thinking the Twentieth Century*. New York: Penguin.

Jungk, Robert. 1958. *Brighter Than a Thousand Suns*. New York: Harcourt, Brace.

Kahn, Roger, and William Bowers. 1970. "The Social Context of the Rank and File Student Activists: A Test of Four Hypotheses." *Sociology of Education* 43 (Winter): 38–55.

Kamens, David H. 1986. "The Importance of Historical Sequencing: Party Legitimacy in the U.S. and Western Europe." In *Comparative Historical Research*, Vol. 9, edited by Richard Tomasson, 301–329. Greenwich, CT: JAI Press.

———. 1988. "Education and Democracy: An Institutional Analysis." *Sociology of Education* 61, no. 2 (Spring): 114–127.

———. 1989. "A Theory of American Political Party Development, 1960–1980." *Journal of Political and Military Sociology* 17, no. 2 (Winter): 263–289.

———. 2009. "The Expanding Polity: Theorizing the Links between Expanded Higher Education and the New Politics of the Post-1970s." *American Journal of Education* 2 (February): 137–180.

———. 2012. *Beyond the Nation-State.* Bingley, UK: Emerald Press.

Kammen, Michael. 1993. "The Problem of American Exceptionalism: A Reconsideration." *American Quarterly* 45, no. 1 (March): 1–43.

Kanter, R. 1978. *Men and Women of the Corporation.* New York: Basic Books.

Kaplan, Robert. 1997. "Was Democracy Just a Moment?" *Atlantic Monthly* (December).

———. 2000. *The Coming Anarchy.* New York: Random House.

Karabel, Zachary. 2014. *The Leading Indicators: A Short History of the Numbers That Rule Our World.* New York: Simon and Schuster.

Katona, Strampel, and E. Zhan. 1971. *Aspirations and Affluence.* New York: McGraw-Hill.

Katz, Elihu, and Daniel Dayan. 1985. "Media Events: On the Experience of Not Being There." *Religion* 15: 305–314.

Katzenstein, Mary F., and Carol Mueller, eds. 1987. *The Women's Movements of Western Europe.* Philadelphia: Temple University Press.

Katzenstein, Peter, 1984. *Corporatism and Change: Switzerland, Austria and the Politics of Industry.* Ithaca, NY: Cornell University Press.

Katznelson, Ira. 2013. *Fear Itself: The New Deal and the Origins of Our Time.* New York: Liveright.

Kaufman, Herbert. 1991. *Time, Chance and Organizations: Natural Selection in a Perilous Environment.* Chatham, NJ: Chatham House.

Kayden, Xandra, and Eddie Mahe, Jr. 1985. *The Party Goes On: The Persistence of the Two Party System.* New York: Basic Books.

Kelley, Stanley. 1984. *Interpreting Elections.* Princeton, NJ: Princeton University Press.

Kenniston, Kenneth. 1968. *Young Radicals: Notes on Committed Youth.* New York: Harcourt, Brace and World.

Kensworthy, Lane. 2014. *Social Democratic America.* New York: Oxford University Press.

Kernell, Sam. 1993. *Going Public: New Strategies of Presidential Leadership.* Washington, DC: Congressional Quarterly Press.

Kerr, Clark. 1963. *The Uses of the University.* Cambridge, MA: Harvard University Press.

Kessel, John. 1977. "The Seasons of Presidential Politics." *Social Science Quarterly* 58, no. 3: 418–435.

Kiewiet, D. Roderick, and Douglas Rivers. 1985. "The Economic Basis of Reagan's Appeal." In *The New Direction in American Politics,* edited by John E. Chubb and Paul E. Peterson, 69–91. Washington, DC: Brookings Institution Press.

Kinder, Don, and Roderick Kiewiet. 1981. "Socio-tropic Politics: The American Case." *British Journal of Political Science* 2, no. 11: 129–161.

Kinder, Donald R., and Lynn M. Sanders. 1996. *Divided by Color: Racial Politics and Democratic Ideals.* Chicago: University of Chicago Press.

King, Anthony, ed. 1990. *The New American Political System,* 2nd ed. Washington, DC: AEI Press.

King, Desmond, and Robert Lieberman. 2007. "Ironies of State Building: A Comparative Perspective on the American State." Paper presented at the annual meeting of the American Political Science Association, Chicago, August 30–September 2.

King, Desmond, Robert Lieberman, Gretchen Ritter, and Lawrence Whitehead. 2009. *Democratization in America: A Comparative-Historical Approach.* Baltimore: Johns Hopkins University Press.

Kitschelt, Herbert. 1986. "Political Opportunity Structures and Political Protest: Anti-Nuclear Movements in Four Democracies." *British Journal of Political Science* 16: 57–85.

Klandermans, Bert, Hanspieter Kriesi, and Sidney Tarrow. 1988. *From Structure to Action: Comparing Social Movement Research Across Cultures,* Vol. 1. Greenwich, CT: JAI Press.

Kleppner, P. 1982. *Who Voted? The Dynamics of Electoral Turnout, 1870–1980.* New York: Praeger.

Kleppner, P., and S. C. Baker. 1980. "The Impact of Voter Registration Requirements on Electoral Turnout, 1900–16." *Journal of Political and Military Sociology* 8: 205–226.

Klinenberg, Eric. 2012a. *Going Solo: The Surprising Rise of Living Alone.* New York: Penguin.

———. 2012b. "Solo Nation: American Consumers Stay Single." http://fortune.com/2012/01/25/solo-nation-american-consumers-stay-single/.

Klingeman, H. D., and D. Fuchs. 1995. *Citizens and the State.* Oxford, UK: Oxford University Press.

Kluckhohn, Clyde. 1958. *Mirror for Man.* New York: Macmillan.

Koopmans, Ruud, and Paul Statham. 1999. "Challenging the Liberal Nation-State? Multiculturalism and the Collective Claims Making of Migrants and Ethnic Minorities in Britain and Germany." *American Journal of Sociology* 105, no. 3 (November): 652–697.

Krippner, Greta. 2011. *Capitalizing on the Crisis: The Political Origins of the Rise of Finance.* Cambridge, MA: Harvard University Press.

Kronberg, Clemens, and Andreas Wimmer. 2012. "Struggling over the Boundaries of Belonging: A Formal Model of Nation Building, Ethnic Closure and Populism." *American Journal of Sociology* 118, no. 1 (July): 176–230.

Krucken, Georg, and Gili Drori. 2009. *World Society: The Writings of John W. Meyer.* New York: Oxford University Press.

Krugman, Paul. 2002. "It's Election Day, and It's Your Duty as a Citizen to Be Irrational." *New York Times,* November 5, A27.

———. 2013. "The Ignorance Caucus." *New York Times,* February 11, A17.

Lachmann, Richard, and Lacy Mitchell. 2014. "The Changing Face of War in Textbooks: Depictions of World War II and Vietnam, 1970–2009." *Sociology of Education,* 87, no. 3: 171–188.

Ladd, E. 1978. *Where Have All the Voters Gone? The Fracturing of American Political Parties.* New York: Norton.

———. 1999. *The Ladd Report.* New York: Free Press.

Ladd, E. C., and K. H. Bowman. 1998. *What's Wrong: A Survey of American Satisfaction and Complaint.* Washington, DC: AEI Press.

Lamont, Michelle. 1997. "The Rhetorics of Racism and Anti-Racism in France and the U.S." New York: Russell Sage.

Lane, Robert E. 1966. "The Decline of Politics and Ideology in a Knowledgeable Society." *American Sociological Review* 31, no. 5: 649–662.

———. 1999. "The Joyless Polity: Contributions of Democratic Processes to Ill Being," 329–371 in Stephen Elkin and Karol Soltan (editors), Citizen Competence and Democratic Institutions, Penn. State University Press: University Park, Pa.

Lapham, Lewis. 2004. "Tentacles of Rage: The Republican Propaganda Mill, A Brief History." *Harper's* 309, no. 1852 (September): 31–43.

Lasch, Christopher. 1979. *The Culture of Narcissism*. New York: Norton.

Laumann, Edward, and David Knoke. 1987. *The Organizational State: A Perspective on Energy and Health Domains*. Madison: University of Wisconsin Press.

———. 1988. "The Increasingly Organizational State." *Society* (January–February): 21–28.

Lauter, David. 1995. "The Smoldering Electorate." *American Prospect* (Fall): 89–95.

Lawson, Kay, and Peter Merkl. 1988. *When Parties Fail*. Princeton, NJ: Princeton University Press.

Lazarsfeld, Paul F., and Wagner Thielens. 1958. *The Academic Mind*. Glencoe, IL: Free Press.

Lehmbruch, G., and P. Schmitter, eds. 1982. *Patterns of Corporatist Policy-Making*. Beverly Hills, CA: Sage.

Lemann, Nicholas. 2005. "Fear and Favor: Why Is Everyone Mad at the Mainstream Media?" *New Yorker* (February 14–21): 168–176.

———. 2013. "The New Deal We Didn't Know." *New York Review of Books* (September 26): 85–92.

Leonhardt, David. 2007. "Has the Jump in Wages Met Its End?" *New York Times*, September 12, C1, C4.

Levin, Yuval. 2016. *The Fractured Republic*. New York: Basic Books.

Lieberman, Jethro. 1981. *The Litigious Society*. New York: Basic Books.

Light, Paul. 1982. *The President's Agenda*. Baltimore: Johns Hopkins University Press.

Lindblom, Charles. 1977. *Politics and Markets*. New York: Basic Books.

Lindert, Peter. 2004. *Growing Public: Social Spending and Economic Growth Since the 18th Century*, Vols. 1 and 2. Cambridge, UK: Cambridge University Press.

———. 2012. "Social Contract Budgeting: Prescriptions from Economics and History." New America, December 17. https://www.newamerica.org/economic-growth/policy-papers/social-contract-budgeting-prescriptions-from-economics-and-history/.

Linz, Juan. 1978. *The Breakdown of Democratic Regimes*. Baltimore: Johns Hopkins University Press.

———. 1993. "Nation Building and State Building." *European Review* 1, no. 4: 355–369.

Lipset, Seymour M. 1963. *The First New Nation*. New York: Basic Books.

———. 1987. "Historical Traditions and National Characteristics: A Comparative Analysis of the U.S. and Canada." In *Patterns of Modernity, Vol. 1: The West*, edited by S. N. Eisenstadt, 60–87. New York: New York University Press.

———. 1990. *Continental Divide*. London: Routledge.

———. 1995. "America Today: Malaise and Resiliency." *Journal of Democracy* 6, no. 3: 3–10.

———. 1996. *American Exceptionalism: The Double Edged Sword*. New York: Norton.

Lipset, Seymour M., and Stein Rokkan. 1967. "Cleavage Structures, Party Systems and Voter Alignments: An Introduction." In *Party Systems and Voter Alignments: Cross National Perspectives*, edited by S. Lipset and S. Rokkan, 1–64. New York: Free Press.

Lipset, Seymour M., and Earl Raab. 1970. *The Politics of Unreason: Right Wing Extremism in America, 1790–1970*. New York: Harper Torchbook.

Lipset, Seymour Martin, and William Schneider. 1983. *The Confidence Gap: Business, Labor, and Government in the Public Mind*. New York: Free Press.

Lipsky, Michael. 1968. "Protest as a Political Resource." *American Political Science Review* 62: 1143–1158.

Loeb, Paul. 1999. *Soul of a Citizen*. New York: St. Martin's Press.

Long, Norton. 1962. *The Polity*. Chicago: Rand McNally.

Longhofer, W., and Evan Schofer. 2011. "National and Global Sources of Environmental Organization." *American Sociological Review* 75, no. 4: 505–534.

Longway, M. Margaret. 1985. *Political Participation in the U.S.* Washington, DC: Congressional Quarterly Press.

Loomis, B. 1984. "Congressional Careers and Party Leadership in the Contemporary House of Representatives." *American Journal of Political Science* 28, no. 1 (February): 108–203.

Loundsbury, Michael, and Mark Ventresca, eds. 2002. *Social Structure and Organizations Revisited*, Vol. 19. London: Elsevier Science.

Lowery, David, and William Berry. 1981. "The Growth of Government in the U.S." *American Journal of Political Science* 27, no. 4: 665–694.

Lowi, Theodore. 1967. "The Public Philosophy: Interest Group Liberalism." *American Political Science Review* 61: 5–24.

———. 1969. *The End of Liberalism*. New York: Norton.

———. 1978a. *Comparing Public Policies*. Beverly Hills, CA: Sage.

———. 1978b. "Europeanization of America? From United States to United State." In *Nationalizing Government*, edited by T. Lowi and A. Stone, 15–29. Beverly Hills, CA: Sage.

———. 1985. *The Personal President*. Ithaca, NY: Cornell University Press.

———. 1996. *The End of the Republican Era*. Norman: University of Oklahoma Press.

Lowi, Theodore, and Benjamin Ginsberg. 1996. *American Government*. New York: Norton.

Lubell, Samuel. 1970. *The Hidden Crisis in American Politics*. New York: Norton.

Luhrman, Tanya M. 2012. "Living with Voices." *American Scholar* (Summer): 49–60.

———. 2013. "The Violence in Our Heads." *New York Times* September 20, A27.

Lunch, William M. 1988. *The Nationalization of American Politics*. Berkeley: University of California Press.

Luttbeg, N. P. 1984. "Differential Voting Turnout in the American States, 1960–1982." *Social Science Quarterly* 65, no. 1: 60–73.

Luttwak, Edward. 1999. *Turbo Capitalism: Winners and Losers in the Global Economy*. New York: HarperCollins.

Macrae, Norman, 1976. *America's 3rd Century*. New York: Harcourt, Brace.

Madrick, Jeff. 2007. "Goodbye, Horatio Alger." *The Nation*, February 5.

Madsen, Richard. 1991. *America at Century's End*. Berkeley: University of California Press.

Magnus, George. 2011. "Crisis Convergence." *Foreign Policy*, August 31. https://foreignpolicy.com/2011/08/31/crisis-convergence/.

Mann, Michael. 1986. *The Sources of Social Power*, Vol. 1. New York: Cambridge University Press.

———, ed. 1990. *The Rise and Decline of the Nation State*. London: Blackwell.

———. 1997. "Has Globalization Ended the Rise and Rise of the Nation-State?" *International Review of Political Economy* 4, no. 3 (Autumn): 472–496.

———. 2005. *Incoherent Empire*. New York: Verso Books.

———. 2011. *Power in the 21th Century: Conversations with John Hall*. New York: Polity Press.

———. 2012. *The Sources of Social Power.* Vol. 3, *Global Empires and Revolution, 1890–1945.* New York: Cambridge University Press.

———. 2013. *The Sources of Social Power.* Vol. 4, *Globalizations, 1945–2011.* New York: Cambridge University Press.

Manza, Jeff, and Clem Brooks. 1997. "The Religious Factor in U.S. Presidential Elections, 1960–1992." *American Journal of Sociology* 103, no. 1 (July): 38–82.

Manza, Jeff, Jennifer Heerwig, and Brian McCabe. 2012. "Public Opinion in the Age of Reagan: Political Trends 1972–2006." In *Social Trends in American Life: Findings from the General Social Survey Since 1972,* edited by Peter Marsden, 117–144. Princeton, NJ: Princeton University Press.

March, J. G., and J. Olsen. 1983a. "The New Institutionalism: Organizational Factors in Public Life." Paper presented at the annual meeting of theAmerican Political Science Association, Chicago, September 1–4.

———. 1983b. "Organizing Political Life: What Administrative Reorganization Tells Us About Government." *American Political Science Review* 77: 281–296.

———. 1989. *The Organizational Basis of Politics.* New York: Free Press.

Markoff, John. 1996. *Waves of Democracy.* Thousand Oaks, CA: Pine Forge Press.

Marks, Gary, Heather Mbaye, and Hyung Min Kim. 2009. "Radicalism or Reformism: Socialist Parties Before World War I." *American Sociological Review* 74, no. 4 (August): 615–636.

Markus, G. 1983. "Dynamic Modeling of Cohort Change: The Case of Political Partisanship." *American Journal of Political Science* 27, no. 4: 717–740.

Marsden, Peter, ed. 2012. *Social Trends in American Life: Findings from the General Social Survey Since 1972.* Princeton, NJ: Princeton University Press.

Marsden, Peter, and Sameer Srivastava. 2012. "Trends in Informal Social Participation, 1974–2008." In *Social Trends in American Life: Findings from the General Social Survey Since 1972,* edited by Peter Marsden, 240–262. Princeton, NJ: Princeton University Press.

Marsh, Alan. 1997. *Political Action in Europe and the USA.* New York: Macmillan.

Marshall, T. H. 1963. *Class, Citizenship and Social Development.* New York: Doubleday.

Martinelli, Alberto. 2003. "Global Order or Divided World? Introduction." *Current Sociology* 51, no. 2: 95–100.

———. 2008. *Trans-Atlantic Divide.* Oxford, UK: Oxford University Press.

Massey, Douglas, Camille Charles, Garvey F. Lundy, and Mary Fischer. 2003. *The Source of the River: The Social Origins of Freshmen at America's Selective Colleges and Universities.* Princeton, NJ: Princeton University Press.

Massey, Douglas, and Nancy Denton. 1993. *American Apartheid: Segregation and the Making of the Underclass.* Cambridge, MA: Harvard University Press.

Mayer, Jane. 2011. "State for Sale." *New Yorker* (October 10): 1–20.

McAdam, Doug. 1982. *Political Development and Black Insurgency: 1930–1970.* Chicago: University of Chicago Press.

———. 1988. "Micro Mobilization Contexts and Recruitment to Activism." In *Supplement to Research in Social Movements, Conflicts and Change,* 125–154. Greenwich, CT: JAI Press.

McAdam, Doug, and W. Richard Scott. 2002. "Organizations and Movements." Paper presented at the annual meeting of the American Sociological Association, New York, August 20.

McCann, James G. 2012. "The Leading Public Policy Research Organizations in the World: The Global Go To Think Tanks Report, 2011." Think Tanks and Civil Societies Program, University of Pennsylvania.

McCarthy, John, and M. Zald. 1973. *The Trend of Social Movements in America: Professionalization and Resource Mobilization*. Morristown, NJ: General Learning Press.

McChesney, Robert. 2004. *The Problem of the Media*. New York: Monthly Review Press.

McCleskey, C. 1981. "The De-Institutionalization of Electoral Politics." In *A Tide of Discontent: The 1980 Elections and Their Meaning*, edited by E. Sandoz and C. Crabb, Jr., 113–139. Washington, DC: Congressional Quarterly Press.

McClosky, Herbert, and John Zaller. 1986. *The American Ethos: Public Attitudes Toward Democracy*. Cambridge, MA: Harvard University Press.

McElwee, Sean. 2015. "Review of *Saving Our Kids*." *Contexts* 14, no. 3: 59–61.

McFarland, Andrew. 1976. *The Public Interest Lobbies*. Washington, DC: American Enterprise Institute.

McGrath, Ben. 2010. "The Movement: The Rise of Tea Party Activism." *New Yorker* (February 1): 41–49.

McKay, Robert. 1977. *Nine for Equality Under Law: Civil Rights Litigation*. New York: Ford Foundation.

McKenzie, Robert, and Allan Silver. 1968. *Angels in Marble: Working Class Conservatives in Urban England*. Chicago: University of Chicago Press.

Meacham, Jon. 2008. *American Lion: Andrew Jackson in the White House*. New York: Random House.

Meaney, Thomas. 2012. "The Generalist," review of *In the Shadow of the General: Modern France and the Myth of de Gaulle*, by Sudhir Hazareesingh. *The Nation* (October 1): 27–32.

Meier, Kenneth, 1975. "Representative Democracy: An Empirical Analysis." *American Political Science Review* 69, no. 2: 526–542.

Menand, Louis. 2007. "Bryan Caplan's The Myth of the Rational Voter." *New Yorker* (July 9–16): 88–91.

Mettler, Suzanne. 2011. *The Submerged State: How Invisible Government Policies Undermine American Democracy*. Chicago: University of Chicago Pres

Meyer, John W. 1970. "'The Charter': Conditions of Diffuse Socialization in Schools." In *Social Processes and Social Structure*, edited by W. R. Scott, 564–579. New York: Holt, Rinehart and Winston.

———. 1977. "The Effects of Education as an Institution," *American Journal of Sociology* 83: 55–78.

———. 1985. "Decentralization and Legitimacy in Public Organization." Paper presented at the Research Meetings on Organization Theory, Norway and Sweden, August.

———. 1986. "Myths of Socialization and Personality." In *Reconstructing Individualism*, edited by T. Heller, M. Sonna, and D. Wellbery, 212–225. Stanford, CA: Stanford University Press.

Meyer, John W., John Boli, George M. Thomas, and Francisco O. Ramirez. 1997. "World Society and the Nation-State." *American Journal of Sociology* 103, no. 1: 144–181.

Meyer, John W., and Michael Hannan, eds. 1979. *National Development and the World System*. Chicago: University of Chicago Press.

Meyer, John W., and Ronald Jepperson. 2000. "The 'Actors' of Modern Society: The Cultural Construction of Social Agency." *Sociological Theory* 18, no. 1: 100–120.

Meyer, John W., Francisco Ramirez, and Yasmin Soysal. 1992. "World Expansion of Mass Education, 1870–1980." *Sociology of Education* 65, no. 2 (April): 128–149.

Meyer, John W., and James Roth. 1970. "A Reinterpretation of American Status Politics." *Pacific Sociological Review* 13, no. 2 (Spring): 95–102.

Meyer, John W., and Brian Rowan. 1977. "Institutionalized Organizations: Formal Structure as Myth and Ceremony." *American Journal of Sociology* 83, no. 2 (September): 340–363.

Meyer, John W., and W. Richard Scott. 1983. *Organizations and Environments: Ritual and Rationality.* Beverly Hills, CA: Sage.

Meyer, David, and David Tarrow. 1998. *The Social Movement Society.* Oxford, UK: Rowman and Littlefield.

Meyerson, Harold. 2012. "Makers Beat Takers." *Washington Post*, December 5, A21.

———. 2013. "America Flunks Its Checkup," *Washington Post*, January 16, A15.

Micklethwait, John, and Adrian Wooldridge. 2004. *The Right Nation.* New York: Penguin.

Miller, Arthur H. 1974. "Political Issues and Trust in Government: 1964–1970." *American Political Science Review* 68: 951–972.

Miller, Arthur H., Edie Goldenberg, and Lutz Erbring. 1983. "Is Confidence Rebounding?" *Public Opinion Quarterly* 6: 16–20.

Miller, William, and Richard Niemi. 2002. "Voting, Choice, Conditioning and Constraint." In *Comparing Democracies* 2, edited by L. LeDuc, R. Niemi, and P. Norris, 169–188. London: Sage.

Mitchell, Joyce, and William Mitchell. 1968. "The Changing Politics of American Life." In *Indicators of Social Change: Concepts and Measurements*, edited by Eleanor Sheldon and Wilbert Moore, 247–294. New York: Russell Sage.

Mirel, Jeffry. 2010, *Patriotic Pluralism: Americanization, European Immigrants and Education.* Cambridge, MA: Harvard University Press.

Mizruchi, Mark. 2013. *The Fracturing of the Corporate Elite.* Cambridge, MA: Harvard University Press.

Moe, Terry. 1985. "The Politicized Presidency." In *The New Direction in American Politics*, edited by John E. Chubb and Paul E. Peterson, 235–273. Washington, DC: Brookings Institution Press.

Mollenkopf, John. 1983. *The Contested City.* Princeton, NJ: Princeton University Press.

Mosher, Michael. 1985. "Explaining Contemporary America: An Analysis of a Disjuncture Country." Published as "America: its Four Corners of Difference" in *Chuo Koron (Central Public Arguments)* 101, no. 4: 161–186.

Moynihan, Patrick. 1996. *Miles to Go.* Cambridge, MA: Harvard University Press.

Muller, Edward, Thomas Jukam, and Mitchell Seligson. 1982. "Diffuse Political Support and Anti-System Political Behavior: A Comparative Analysis." *American Journal of Political Science* 26: 240–264.

Murray, Charles. 2011. *Coming Apart: The State of White America, 1960–2010.* New York: Crown Forum.

Myrdal, Gunnar. 1944. *An American Dilemma: The Negro Problem and Modern Democracy.* New York: Harper.

Nachmias, David, and David Rosenbloom. 1980. *Bureaucratic Government USA.* New York: St. Martin's Press.

National Committee for Responsive Philanthropy. 1995. "Foundations in the Newt Era." Draft report. Washington, DC: National Committee for Responsive Philanthropy.

———. 1997. "Moving a Public Policy Agenda: The Strategic Philanthropy of Conservative Foundations." Washington, DC: National Committee for Responsive Philanthropy.

———. 2004. "Axis of Ideology: Conservative Foundations and Public Policy." Draft report. Washington, DC: National Committee for Responsive Philanthropy.

Natter, G. Warren. 1978. *Growth of Government in the West*. Washington, DC: American Enterprise Institute.

Neely, Richard. 1981. *How Courts Govern America*. New Haven, CT: Yale University Press.

Nelles, H. V. 1997. "Review Essay: American Exceptionalism: A Double-Edged Sword." *American Historical Review* 102: 749–757.

Nettl, J. P. 1968. "The State as a Conceptual Variable." *World Politics* 20: 559–592.

Nie, Norman, Jane Junn, and Kenneth Stehlik-Berry. 1996. *Education and Democratic Citizenship in America*. Chicago: University of Chicago Press.

Nie, N., S. Verba, and J. Petrocik. 1979. *The Changing American Voter*. Cambridge, MA: Harvard University Press.

Norris, Pippa. 1999. *Critical Citizens*. Oxford, UK: Oxford University Press.

———. 2017. *Why American Elections Are Flawed (and How to Fix Them)*. Ithaca, NY: Cornell University Press.

Norris, Pippa, and Ronald Inglehart. 2009. *Cosmopolitan Communications: Cultural Diversity in a Globalized World*. New York: Cambridge University Press.

Novak, William J. 2010. "Law and the Social Control of Capitalism." *Emory Law Journal* 60: 377–405.

NSF (National Science Foundation). 2010. "Globalization of Science and Engineering Research: A Companion to Science and Engineering Indicators." https://www.nsf.gov/publications/pub_summ.jsp?ods_key=nsb1003.

Nye, J. S., P. D. Zeilikow, and David King, eds. 1997. *Why People Don't Trust Government*. Cambridge, MA: Harvard University Press.

Oberschall, Anthony. 1973. "Mobilization, Leaders and Followers in the Civil Rights Movement in the U.S., 1950–1970." In *Social Conflict and Social Movements*, 204–242. Englewood Cliffs, NJ: Prentice-Hall.

Offe, C. 1981. "The Attribution of Public Status to Interest Groups: Observations on the West German Case." In *Organizing Interests in Western Europe*, edited by S. Berger, 123–158. New York: Cambridge University Press.

Olsen, J. 1981. "Integrated Organizational Participation in Government." In *Handbook of Organizational Design*, edited by P. Nystrom and W. Starbuck, 492–517. Chicago: Rand McNally.

Olsen, Mancur. 1971. *The Logic of Collective Action*. Cambridge, MA: Harvard University Press.

Orren, Karen, and Stephen Skowronek. 2004. *The Search for American Political Development*. Cambridge, MA: Cambridge University Press.

Padavic, Irene, and Barbara Reskin. 2002. *Women and Men at Work*, 2nd ed. Thousand Oaks, CA: Pine Forge Press.

Page, B. I., and Shapiro, R. Y. 1992. *The Rational Public: Fifty Years of Trends in Americans' Policy Preferences*. Chicago: University of Chicago Press.

Page, Benjamin, Larry Bartels, and Jason Seawright. 2011. "Democracy and the Policy Preferences of Wealthy Americans." Paper presented at the annual meeting of the American Political Science Association, August 31–September 4 (rev. September 29, 2011).

Paxton, Pamela. 1999. "Is Social Capital Declining in the United States? A Multiple Indicator Assessment." *American Journal of Sociology* 105, no. 1 (July): 88–127.

Pearlstein, Steven. 2012. "The Judicial Jihad Against the Regulatory State." *Washington Post*, October 14, sec. G, 1, 6.

Peterson, Paul. 1985. "The New Politics of Deficits." In *The New Direction in American Politics*, edited by John E. Chubb and Paul E. Peterson, 365–399. Washington, DC: Brookings Institution Press.

Petracca, Mark P. 1990. "Politics Beyond the End of Liberalism." *PS: Political Science and Politics* 23, no. 4: 566–569.

Petrocik, John R. 1981. *Party Coalitions: Realignments and the Decline of the New Deal Party System*. Chicago: University of Chicago Press.

———. 1982. *The Electorate in 1980*. Beverly Hills, CA: Sage.

Pew Research Center. 2010, "Millennials: Portrait of a Generation: Confident, Connected and Open to Change." http://www.pewresearch.org/wp-content/uploads/sites/3/2010/10/millennials-confident-connected-open-to-change.pdf.

Pew Research Center. 2014. "Political Polarization in the American Public." http://www.people-press.org/2014/06/12/political-polarization-in-the-american-public.

Pew Research Center. 2015. "Beyond Disrust; How Americans View their Government." http://www.people-press.org/2015/11/23/beyond-distrust-how-americans-view-their-government/.

Pew Research Center. 2017. "Political Polarization, 1994–2017." http://www.people-press.org/interactives/political-polarization-1994-2017/.

Pew Research Center, 2018. "The Age Gap in Religion Around the World." http://www.pewforum.org/2018/06/13/young-adults-around-the-world-are-less-religious-by-several-measures/

Pew Research Center for People and the Press. 2004a. "New Audiences Increasingly Polarized." Washington, DC.

———. 2004b. "The State of the News Media, 2004: Annual Report on American Journalism." Washington, DC.

Pharr, Susan, and Robert Putnam, eds. 2000. *Disaffected Democracies*. Princeton, NJ: Princeton University Press.

Phillips, Kevin. 1994. *Arrogant Capital*. Boston: Little, Brown.

Phillips, Kevin P., and Paul H. Blackman. 1975. *Electoral Reform and Voter Participation: Federal Registration, A False Remedy for Voter Apathy*. AEI-Hoover Policy Study 14. Washington, DC: American Enterprise Institute.

Pierson, Paul. 1998. "Irresistible Forces, Immovable Objects: Post Industrial Welfare States Confront Permanent Austerity." *Journal of European Public Policy* 5, no. 4: 539–560.

———. 2004. *Politics in Time: History, Institutions and Social Analysis*. Princeton, NJ: Princeton University Press.

———. 2007. "The Rise and Reconfiguration of Activist Government." In *The Transformation of American Politics: Activist Government and the Rise of Conservatism*, edited by Paul Pierson and Theda Skocpol, 19–39. Princeton, NJ: Princeton University Press.

Pierson, Paul, and Theda Skocpol, eds. 2007. *The Transformation of American Politics: Activist Government and the Rise of Conservatism*. Princeton, NJ: Princeton University Press.

Piven, Frances Fox, and Richard Cloward. 1971. *Regulating the Poor: The Functions of Public Welfare*. New York: Vintage Books.

———. 1988. *Why Americans Don't Vote.* New York: Pantheon Books.

Poggi, Gianfranco. 1990. *The State: Its Nature, Development and Prospects and Development.* Stanford, CA: Stanford University Press.

Pollock, Phillip H. III. 1982. "Organizations as Agents of Mobilization: How Does Group Activity Affect Political Participation?" *American Journal of Political Science* 26, no. 3 (August): 485–504.

Polsby, Nelson W. 1981–82. "Contemporary Transformations of American Politics: Thoughts on Research Agendas." *Political Science Quarterly* 96, no. 4: 551–571.

Polsby, Nelson W., and Aaron Wildavsky. 1976. *Presidential Elections: Strategies of American Electoral Politics,* 4th ed. New York: Scribner.

Pool, Ithiel de Sola. 1976. "Government and the Media." *American Political Science Review* 70: 1234–1241.

Powell, G. Bingham. 1980. *Electoral Participation.* Beverly Hills, CA: Sage.

———. 1986. "American Voter Turnout in Comparative Perspective." *American Political Science Review* 80, no. 1: 17–45.

Powell, Lewis F. 1971. "Confidential Memorandum: Attack on American Free Enterprise System." August 23. https://www.thwink.org/sustain/articles/017_PowellMemo/PowellMemoReproduction.pdf.

Prasad, Monica. 2005. "Why Is France So French? Culture, Institutions and Neo-Liberalism, 1974–1981." *American Journal of Sociology* 111, no. 2 (September): 357–408.

———. 2006. *The Politics of Free Markets.* Chicago: University of Chicago Press.

Putnam, Robert. 1995. "Tuning In, Tuning Out: The Strange Disappearance of Social Capital in America." *PS: Political Science and Politics* 28, no. 4: 664–683.

———. 1996. "Robert Putnam Responds." *American Prospect,* no. 25: 26–28.

———. 2000. *Bowling Alone: The Collapse and Revival of American Community.* New York: Simon and Schuster.

———. 2002a. "Bowling Together: The United State of America." *American Prospect* 13 (February 11): 20–22.

———, ed. 2002b. *Democracies in Flux.* Oxford, UK: Oxford University Press.

———. 2007. "E Pluribus Unum: Diversity and Community in the 21st Century. The 2006 Johan Skytte Prize Lecture," *Scandinavian Political Studies* 30, no. 2: 137–174.

Putnam, Robert. 2015. *Our Kids: The American Dream in Crisis.* New York: Simon and Schuster.

Putnam, Robert, and David Campbell. 2010. *American Grace.* New York: Simon and Schuster.

Putnam, Robert, Robert Leonardi, and Raffaella Nanetti. 1993. *Making Democracy Work: Civic Traditions in Modern Italy.* Princeton, NJ: Princeton University Press.

Rainwater, Lee, and Martin Rein. 1983. *Evaluating the Welfare State.* New York: Academic Press.

Ramirez, Francisco. 1981. "Comparative Social Movements." *International Journal of Comparative Sociology* 22, no. 1–2: 3–21.

———. 2006a. "From Citizen to Person: Rethinking Education as Incorporation." In *The Impact of Comparative Education Research on Institutional Theory,* edited by David Baker and Alexander Wiseman, 367–389. Amsterdam: Elsevier.

———. 2006b. "Review of Islamic Identity, Post-Coloniality and Educational Policy." *Comparative Education Review* 50, no. 3: 533–535.

————. 2012. "The World Society Perspective: Concepts, Assumptions and Strategies." *Comparative Education Review* (forthcoming).

Ramirez, Francisco, and John Boli. 1987. "On the Union of States and Schools." In *Institutional Structure: Constituting State, Society and the Individual*, by George Thomas, John Meyer, Francisco Ramirez, and John Boli, 173–198. Beverly Hills, CA: Sage.

Ramirez, Francisco, and John Boli-Bennett. 1982. "Global Patterns of Educational Institutionalization." In *Comparative Education*, edited by P. Altbach, G. Kelly, and R. Arnove, 15–36. New York: Macmillan.

Ramirez, Francisco O., David Suarez, and John W. Meyer. 2006. "The Worldwide Rise of Human Rights Education." In *School Knowledge in Comparative and Historical Perspective*, edited by Aaron Benavot and Cecilia Braslavsky, 35–55. Hong Kong, Springer.

Ranney, Austin. 1983. *Channels of Power: The Impact of Television on American Politics.* New York: Basic Books.

————. 1994. *The New American Political Order.* Berkeley: University of California Press.

Ranney, Austin, P. Bonomi, and J. M. Burns. 1981. *The American Constitutional Systems Under Strong and Weak Parties.* New York: Praeger.

Rapoport, Ronald B., and Walter J. Stone. 2005. *Three's a Crowd: The Dynamic of Third Parties, Ross Perot and Republican Resurgence.* Ann Arbor: University of Michigan Press.

Reich, Robert. 1994. *The Work of Nations.* New York: Knopf.

————. 2007. *Supercapitalism: The Transformation of Business, Democracy and Everyday Life.* New York: Vintage Books.

————. 2012. "The Ryan Choice." August 11. http://robertreich.org/post/29215926175.

Reichley, H. James. 1985. "The Rise of National Parties." In *The New Direction in American Politics*, edited by John E. Chubb and Paul E. Peterson, 175–203. Washington, DC: Brookings Institution Press.

Reid, T. R. 2009. *The Healing of America: A Global Quest for Better, Cheaper and Fairer Health Care.* New York: Penguin.

Riddle, Phyllis. 1990. "University and State: Political Competition and the Rise of Universities, 1200–1985." Ph.D. diss., Stanford University.

————. 1993. "Political Authority and University Formation in Europe, 1200–1800." *Sociological Perspectives* 36, no. 1 (Spring): 45–62.

Roazen, Paul. 1988. "Louis Hartz's Teaching." *VQR* (Winter). https://www.vqronline.org/essay/louis-hartz%E2%80%99s-teaching.

Robinson, Michael J. 1976. "Public Affairs Television and the Growth of Political Malaise: The Case of 'The Selling of the Pentagon.'" *American Political Science Review* 70, no. 2: 409–432.

Rose, Richard. 1984. *Understanding Big Government: The Program Approach.* Beverly Hills, CA: Sage.

————. 1985a. *Centre-Periphery Relations in West Europe.* Stanford, CA: Hoover Institution.

————. 1985b. "How Big Is American Government? And How Distinctive?" Paper presented at the annual meeting of the American Political Science Association, New Orleans, August 30.

Rose, Richard, and Terrence Karan. 1984. *Comparative Resource Allocation.* Beverly Hills, CA: Sage.

Rose, Richard, and Guy Peters. 1978. *Can Government Go Bankrupt?* New York: Basic Books.

Rosen, Christine. 2005. "The Over-Praised American." *Policy Review* (October 1). https://www.hoover.org/research/overpraised-american.

Rosenmund, Moritz. 2006. "The Current Discourse on Curriculum Change: A Comparative Analysis of National Reports on Education." In *School Knowledge in Comparative and Historical Perspective*, edited by Aaron Benavot and Cecilia Braslavsky, 173–195. Hong Kong: Springer.

Rosenstone, Steven, Roy L. Behr, and E. Lazarus. 1996. *Third Party Movements: Citizen Response to Major Party Failure*. Princeton, NJ: Princeton University Press.

Rosenstone, Steven J., and John M. Hansen. 1993. *Mobilization, Participation and Democracy in America*. New York: Macmillan.

Ross, Alex. 2007. "Appalachian Autumn: Aaron Copland Confronts the Politics of the Cold War." *New Yorker* (August 27): 34–44.

Rothstein, Bo. 1999. "Trust, Social Dilemmas and the Strategic Construction of Collective Memories." New York: Russell Sage.

Rubin, Beth. 1996. *Shifts in the Social Contract*. Thousand Oaks, CA: Pine Forge Press.

Sachs, Jeffrey. 2000. "Sacks on Globalization: A New Map of the World." *The Economist*, June 22, 81–83.

———. 2012. "Election-IV." *New York Review of Books* (November 8): 64–65.

Sanders, David, David March, and Hugh Ward. 1993. "The Electoral Impact of Press Coverage of the British Economy, 1979–87," *British Journal of Political Science* 23, no. 2: 175–210.

Saunders, Kyle, and Alan Abramovitz. 2003. "Ideological Realignment and Active Partisans in the American Electorate," *American Politics Research* 31, no. 10: 1–25.

Schattschneider, E. E. 1960. *The Semi Sovereign People: A Realist's View of Democracy in America*. New York: Holt, Rinehart and Winston.

Schlesinger, Joseph A. 1984. "On the Theory of Party Organization." *Journal of Politics* 46, no. 2 (May): 369–401.

———. 1985. "The New American Political Party." *American Political Science Review* 79, no. 4: 1152–1170.

Schlozman, Kay L., and John Tierney. 1983. "More of the Same: Washington Pressure Group Activity in a Decade of Change." Journal of Politics, 45: 351–377.

———. 1984. "What Accent the Heavenly Chorus: Political Equality and the Contours of the Pressure System." *Journal of Politics* 46, no. 4 (November): 1006–1032.

———. 1986. *Organized Interests and American Democracy*, New York: Harper and Row.

Schofer, Evan, and M. Fourcade-Gourinchas. 2001. "The Structural Contexts of Civic Engagement: Voluntary Association Membership in Comparative Perspective," *American Sociological Review* 66, no. 6 (December): 806–828.

Schofer, Evan, and John Meyer. 2005. "The Worldwide Expansion of Higher Education in the Twentieth Century." *American Sociological Review* 70, no. 6 (December): 898–920.

———. 1994. *Institutional Environments and Organizations*. Thousand Oaks, CA: Sage.

Schrag, Peter. 1998. *Paradise Lost: California's Experience, America's Future*. Berkeley: University of California Press.

———. 2000. "Where the Right Lost." *Public Interest* (December): 14–16.

Schudson, Michael. 1978. *Discovering the News: A Social History of American Newspapers*. New York: Basic Books.

———. 1991. "National News Culture and the Rise of the Informational Citizen." In *America at the Century's End*, edited by Alan Wolfe. Berkeley: University of California Press.

———. 1996a. *The Power of News*. Cambridge, MA: Harvard University Press.

———. 1996b. "What If Civic Life Didn't Die?" *American Prospect*, no. 25: 17–20.

———. 1998a. *The Good Citizen: a History of American Civic Life*. New York: Kessler Books.

———. 1998b. "The Silent New Deal and the Widening Web of Citizen Rights, 1964–1975." In *The Good Citizen*, 240–294. New York: Kessler Books.

———. 1999. "Is Our Civic Life Really in Decline? Citizen Involvement in Government Surpasses Dreams of Founding Fathers." *American Heritage* 50, no. 6: 53–60.

———. 2000. "America's Ignorant Voters." *Wilson Quarterly* 24, no. 2: 16–25.

Schulman, Beth. 1995. "Foundations for a Movement: How the Right Wing Subsidizes Its Press." *Extra!* (March–April).

Schultz, T. 1961. "Investment in Human Capital." *American Economic Review* 51, no. 1: 1–17.

Schuman, Howard, and Shirley Hatchett. 1974. *Black Racial Attitudes*. Ann Arbor, MI: Institute for Social Research.

Schuman, Howard, Charlotte Steeh, and L. Bobo. 1985. *Racial Attitudes in America*. Cambridge, MA: Harvard University Press.

Science Progress. 2011. "U.S. Scientific Research and Development 101." February 16. https://scienceprogress.org/2011/02/u-s-scientific-research-and-development-101/.

Scott, Richard, and John W. Meyer. 1983. "The Organization of Societal Sectors." In *Organizational Environments: Ritual and Rationality*, 129–154. Beverly Hills, CA: Sage.

Seidman, Harold, and Robert Gilmour. 1986. *Politics, Position and Power: From the Positive to the Regulatory State*. Oxford, UK: Oxford University Press.

Seligman, Lester. 1978. "The Presidential Office and the President as Party Leader (with a Postscript on the Kennedy-Nixon Era." In *Parties and Elections in an Anti-Party Age*, edited by Jeff Fishel, 295–300. Bloomington: Indiana University Press.

Shafer, Byron. 1981. *Anti-Party Politics*. New York: Public Interest Press.

Shapiro, Robert, and Y. Elkon. 2006. "Political Polarization and the Rational Public." Paper presented at the annual meeting of the Association of American Public Opinion Research, Montreal, Canada, May 18–21.

Shavit, Yossi, Richard Arum, and Adam Gamoran, eds. 2007. *Stratification in Higher Education*. Stanford, CA: Stanford University Press.

Shea, Daniel, and Alex Sproveri. 2012. "The Rise and Fall of Nasty Politics in America." *PS: Political Science and Politics* 45, no. 3 (July): 416–421.

Shefter, Martin. 1977. "Party and Patronage: Germany, England and Italy." *Politics and Society* 4: 403–451.

———. 2002. "War, Trade and U.S. Party Politics." In *Shaped by War and Trade*, edited by Ira Katznelson and Martin Shefter, 118–133. Princeton, NJ: Princeton University Press.

Shefter, Martin, and Benjamin Ginsberg. 1985. "Institutionalizing the Reagan Regime." Paper presented at the annual meeting of the American Political Science Association, New Orleans, August 29–September 2.

Sheldon, Eleanor, and Wilbert Moore, eds. 1968. *Indicators of Social Change: Concepts and Measurements*. New York: Russell Sage.

Sherkat, Darren. 2012. "Review of *American Grace*." *American Journal of Sociology* 117, no. 4: 1264.

Shienbaum, C. 1984. *Beyond the Electoral Connection: A Reassessment of the Role of Voting in Contemporary American Politics*. Philadelphia: University of Pennsylvania Press.

Shils, Edward A. 1958. "The Concentration and Dispersion of Charisma." *World Politics* 1 (October): 101–120.

———. 1971. "No Salvation Outside of Higher Education." *Minera* 6: 313–321.

Shortridge, R. M. 1981. "Estimating Voter Participation." In *Analyzing Electoral History: A Guide to the Study of American Voter Behavior*, edited by Jerome M. Clubb, William H. Flanigan, and Nancy H. Zingale, 137–152. Beverly Hills, CA: Sage.

Silberman, Matthew. 1985. *The Civil Justice Process: A Sequential Model of the Mobilization of Law.* New York: Academic Press.

Silver, Nate. 2016. "2016 Election." FiveThirtyEight, November 22. https://fivethirtyeight.com/features/education-not-income-predicted-who-would-vote-for-trump/.

Singer, Audrey, Susan Hardwick, and Caroline Breitell, eds. 2008. *Twenty-First Century Gateways: Immigrant Incorporation in Suburban America.* Washington, DC: Brookings Institution Press.

Skidelsky, Robert. 2009. "The World Financial Crisis and the American Mission." *New York Review of Books* (July 16): 31–33.

Skocpol, Theda. 1992. *Protecting Soldiers and Mothers.* Cambridge, MA: Harvard University Press.

———. 1996. "Unraveling from Above." *American Prospect*, no. 25: 20–25.

———. 1997. "Building Community Top-down or Bottom-up? America's Voluntary Groups Thrive in a National Network." *Brookings Review* 15, no. 4: 16–29.

———. 1999. "How Americans Became Civic." In *Civic Engagement in American Democracy*, edited by Theda Skocpol and Morris Fiorina, 27–81. Washington, DC: Brookings Institution Press.

———. 2002. "U.S.: From Membership to Advocacy." In *Democracies in Flux*, edited by Robert Putnam, 103–136. Oxford, UK: Oxford University Press.

———. 2003. *Diminished Democracy: From Membership to Management in American Civic Life.* Norman: University of Oklahoma Press.

———. 2012. "The Gravitational Force in the Republican Party." February 16. https://mobilizingideas.wordpress.com/2012/02/16/the-gravitational-force-in-the-republican-party/.

Skocpol, Theda, and Kenneth Finegold. 1982. "State Capacity and Economic Intervention in the Early New Deal." *Political Science Quarterly* 97, no. 2: 255–278.

Skocpol, Theda, and Morris Fiorina, eds. 1999. *Civic Engagement in American Democracy.* Washington, DC: Brookings Institution Press.

Skocpol, Theda, and John Ikenberry. 1982. "The Political Formation of the U.S. Welfare State in Comparative and Historical Perspective." Paper presented at the annual meeting of the American Sociological Association.

Skocpol, Theda, and Vanessa Williamson. 2012. *The Tea Party and the Remaking of Republican Conservatism.* Oxford, UK: Oxford University Press.

Skowronek, Stephen. 1982. *Building a New American State.* New York: Cambridge University Press.

Smith, Rogers, 1997. *Civic Ideals: Conflicting Visions of Citizenship in U.S. History.* New Haven, CT: Yale University Press.

Smith, Timothy. 1957. *Revivalism and Social Reform: American Protestantism on the Eve of the Civil War.* New York: Harper Torch Books.

Smith, Tom. 1989. "Liberal and Conservative Trends in the U.S. Since World War II." GSS Social Change Report No. 29, May. Chicago: NORC, University of Chicago.

———. 2007. "Religion and Civic Engagement in the U.S., 1972–2006." Report prepared for the Heritage Foundation.

———. 2012. "Trends in Confidence in Institutions, 1973–2006." In *Social Trends in American Life: Findings from the General Social Survey Since 1972*, edited by Peter Marsden, 177–210. Princeton, NJ: Princeton University Press.

Smith, Tom. 2015. "Trends in Gun Ownership in the United States, 1972–2014." NORC, March. http://www.norc.org/PDFs/GSS%20Reports/GSS_Trends%20in%20Gun%20Ownership_US_1972-2014.pdf.

Smith, Tom, and Son Jaesok. 2015. "Question: Do You Happen to Have in Your Home (or Garage) Any Guns or Revolvers?" General Social Survey: Trends in Gun Ownership in the United States, 1972–2014 (Table 1), p. 3. Chicago, IL: NORC. March 1. https://www.gunpolicy.org/firearms/citation/quotes/8323.

Sniderman, Paul. 1981. *A Question of Loyalty*. Berkeley: University of California Press.

Snyder, David, and Charles Tilly. 1972. "Hardship and Collective Violence in France, 1830–1960." *American Sociological Review* 37, no. 5: 520–533.

Somers, Margaret, and Fred Block. 2005. "From Poverty to Perversity: Ideas, Markets and Institutions over 200 Years of Welfare Debate." *American Sociological Review* 70, no. 2 (April): 260–288.

Soss, Joe, Jacob S. Hacker, and Suzanne Metler, eds. 2007. *Remaking America Democracy and Public Policy in an Age of Inequality*. New York: Russell Sage.

Stanley, Harold. 1987. *Voter Mobilization and the Politics of Race*. New York: Praeger.

Stanley, Harold, and Richard Niemi. 2006. *Vital Statistics on American Politics, 2005–2006*. Washington, DC: Congressional Quarterly Press.

Stark, Rodney. 2005. *The Victory of Reason: How Christianity Led to Freedom, Capitalism and Western Success*. New York: Random House.

Stark, Rodney, and William S. Bainbridge. 1985. *The Future of Religion: Secularization, Revival and Cult Formation*. Berkeley: University of California Press.

Steensland, Brian. 2006. "Cultural Categories and the American Welfare State: The Case of Guaranteed Income Policy." *American Journal of Sociology* 111, no. 5 (March): 1273–1326.

Steinberg, Stephen. 2011. "Medicare and the Lessons of History." *Contexts* 10, no. 4: 62–63.

Steinmetz, George. 2005. "Return to Empire: The U.S. Imperialism in Comparative, Historical Perspective." *Sociological Theory* 23, no. 4: 339–367.

Steinmo, Sven. 2010. *The Evolution of Modern States*. London: Cambridge University Press.

Steuerle, C. Eugene, Edward Gramlich, Hugh Heclo, and Demetra Nightingale. 1998. *The Government We Deserve*. Washington, DC: Urban Institute Press.

Stiglitz, Joseph E. 2003. *Globalization and Its Discontents*. New York: Norton.

Stinchcombe, Arthur. 1965. "Social Structure and Organizations." in *Handbook of Organizations*, edited by James March, 142–193. Chicago: Rand McNally.

———. 1968. *Constructing Social Theory*. Chicago: University of Chicago Press.

Sugie, Naomi. 2018. "Work as Foraging: A Smartphone Study of Job Search and Employment After Prison." *American Journal of Sociology* 123, no. 5 (March): 1453–1491.

Sundquist, James L. 1968. *Politics and Policy: The Eisenhower, Kennedy and Johnson Years*. Washington, DC: Brookings Institution Press.

———. 1981. *The Decline and Resurgence of Congress*. Washington, DC: Brookings Institution Press.

———. 1983–88. "Whither the American Party System? Revisited." *Political Science Quarterly* 98, no. 4: 573–598.

Swidler, Ann. 2001. *Talk of Love*. New York: Basic Books.

Taub, Richard, Garth Taylor, and Jan Dunham. 1984. *Paths of Neighborhood Change*. Chicago: University of Chicago Press.

Teixeira, Ruy. 1987. *Why Americans Don't Vote: Turnout Decline in the U.S. 1960–1984*. Chicago: Greenwood Press.

———. 1990. "Things Fall Apart: Americans and their Political Institutions, 1960–1988." In *Change in Societal Institutions*, edited by Maureen T. Hallinan, David M. Klein, and Jennifer Glass. New York: Plenum Press.

Teixeira, Ruy, and Joel Rogers. 2000. *America's Forgotten Majority: Why the White Working Class Still Matters*. New York: Basic Books.

Thomas, George I. 1989. *Revivalism and Cultural Change: Christianity, Nation Building and the Market in the Nineteenth Century U.S.* Chicago: University of Chicago Press.

Thompson, Daniel. 1986. *A Black Elite*. New York: Greenwood Press.

Thurgood, Lori, Mary J. Golladay, and Susan T. Hill. 2006. *U.S. Doctorates in the 20th Century*. Special report, Division of Science Resources Statistics, Directorate for Social, Behavioral, and Economic Sciences. Washington, DC: National Science Foundation.

Tilly, Charles. 1979. "Repertoires of Contention in America and Great Britain, 1750–1830." In *Dynamics of Social Movements*, edited by M. Zald and J. McCarthy. Cambridge, MA: Winthrop Press.

Tocqueville, Alexis de. 1945. *Democracy in America*, Vol. 1. New York: Vintage Books.

Tolbert, Pamela, and Lynn Zucker. 1983. "Institutional Sources of Change in the Formal Structure of Organizations: The Diffusion of Civil Service Reform, 1880–1935." *Administrative Science Quarterly* 30: 1–13.

Tomasky, Michael. 2008. "How Historic a Victory?" *New York Review of Books* (December 18): 44–47.

Tomkins, Calvin. 2007. "The Turnaround Artist." *New Yorker* (April 27): 58–68.

Tornry-Purta, Judith, John Schville, and Jo-Ann Amadeco. 1999. *Civic Education Across Countries: 24 National Case Studies from the IEA Civic Education Project*. Amsterdam: International Association for the Evaluation of Educational Achievement.

Tulis, Gregory. 1988. *The Rhetorical Presidency*. Princeton, NJ: Princeton University Press.

Turner, Ralph. 1969. "The Public Perception of Protest." *American Sociological Review* 34, no. 6: 815–831.

Tuveson, Ernest Lee. 1968. *Redeemer Nation: The Idea of America's Millennial Role*. Chicago: University of Chicago Press.

Twenge, J. M. 2006. *Generation Me*. New York: Free Press.

Tyack, David. 1975. *The One Best System*. Cambridge, MA: Harvard University Press.

Tyack, David, and Larry Cuban. 1995. *Tinkering Toward Utopia: A Century of Public School Reform*. Cambridge, MA: Harvard University Press.

Tyack, David, James Lowe, and Aaron Benavot. 1986. *Law and Education in the U.S.* Madison: University of Wisconsin Press.

Tyrrell, Ian. 1991. "American Exceptionalism in an Age of International History." *American Historical Review* 96, no. 4: 1031–1055.

U.S. Census. 2016. *Population of the United States*. Washington, DC: U.S. Government Printing Office.

Valelly, Richard M. 1996. "Couch-Potato Democracy?" *American Prospect* no. 25 (March–April): 25–26.

Varenne, Herve. 1977. *Americans Together*. New York: Teachers College Press.

Verba, Sidney, and Norman Nie. 1992. *Participation in America*. Chicago: University of Chicago Press.

Verba, Sidney, and Gary Orren. 1986. *Equality in America: The View from the Top*. Cambridge, MA: Harvard University Press.

Verba, Sidney, Kay Schlozman, and Henry Brady. 1995. *Voice and Equality: Civic Voluntarism in American Politics*. Cambridge, MA: Harvard University Press.

Walker, Jack. 1969. "The Diffusion of Innovations Among the States." *American Political Science Review* 63: 880.

———. 1991. *Mobilizing Interest Groups in America*. Ann Arbor: University of Michigan Press.

Wallerstein, Immanuel. 1995. *Unthinking Social Science: The Limitations of 19th Century Paradigms*. Cambridge, UK: Polity Press.

Walters, Suzanna D. 2001. *The Story of Gay Visibility in America*. Chicago: University of Chicago Press.

Walton, John. 1993. *Sociology and Critical Inquiry*. Belmont, CA: Wadsworth.

Warwick, Donald. 1975. *A Theory of Public Bureaucracy*. Cambridge, MA: Harvard University Press.

Wattenberg, Martin. 1996. *The Decline of American Political Parties, 1952–1994*. Cambridge, MA: Harvard University Press.

Weber, Eugene. 1979. *Peasants into Frenchmen*. Stanford, CA: Stanford University Press.

Weber, Max. (1922) 1963. *The Sociology of Religion*. Boston: Beacon Press.

Weinstein, James. 1968. *The Corporate Ideal in the Liberal State, 1900–1918*. Boston: Beacon Press.

Weir, Margaret, ed. 1998. *The Social Divide: Political Parties and the Future of Activist Government*. Washington, DC: Brookings Institution Press.

Weir, Margaret, Ann Orloff, and Theda Skocpol. 1988. *The Politics of Social Policy in the U.S.* Princeton, NJ: Princeton University Press.

Wilensky, Harold. 2002. *Rich Democracies*. Berkeley: University of California Press.

Wilentz, Sean. 2005. *Andrew Jackson*. New York: Times Books.

———. 2016. *The Politicians and the Egalitarians: The Hidden History of American Politics*. New York: Norton.

Williams, Philip. 1985. "Party Realignment in the United States and Britain." *British Journal of Political Science* 15, no. 1: 97–115.

Williams, Rhys, ed. 1997. *Culture Wars in American Politics*. New York: Aldine de Gruyter.

Wills, Gary. 2000. "Putnam's America." *American Prospect* 11, no. 16: 34–37.

Wilson, G. 1982. "Why Is There No Corporatism in the U.S.?" In *Patterns of Corporatist Policy-Making*, edited by G. Lehmbruch and P. Schmitter, 219–236. Beverly Hills, CA: Sage.

Wilson, James Q. 1981. "The Rise of the Bureaucratic State." *Public Interest* 41: 77–101.

———. 2006. "The Rise of the Bureaucratic State." In *Readings in American Government*, edited by Peter Woll, 357–363. New York: Pearson Longman.

Wilson, John. 2001. "Dr. Putnam's Social Lubricant." *Contemporary Sociology* 30, no. 3 (May): 225–227.

Wilson, William J. 1978. *The Declining Significance of Race*. Chicago: University of Chicago Press.

Winship, Scott. 2011. "Mobility Impaired." National Review (November 7). http://www.nationalreview.com/articles/282292/mobility-impaired-scott-winship.

Wolff, K. 1950. *The Sociology of Georg Simmel*. New York: Free Press.

Wolfinger, Raymond, and S. Rosenstone. 1980. *Who Votes?* New Haven, CT: Yale University Press.

Woll, Peter. 2006. *American Government*. New York: Pearson Longman.

Wong, Suk Ying. 1991. "The Evolution of Social Science Instruction. 1900–1986: A Cross National Study." *Sociology of Education* 64, no. 1 (January): 33–47.

Wright, Robert. 2010. "The Internet vs. Obama." *New York Times*, February 2. https://opinionator.blogs.nytimes.com/2010/02/02/obamas-modern-predicament/.

Wuthnow, Robert. 1980. "World Order and Religious Movements." In *Studies of the Modern World System*, edited by Albert Bergesen, 57–76. New York: Academic Press.

———. 1987a. "American Democracy and the Democratization of American Religion." *Politics and Society* 15, no. 2: 223–234.

———. 1987b. "America's Legitimating Myths: Continuity and Crisis." In *America's Changing Role in the World System*, edited by Terry Boswell and Albert Bergesen, 235–255. New York: Praeger.

———. 1987c. *Meaning and Moral Order: Explorations in Cultural Analysis*. Berkeley: University of California Press.

———. 1988. *The Restructuring of American Religion*. Princeton, NJ: Princeton University Press.

———. 1999. "Mobilizing Civic Engagement: The Changing Impact of Religious Involvement." In *Civic Engagement in American Democracy*, edited by Theda Skocpol and Morris Fiorina, 331–366. Washington, DC: Brookings Institution Press.

———. 2002. "The U.S.: Bridging the Privileged and the Marginalized." In *Democracies in Flux*, edited by Robert Putnam, 59–102. Oxford, UK: Oxford University Press.

Wyatt, Ian, and Daniel Hecker. 2006. "Occupational Changes During the 20th Century." *Monthly Labor Review* (March): 35–57.

Yglesias, Matthew. 2015. "American Democracy Is Doomed." *Vox* (March 2). https://www.vox.com/2015/3/2/8120063/american-democracy-doomed.

Young, Michael. 1958. *The Rise of Meritocracy*. London: Penguin.

Zald, Mayer N., and John D. McCarthy. 1987. *Social Movements in an Organizational Society*. New Brunswick, NJ: Transaction Books.

Zelinsky, Wilbur. 1988. *Nation into State: The Shifting Symbolic Foundations of American Nationalism*. Chapel Hill: University of North Carolina Press.

Zemans, Frances Kahn. 1983. "Legal Mobilization: The Neglected Role of Law in the Political System." *American Political Science Review* 77, no. 3: 690–704.

Zinger, James, and Paul Dawson. 1979. "Encouraging Voter Participation." In *Political Finance*, edited by H. Alexander. Beverly Hills, CA: Sage.

Zolberg, Aristide. 2002. "International Engagement and American Democracy: A Comparative Perspective." In *Shaped by War and Trade*, edited by Ira Katznelson and Martin Shefter, 24–54. Princeton, NJ: Princeton University Press

Zukin, Cliff, Scott Keeter, Molly Andolina, Krista Jenkins, and Michael Carpini. 2006. *A New Engagement? Political Participation, Civic Life, and the Changing Citizen*. Oxford, UK: Oxford University Press.

Index

Page numbers followed by f or t indicate material in figures or tables.

deregulation of economy, 74, 149–153, 192, 206–209, 227, 229–234, 253n4
deregulation of media, 213–214, 218
deregulation of morality, 227–229
DiMaggio, Paul, 169
direct popular referenda, 189, 200
diversity: Americans versus European views of, 27; as corporate goal, 121; within political parties, 153; social rituals and, 222; as threat, 22, 24, 186. *See also* melting pot narrative; multiculturalism
Dodd-Frank Act (U.S.), 50, 232
Domesday Book, 79
donor class, 108, 130–131, 134–135, 157–158, 190, 231
downsizing democracy, government, 2, 58, 64, 132
Dukakis, Michael, 150
Durkheim, Émile, 5, 100, 119
dutiful citizenship, 6, 108, 180

economic: collectivism, 69; deregulation, 74; division in U.S., 201; globalization, 162–163; human capital, 102; inequality, 156, 164, 224–225, 230; libertarianism, 146, 156; moralism, 132; regulation or deregulation, 227, 231; role of government, 233–234
education: and 2016 presidential election, 193–194; attacks on, 172–173, 179; centered on individual, 105; closing of schools, 134; cost of, 16; decreasing public funding for, 3, 173–175 (174t); enhanced significance of, 12–13, 156; expansion of college, 86–89 (87t), 94; importance of universities, 82; increasing specialization in, 15; as individual social duty, 13–15; less-educated voters, 230–231; limits of impact of, 233; and national defense, 16; nontaxpayers' right to, 183–184; private and charter schools, 136, 202; as right and obligation, 5; rise of common schools, 29; as societal dividing line, 194; states' rights and, 184; state support for, 85

egalitarianism, 33–34, 78–79, 153t, 159, 232–233, 236–237
Eisenhower, Dwight, 75–76, 82, 95, 127, 139, 213, 237
embeddedness of state, 43–45, 114
English language, 26, 183, 186
environmental protection, 110, 125, 179
ethnicity: diversity and identity politics, 23–24; intermarriage, 113; as personal adornment, 118
Europe/Europeans: Brexit, 9; differences with Americans, 7–8, 21–22, 27, 33, 38–42; European Coal and Steel Community, 69; European Union, 23, 114, 238; immigration quotas favoring, 26; views of immigrants, 19, 21–22, 188
evangelical religion: alliance with conservative groups, candidates, 128; and government regulation of morality, 127; and immigration, 186; and materialism, 30; and multiculturalism, 185; and neoliberalism, 17; opposing libertarianism, 147, 204; political orientation of, 153–156 (153t); poverty seen as natural, 57; and Republican Party, 13; and revivalism, 29; and science, 34, 110, 173, 179, 248n2 (ch6); United States as Christian nation, 161
exceptionalism, American, viii, 43; challenged by Depression, 10, 65; conservative belief in, 159; in Constitution, 46–47; current evidence for, 38–42 (39t); leading to gridlock, 59; and nationalism, 9–10; and radical populism, 131; voluntarism as part of, 196
experimentation, eras of, viii, 63–66, 68–69, 75
experts: rejection of, 177–178, 183, 195, 199; role of, 6, 9, 17, 49, 68, 79, 81, 97, 110, 134
Export-Import Bank, 58

F-35 fighter, 53
Facebook, 196, 216–218, 251n10

War, 243–244n2; Progressive Era, 62; and religion, 155–156; role reversal with Democrats, 206; and state government, 173; and taxes, 51, 162; and tech elites, 157; White Southerners' joining, vii, 85

"respect" in corporate world, 222

responsibilities versus options, ix

revitalization movements, 10, 29, 35–36, 134, 148, 165–166, 190

revival religion, 29–31

Riddle, Phyllis, 82

Riesman, David, 181

rights revolution, 96, 125, 160

right-wing, 1; populism/neopopulism, 9, 185, 188, 191, 194; radio/TV networks, 213–216

rituals of solidarity, 112, 120–122, 142, 221, 225

Road to Serfdom, The (Hayek), 181

Romney, Mitt, 150, 197, 205, 249n5 (ch7)

Roosevelt, Franklin D., 63, 65–66, 210, 212, 216

Roosevelt, Theodore, 237

"Rum, Romanism and Rebellion" slogan, 32

rural issues, 150, 155, 198

Russia, 64, 163, 196, 237, 238

Sachs, Jeffrey, 46–47, 244n6

same-sex marriage, 102

Sanders, Bernie, 111, 134, 152–153, 156, 165, 187

saturation, 80–83

Save the Children (U.S.), 54

Saving Private Ryan film, 108

Scalia, Antonin, 210

Scandinavia, 39, 56, 176, 185, 196, 246n9

scapegoating, 35, 70, 72

schizophrenics in United States versus India, 243n5

Schlozman, Kay L., 128

schools: desegregation of, 213; failed school closings, 134; importance of, 82; increase in private/charter, 136, 202; and socialization, 104; textbooks, curriculum, 14, 107, 139;

trust in, 136, 168, 201–202. *See also* college education; universities

science: attacks on, 3, 6, 9, 28, 110, 172–173; big science/knowledge society, 77–83; climate change/global warming, 28, 34, 110, 172, 179, 183, 199, 219; government support for, 85–92 (87t, 91t); objectivity of, 179, 211

Sea of Japan, 238

SEC (Securities and Exchange Commission), 149

secularization, 4–5, 16, 33, 223

self-censorship by mass media, 243n1

self-help versus state support, 39t, 40–41

sensitivity training, 121, 137

"separate but equal" doctrine, 78, 95

separation of church and state, 24, 39–40

Sessions, Jeff, 254n10

sexism, 137, 147, 152, 195

sexting, 106, 222

sexuality and sexual identity, 103, 151, 155, 185, 206, 228

Shakers, 36

Shea, Daniel, 171

Shils, Edward A., 12

shrinking middle, 207

siege mentality, 203

silent majority, 159, 205

Silicon Valley, 154, 157–158, 195–196, 229, 234

Silver, Nate, 193–194

single-parent families, 102–103

singles, 104–105

60 Minutes, 214

Skocpol, Theda, 138, 244–245n7

slang, 222

slavery, 29, 36, 96

Smith, David H., 117

Snyder, Timothy, 198

social and psychological science, 117

social contract, 30, 37, 200, 204

Social Darwinism, 32, 34, 164, 197, 244–245n7

"social gospel," 32, 62

social indicators, 79–80

socialism, 51, 64, 66, 151

temperance movement, 29–30
term limits, 54, 200
textbooks, 14, 107
Thatcher, Margaret, 25, 101
theoretical stance, 4–7
think tanks, 81, 89, 129 (129t)
third-party movements, 117, 182
Thomas, Norman, 64, 66
Tierney, John, 128
tobacco danger, 28
Tocqueville, Alexis de, 28, 34, 212, 236, 250n6 (ch8)
"too big to fail," 76, 127
Traffic Safety Act (1961), 125
Treasury securities, 162–163
tribalism, 148
truancy, 13, 246n1
Trump, Donald, 237–238; authoritarianism of, 236; civil rights under, 239; economic policies of, 156, 165, 234, 237; election percentage, 240; on law and order, 204; "make America great again," 193; misogyny of, 192; national science advisor role, 3–4, 92; nativism and white nationalism of, 31, 150–151, 156, 165; presidential campaign of, 191–195, 200, 216, 235; rallies for and against, 194; sloganeering by, 193; supporters of, 150, 172, 191–195, 198, 204, 225, 230, 236; use of media by, 111, 216, 236
Tufekci, Zeynep, 217
Twitter, 216, 218
tyranny, U.S. fear of, 43

"un-American," viii; bank regulation as, 206; communists as, 145; gays as, 204; immigrants as, 31; liberals as, 204; Native Americans, Catholics as, 13, 32; New Deal as, 145; non-Christians as, 31, 32, 183; Obama reforms as, 151; right-wing views on, 9; state itself as, 142; various wars declaimed as, 203
"undeserving" groups, 185, 197, 225, 245n7
unemployment/underemployment, 66, 77, 140, 150, 186, 197, 224

unionism, 145; becoming anti-communist, 145; during Cold War, 70; decline of, 187; during/after Depression, 64, 66; need for government support, 229; Supreme Court actions against, 232; tech elites opposing, 157, 230; as "un-American," 32, 72
United States: as center-right or -left, 153–154; as Christian nation, 24–29, 161, 183, 223–224; contrasts with Europe, 7–9; declining hegemony, 158–159; founding narrative of, 23; as moral leader, 84; myth of peaceful past, 243n1; as nation-state, 22; "under God," 28–29. See also Congress, U.S.
universities: conservative critiques of, 148, 168, 172–173, 179, 239; defunding of, 174–176 (174t); role of, 81–89 (88t), 136. See also college education

Venezuela, 238
Verba, Sidney, 2, 8, 11, 21
veteran's benefits, 58, 70, 140, 245n7
Vietnam War: as activist government, 95; "body count" metric in, 72; defective weapons in, 53; draft, 16; as nation building, 30; news media on, 210, 213; political divisions over, 147, 159, 181, 203
virtual reality, 110, 117, 190
voluntarism, 25, 34, 108, 112, 115, 220
voting: as community ritual, 220; decreasing turnout, vii, ix, 2, 108, 112, 221; electoral incentives for, 141–144; by ex-felons, 152; lack of transparency in, 240–241; party line, 168; polling place issues, 240; social movements replacing, 221; suppression of, 190, 233, 235, 239–240; voter ID laws, 240. See also young voters

wages: low-wage workers, 150, 186, 234; minimum wage, 152, 212, 225, 231; stagnation of, 148, 154, 156, 160, 165, 182, 187
Wall Street, 234; conservatist alignment with, 155, 188, 190; cultural